Sir John Budd Phear

The Aryan Village in India and Ceylon

Sir John Budd Phear

The Aryan Village in India and Ceylon

ISBN/EAN: 9783337243548

Printed in Europe, USA, Canada, Australia, Japan

Cover: Foto ©Andreas Hilbeck / pixelio.de

More available books at **www.hansebooks.com**

THE ARYAN VILLAGE

IN

INDIA AND CEYLON.

BY

Sir JOHN B. PHEAR.

London:

MACMILLAN AND CO.

1880.

The Right of Translation and Reproduction is Reserved.

CONTENTS.

INTRODUCTION . . .   PAGE vii

MODERN VILLAGE LIFE IN BENGAL.

I.

INS AND OUTS OF THE VILLAGE 3

II.

ZAMINDAR AND MAHĀJAN 47

III.

DOMESTIC LIFE . . . 68

IV.

GRAVE AND GAY 88

V.

RURAL CRIME .   PAGE 102

VI.

ADMINISTRATION AND LAND LAW   124

VII.

WAYS AND MEANS   160

THE AGRICULTURAL COMMUNITY IN CEYLON.

I.

THE VILLAGE ECONOMY   173

II.

LAND TENURE AND STATE ECONOMY .   197

III.

CEYLON AND BENGAL 206

IV.

THE GRAIN TAX 214

EVOLUTION OF THE INDO-ARYAN SOCIAL AND LAND SYSTEM.

FROM THE JOINT FAMILY TO THE VILLAGE   233

APPENDIX—Note A.   275

  ,,   Note B.   285

GLOSSARY   289

INTRODUCTION.

DURING the last forty or fifty years an immense wealth of facts, previously unascertained, has been amassed within the provinces of archæology, philology, and geology. By inference from these, and by reasoning upon the data furnished by them, the conviction is arrived at that man made his first appearance upon the earth very many ages ago, during a period of time when probably the physical conditions of the world were in important respects considerably different from those which obtain at present.

So far, also, as can be judged from these materials, the human race at its commencement was in the lowest conceivable condition of civilization. Its progress upwards to that state of comparatively advanced culture, which is observed to generally prevail at the dawn of history, must probably have passed through at least three or four principal well-marked stages.

It is almost stating an axiom to say that human life can only be maintained by the continued use and consumption of material products of Nature, prepared, fashioned, and modified for the purpose by the application of human labour and skill.

Moreover, during man's lowest or least developed stage of civilization the animals and vegetables on which he feeds are both alike in a wild condition; he has not yet succeeded in domesticating either. The instruments, also, by which he catches and battles with the one, and gathers or roots up the other, are rude and inefficient—wooden clubs, bows with flint-tipped arrows, creeper-made cords, springes of fibre, stone-flakes, and such like things. His clothing is furnished from the skins of the beasts which he slays. His dwelling is a cave, or other natural shelter, supplemented by branches of trees, skins, and clay or stonework. His fire, if any, is produced in a most laborious manner by friction. The family group is the limit of his society; and it is not too much to say that under the foregoing conditions the daily subsistence and protection of that group is only ensured by the incessant labour and anxious attention of every member of it, male and female

In this state of things it is obvious there is little to favour improvement. The manner of life is necessarily erratic. As the jungle gets exhausted of its edible products, and the wild animals are killed down before their human persecutor, he must move on to new grounds. There is doubtless unity of purpose and co-operation inside each family circle. The father and the mother fight the battle of life for their progeny, as the lion and lioness for their cubs; and the children, as soon as may be, participate with them in the struggle. Collateral descendants from a near common ancestor, or even wife-connections, may sometimes be included in the community. But all others are enemies—little better, if at all, than the beasts of the forest—competitors for the necessaries of existence, and therefore to be avoided, kept at a distance, destroyed. From such circumstances ensued chronic hostility to all outsiders, as well as exigencies of self-defence, which gradually, though perhaps very slowly, led to the aggregation of families of the same blood into tribes.

There seems good reason to believe that for many ages man lived, sparsely scattered over the face of the earth, very much in the manner just attempted to be sketched. Small tribes of hunters, skin-clad and ill-armed, wandered from place to place, winning by their own strong arms a hard and precarious subsistence from the forest and the plain.

Evidently, the greater the advance made by any tribe through the means of superior intelligence and physique, and the improvement of arms, and the greater, consequently, its success in war and the chase, the larger in proportion would be the extension of its hunting-grounds and the diminution of any other outside population.

For any further material progress of civilization the introduction of a new element is required, and apparently this first came in the shape of domesticated sheep and oxen. With this addition the hunter became changed into the pastoral nomad; the means of subsistence was better assured; life was less hard; the idea of property developed itself; there grew to be those who had much—many cattle—and those who, having little or nothing, necessarily become attached, as dependents, to those who had. The care of flocks and herds gave rise to the relation of master and servant—owner and dependent—superior and inferior. Small crafts sprang out of the needs of cattle-tending, the requirements of the camp, and the textile capabilities of wool. The incidental manual labour fell to the dependent and the younger members of the pastoral group; the superintendence and control to the family chief; and the differentiation of the propertyless worker from the leisured capitalist commenced.

It is worth while to compare for a moment the two stages of human culture which have just been touched upon.

In the hunter stage man only barely manages to appropriate such and so much of the products of nature (or in other words, materials not produced or modified by human agency) as he needs for existence, and no more; and the attainment of this end calls for the unintermittent exertion of physical labour and anxious care on the part of every member of the hunting society.

By the advance to the pastoral stage man's dominion over natural products is largely extended. Better and more plentiful food, greatly improved clothing and articles of various degrees of fabrication enormously ameliorate his condition of life, and conduce to his welfare. Yet the labour requisite for these results is sufficiently furnished by a portion only of the community; and proprietors, as distinguished from non-proprietors, are at least partially relieved from it.

A third great step in the course of human progress is distinguished by the cultivation of cereals, which obviously necessitates the more or less permanent sojourn of the cultivating community in one place, the prehension and clearing of a definite tract of ground, and some communal arrangements for tilling and depasturing it. Out of these circumstances grows a village organization embracing independent households and characterized by differences in social status, privilege, and occupation. With the ancestors of the peoples who are the principal subject of the following papers, there is in the cultivating group the leading man of the community, or village chief, having his share of the communal land, and maintained in a position of pre-eminence, authority, and leisure by the variously rendered service of the other members of the commune; there is the depositary and expounder of ceremonial rules and observances, who has similar advantages, only less in degree; there is the husbandman cultivating his plot, and discharging his measure of duty to the chief; and the craftsman, no longer an ingredient in each family, but become by division of labour a distinct entity of the village, exchanges the results of his handywork and specially acquired skill against a share of the produce on the threshing-floor of his neighbours.

In regarding a social system of this kind one cannot fail to recognise the great advance which has been made upon the preceding stages in the economic application of human labour and intelligence to the reducing of natural products into possession, and the manufacturing or adaptation of them to the use of man. The aggregate of the articles brought within the reach of man and made available for his use and requirements is greatly larger in proportion to the numbers of the community than it was under either of the preceding conditions of life. This aggregate—in modern phraseology the wealth of the community—is distributed by a process of exchange, which may be deemed in a certain sense the beginning of trade, but which yet is not trade. The cultivator, the miller, the carpenter, the potter, the weaver, each does his part in maintaining the out-turn of usable products, raw and manufactured, and so far as he produces in excess of his own household's wants he does so for the benefit of his neighbours, on the understood but not expressed consideration of getting in return for it shares of their respective productions.

It is especially to be observed that in its earliest form this peculiar sort of barter is regulated by custom, and is not a system of bargaining. It may be conceived of as having grown naturally out of the prior order of things. Antecedent to the times of the village settlement, those members of the nomad family group, who did the weaving, or the carpentering, or the tent-work, or kept up the cattle furniture, &c., simply performed the tasks which fell to them in ordinary course, and participated each according to his status in the community of goods, which was the product of their joint labours. After the cultivating settlement had come into being, the tilling of the soil and the various artizan crafts became, probably by a slow process of gradual change, the separate occupations of independent households; but the old family principle only thereby experienced a new development: each occupation was directed to and limited by the wants of the whole village, and each craftsman in return for the results of his labour and skill in his own specialty received a customary share of all the other villagers' productions. The miller, for example, ground the corn of the village chief, and perhaps of the religious teacher, or wisdom man, upon an obligation of duty to a superior; he ground the corn of the watchman in return for the benefit of his service; of the potter for the needful supply of cooking and domestic vessels; of the cultivator for an ascertained quantity of grain at harvest time. In like manner the cultivator contributed a share of the produce of his threshing-floor to the chief and other privileged persons of the village (if any) as a duty, to the watchman in return for his service, to the barber for his shaving, to the miller for his grinding; while the barber on his part shaved the miller's household for his grinding, the carpenters for a portion of the grain which the latter earned from the cultivators. And the other links of the village nexus, if pursued, yield a repetition of these illustrations.

It is a principal feature of this form of primitive village communism that the just-mentioned interchange of benefits or distribution of commodities is not effected through any process of competition, but is regulated by custom, which, in case of question, is determined either by the village chief alone, or by a village assembly.

And the spirit of enmity to all outsiders, which marked alike the hunter's family and the nomad camp, animated in a still greater degree, if possible, each separate village society. Except so far as community of blood, or other strong influence, favoured the defensive combination of villages against common dangers, and so led practically to an enlargement of the commonwealth, each village community stood alone, self-sufficient and unyielding in its hostility to all that lay outside its own pale.

These two early communistic principles, last mentioned, have survived very persistently into the later stages of society; and their influence can be unmistakably traced in the land-economies of modern Europe.

The hostility, in particular, ripening eventually into militancy (to use an apt term of Mr. Herbert Spencer's), was the means of bringing about the next great change in the evolution of human society. The individual primitive man, in like manner, as he killed and eat such wild animals as he could reach and overcome, appropriated, without being troubled by any notions of right and wrong in the matter, the goods of such men as he encountered outside his own circle and was able to overpower.

The one was as legitimate prey as the other. And the combined force of the village, under the leadership of its chief, or perhaps a member of his family, naturally acted in a similar way towards other villages. From this root sprang the domination of a fighting class over an aggregation of villages, and so initiated the formation and growth of political communities; while the acquisition of the better weapons and other advantages tending to the increase of physical force, led in the end to the diffusion and predominance of the stronger peoples, and to the development of national feeling and power as we see it manifested in history.

How remote from the present times was the apparent beginning of the human race, from which the foregoing, in large measure imaginary, course of evolution has been followed, can only be realized by briefly passing under review so much, little though it be, as is known of the successions of men which have since occurred.

The long series of ages which in geology is

termed the pleistocene period of the earth's history, is, it need hardly be remarked, distinguished from the periods which preceded it by the circumstance that a very large proportion of all the species of mammals prevalent during its currency have remained unchanged to the present day, and are at this time flourishing contemporaneously with man on the face of the globe. And only one species of mammal,[1] namely, the African hippopotamus, out of those few which survived from an earlier period into the pleistocene period, has succeeded in maintaining its place in the terrestrial fauna under the existing order of things. Moreover, no traces of man have yet been found which can certainly be attributed to any earlier date. And it therefore seems a fair inference to conclude that previously to the commencement of the pleistocene period the conditions of life on the globe were

---

[1] It will be seen that in the short survey of geological and ethnological facts which here follows, the views of Professor Boyd Dawkins and of the late M. Paul Broca, have been adopted.

not such as to favour the existence of man, while during that period conditions which suited a large number of the present contemporaries of the human mammal would probably offer no obstacle to his appearance.

The available geological evidence bearing on the point seems to establish man's existence at a time when enough of the pleistocene period had elapsed to suffice for the occurrence therein of considerable change in the physical circumstances of the earth and in the composition of its fauna and flora. In the earlier portion of the period the British Isles were a constituent part of the continent of Europe; and both Spain and Italy were probably connected with Africa. The climate of the European area was such as to enable the leopard to range as far north as the Mendip hills, the lion to frequent Yorkshire, and the porcupine to live in Belgium.

Then, as now, however, arctic conditions obtained in the polar regions; and as time went on these spread southward. Several systems of glaciers grew up on the northern tracts of Britain, serving to cover Scotland and much of England under a sheet of ice. And this state of things prevailed for a long period of time. Afterwards, the rigour of the climate abated; temperate conditions came in; and the southern limit of ice and snow retreated northward.

Again, after an interval of the temperate *régime* which thus ensued, snow and ice once more resumed their sway over England and Mid-Europe for a period, which the effects produced by their agency prove to have been very considerable. And lastly, the ice and snow for a second time retreated from the south, giving place gradually to the temperate climate of historic days.

As the arctic climate, on the first occasion, came southwards, the hot country mammals left our latitudes for warmer regions, and were replaced by mammals of a temperate zone. These latter seem to have mostly come in from the east, doubtless driven from Central Asia by the advancing cold on the north and finding the only practical outlets for them open towards the plains of Europe. These, too, in turn, were driven more southward as the arctic conditions continued to progress into lower latitudes. On the return of the ice-line the proceeding was reversed. And a like series of events, differing perhaps in degree, occurred at each oscillation.

During this long lapse of time new forms entered on the scene and the several successions of fauna backwards and forwards over the same ground gave rise to a very complex state of animal life. So far as the evidence at present extends, man was existing in England during the temperate interval which separated the two ice invasions. He was seemingly in the lowest stage of human civilization, possessing only the rudest and least effective stone implements and weapons. Professor Boyd Dawkins states[1] the effect

[1] *Early Man in Britain*, p. 137.

of the evidence to be that "man was living in the valley of the lower Thames before the arctic mammalia had taken full possession of the valley of the Thames, and before the big-nosed rhinoceros had become extinct"; and he adds:—

"The primeval hunter who followed the chase in the lower valley of the Thames, armed with his rude implements of flint, must have found abundance of food and have had great difficulty in guarding himself against the wild animals. Innumerable horses, large herds of stags, uri, and bison, were to be seen in the open country; while the Irish elk and the roe were comparatively rare. Three kinds of rhinoceros and two kinds of elephant lived in the forests. The hippopotamus haunted the banks of the Thames, as well as the beaver, the water rat, and the otter. There were wolves also, and foxes, brown bears and grisly bears, wild cats and lions of enormous size. Wild boars lived in the thickets; and as the night came on the hyænas assembled in packs to hunt down the young, the wounded, and the infirm."

With the advance of the glacial climate man disappeared for a while from southern England; but after this had again given way to temperate conditions his vestiges become very plentiful, and serve to indicate that he was still in the lowest stage of culture. He lived by the chase of wild animals in the southern parts of England, in France and Spain, and throughout the Mediterranean area, as well on the African as the European side, in Palestine and in India—"a nomad hunter poorly equipped for the struggle of life, without knowledge of metals, and ignorant of the art of grinding his stone tools to a sharp edge."[1]

His contemporaries in England, at this era, were the hippopotamus and the straight, tusked elephant, the reindeer, and other arctic animals; in Spain, the African elephant; and in Greece, possibly the pigmy hippopotamus. And there can be little doubt that

[1] *Early Man in Britain*, p. 163.

the period of time, for which this description is applicable, was of very long duration.

The progress of physical change which slowly and gradually led up to the historical state of things on the face of the earth, included change in the human species. The men whose remains are found under the circumstances above described are commonly spoken of as the river-drift men. During the latter part, however, of the pleistocene period these were apparently replaced by men of a somewhat higher type, whom it is convenient to distinguish by the name of the cave-men, and who not only added ingenious and efficient weapons and implements of bone to the rude stone weapons of their predecessors, but exhibited a remarkable talent for ornamenting their various weapons, tools, and implements, with graphic drawings of the animals they hunted and killed.

The geographical range of the cave-men was markedly less than that of the river-drift men. And there appears good ground for supposing that the two groups sprang from different origins, and in particular that the cave-men were allied to, if not identical with, the Eskimo of the present day.

As in the case of the river-drift men the period of time covered by the generations of the cave-men was also very long, terminating only with the pleistocene age.

The era of time, which in chronological order immediately followed the days of the cave-men, and which itself reached to the commencement of history (in a certain manner, indeed, overlapping it), exhibits to us in the area of Europe man in three successive stages of culture, respectively denominated the neolithic, the bronze, and the iron age, all superior to that of the cave-men, and each forming a marked step of human progress in advance of the one which precedes it.

The men of the neolithic, or later stone age, had not discovered the use of the metals. As was the case with their predecessors, the river-drift men and the cave-men, stone was their only cutting and piercing medium; and hence, notwithstanding the considerable interval of time which seems to have separated them from the cave-men, they strictly constitute a member of the stone-using group and are appropriately designated by reference to their position therein. They are, however, sharply distinguished from the earlier members of the same group by the fact that they managed, by grinding, to give polished surfaces and smooth edges to their tools and weapons of stone, thus rendering them greatly more efficient instruments than the rudely chipped instruments of the river-drift men and cave-men could possibly be. They lived in substantially constructed huts, and had attained to some proficiency in the arts of pottery and of weaving. The dog, the sheep, the goat, the ox (short-horn) and the hog, which had not before appeared in the fauna of the earth, were used by them as domestic animals. To some extent, also, they practised agriculture. They cultivated wheat, barley, millet, and peas; and they had their orchards of apples, pears, and bullaces.

Notwithstanding, however, that the men of the neolithic age were thus very far superior to their predecessors, the cave-men, in regard to all the material means of life, they were yet greatly inferior to them in pictorial art; so much so that it seems almost impossible, in reason, to suppose them to be the same people in an advanced state of development. Their distribution over Europe was also much more extensive than that of the cave-men. And. judging from the characteristics of the domestic animals and cereals which everywhere accompanied them, we may safely conclude that they came into Europe from the regions of Central Asia, overpowering or driving out by force of their material advantages the cave-men, who seem to have either merged in them or to have disappeared before them—some of them, perhaps, falling back on the more northern and arctic regions, where the Eskimo now contrive to maintain an unenviable existence.

It is established satisfactorily by ample evidence that the people of at least the earlier portion of the neolithic age were, throughout the British Isles, Mid and South Europe, small in stature, with heads of the peculiar shape termed dolichocephalic—long-skulled. After a time, however, as the obscurity of the later stone age dawns into the grey light of history, it is perceived that there are certainly two very different sets of people in Europe under more or less the same neolithic state of civilization. The earlier long skulled folks seem to have been largely displaced by a tall, broad-skulled (brachycephalic) race, of no higher culture than themselves, who also came westward from the direction of Asia, and who are identified with the Kelts of history. By the greater physical strength, and probably the greater numbers of the latter, the little long skulled men were forced into the rougher and less accessible localities, more or less isolated from each other; and there seems now to be a well-grounded disposition to believe that they are represented in modern times by the various dispersed branches of a family which has sometimes been termed Iberian, such as the Basques of France and Spain, the earlier Bretons, Welsh, Scotch, and Irish, the ancient Ligurians, Etruscans, &c.

Although both these early Iberians and the Kelts (as just distinguished) in their turn, the one after the other, but with a long unknown interval, appear to have come into Europe from Asia, yet the result of all the relevant evidence seems to be that they were radically distinct from each other in language, physique, and other characteristics, and must therefore be attributed to different sources. And the Kelts are now commonly looked upon as having been among the first of the numerous constituent peoples of the great Aryan family to sweep over and settle upon the European area.

The state of civilization, which has been termed

neolithic does not appear to have been materially modified by the ethnical vicissitudes just referred to. It was the civilization of the early Kelts, as well as of their Iberian predecessors; and it prevailed alike for a long duration of time with the inhabitants of Northern Africa, the whole of Europe and Asia, the two Americas, and the islands of the Pacific.

But after a time the knowledge of bronze, the first form under which the metals were used by man as a means of augmenting applied force, became general on the Continent of Europe; and it is noteworthy that when the tall broad-skulled Kelts invaded and swept before them the long-skulled (Iberian) people of the British Isles an event which was posterior—by a long interval of time to the displacement of the cognate people in France and Western Europe—they brought with them weapons and implements of bronze; and they possibly owed much of their success to the superiority over the stone-using islanders which these ancient "arms of precision" must have given them. With the use of bronze, for some cause which remains as yet unexplained, the practice of burning the dead became customary instead of burying. As might have been anticipated, also, the employment of metal in the construction of implements and utensils gave rise to enormous improvement in the conditions of human life, and effected an immense advance in the welfare of man. Of this plentiful evidence remains in every part of Europe. The initial limit of the bronze civilization can, without much difficulty, be very generally ascertained, and it is plain that the date of its commencement is not for all places the same. Great progress, for instance, had been made in bronze industry in the south and south-east of Europe at a time when nothing better than the neolithic culture existed in the west and in the north. Originating in some outside centre-point, the art was probably brought into Europe by some invading people, and became gradually spread from east to west by the two ordinary means of diffusion, namely, commerce (elementary though it then was) and conquest.

The use of iron soon followed that of bronze, and served to mark a still more advanced grade of civilization. Like that of bronze, too, it came into Europe from the outside, and spread gradually from the south and east to the west and north.

At the commencement of the trustworthy history of Europe the small long-skulled pre-Kelts, bearing the locally differing names of Iberians, Vascones (or Basques), Ligurians, and Etruscans, were occupying the western portions of the British Isles and of France, the Spanish peninsula, the seaboard of the Savoy Alps, and the plain of Lombardy; the Kelts were pressing hard upon them in the eastern and northern districts of France; the Belgæ, again, were on the back of these; and the Romans and Greeks respectively inhabited the two Mediterranean peninsulas.

Those movements of the Kelts and Belgæ were then in progress by which the different tribes of the smaller pre-Keltic people were ultimately compressed into the restricted areas which their descendants still occupy. So far as anything was known of Middle and Northern Europe, these regions were at that time sparsely inhabited by tribes in a low state of civilization relative to the Greeks and Romans, who were generally designated by the Latin writers Germans; while in the tract about the mouth of the Danube and the north shore of the Black Sea were an apparently altogether different set of people, called the Scythians. Somewhat later the group of Sclavonians were recognised as a people distinct from the Germans; and we are all familiar with the subsequent westward and southward migrations of the German, Slavonic, and other little-civilized hordes, all proceeding as from the direction of Asia, which resulted in the subversal of the Roman empire, and led to the development of the many diverse nationalities which now cover the European area. The Latins themselves and the Greeks, as well as the Kelts already spoken of, are found, on examination of the relevant evidence, to be only the fruits of earlier migrations from the same quarter. And ethnologists seem to be generally agreed that this group almost certainly came from one and the same mother-source in South-Western Asia as the German and Slavonic groups.

From this same centre also, besides the stream north-westwards into Europe, another stream of peoples flowed south-eastwards, bifurcating so as to give rise to the Iranian group in the south and the Hindu group in the east. The latter division, at several different times, poured into India at its north-west corner, and from thence wave by wave spread down the Indus and the Ganges and up the Assam valley, and overflowed southwards as far as it could over the table-land of Central and Peninsular India, displacing or mixing with the relatively aboriginal peoples which it found upon the ground.

The mass of peoples in Europe and Asia resulting from these several streams of migration, diverging from an apparently common centre, to this day exhibit such very marked affinities in their languages, and in other respects, as serve in the aggregate very convincingly to betoken their community of origin.

National traditions, and other historical materials, bear the same way. They are accordingly classed together by ethnologists under the designation sometimes of the Aryan, sometimes of the Indo-European, and often, by German writers, of the Indo-Germanic family of peoples.[1]

On the outskirts of the area now occupied in Europe by the Aryan nations, as above defined, we find, in the south, one or two small isolated patches of non-Aryan peoples, seemingly the descendants of the neolithic pre-Kelts, with whom we have seen the Kelts in juxtaposition, and on the north the Finns, Lapps, and Samoides. The latter also form a decidedly non-Aryan group, nearly allied to the great yellow-complexioned family of peoples (commonly termed the Turanian or Mongolian family) which is spread over Asia north of the Himalayas. It would seem that the Aryan stream of Kelts, Latins

[1] The term Aryan seems to owe its appropriateness for this purpose to the fact that it is the name by which both the Hindu people and the Iranian people alike are spoken of in their respective scriptures, namely, in the Vedas and the Zendavesta.

Greeks, Germans, Slavonians, &c., in their progressive advance into Europe from the East, encountered on the ground the Iberian pre-Kelt and the Turanian on the south and north respectively, and pushed them on one side or absorbed them. The mixture of the Kelts and Latins with the small brown southern race is still easily recognised in the modern Romanic group of Romanians, Greeks, Italians, Spanish, Portuguese, and the southern French.

In like manner the Iranian stream met, on the south, Arabs and the Mesopotamian ancestors of the Jews, who, with the Phœnicians and the inhabitants of Lower Egypt, and others, all allied to each other, belonged to a third very distinct family, now known as the Semitic. And it also appears, from recent discoveries, that these Semitic Mesopotamians were themselves preceded by a most remarkable people of advanced civilization, who have been distinguished by the name Accadian, and whose language seems to connect them with the Turanian family.

And the Hindu stream of Aryan immigrants, in

their turn, came into conflict with prior occupants of the soil in the river basins and on the peninsular table-land of India. These also appear to have been remotely connected, at least in language, with the Turanian family lying on the north of the Himalayahs. They were, however, very distinct from the latter in complexion (among other physical characteristics), for instead of being yellow they were black. The Kohls, the Ghonds, the Tamils, and the remaining members of the Dravidian or South Indian group are the representatives of these people at the present day, and are all very dark. It does not appear that the darkness of tint is the direct consequence of solar action, but it in some way implies qualities which enable the possessor the better to resist the deleterious conditions of tropical climate. And for this cause, probably, by force of the principle, "survival of the fittest," the Hindu population of the Indian peninsula, resulting from the greater or less mixture of immigrant with indigenous blood, is more purely Aryan in the neighbourhood of the place of entrance, and manifests a gradual shading off of the Aryan type as one pursues the course of the stream's advance to its further tropical extreme. Kabul and the Punjab everywhere afford fine examples of the comparatively unmodified Aryan; but at a glance the ordinary Bengali of the Delta, or the Uriya of Orissa, is perceived to be of mixed origin. The lips, the nose, and the cheek-bones betray a foreign ingredient; and, above all, the darkened tint of the skin shows the infiltration from without of a very strong colouring material: the Kabuli is almost, if not quite, as fair as an Englishman, while the lower-caste Bengali very nearly approaches the negro in blackness. Thus it happens that within the limits of the Hindu branch of the Aryan family of peoples the utmost diversity of national character and feature is to be observed, a diversity which is especially striking in regard to the colour of the skin. The like occurs, though to a very much less extent, in the Iranian and European branches. But, notwithstanding the very remarkable differences which serve to distinguish many members of the widely distributed Aryan family (as above described) from the rest, full consideration of all the relevant facts leaves little or no room for doubt that they are all, as a whole, sprung from, or rather developed in the manner indicated out of, a common origin, the local site of which was in the south-western highlands of Asia.

The great Turanian and Mongolian family of peoples who still cover the larger part of Asia and China is more numerous than the Aryan; and may be said to exhibit no sort of community with it.

And the Semitic again, in the present state of the information bearing upon the point, cannot be assigned a community of origin with either of the other families.

This survey, most incomplete though it be, of the career of the human race, reaching from the point of time when its appearance in the world can be first made out, down to historical times, renders it plain that the existing state of mankind on the face of the globe, marvellously perfect as it seems to be in some quarters, has only been arrived at by a slow and tedious course of progression, not easily to be realized in conception, commencing with a stage little if at all in advance of that of the most intelligent beasts of the forest, and continued through a long series of ages which lie at present beyond measurable computation.

The spread of the ill-provided river-drift men in association with a hot-country fauna over the greater part of the known globe must itself have required a very long lapse of time. And the terrestrial and other physical changes, which took place while the river-drift men and the cave-men were living, evidently effected as they were by the slow action of the natural causes with which we are familiar, tell the same tale. Again, the total disappearance everywhere on the earth of the river-drift men, followed by their partial replacement in Europe by the cave-men, who, though still a hunting people, were of a markedly higher culture than their predecessors, betraying an essentially different (probably a cold country) derivation, seems to point to an intervening long gap of time, as to the duration of which we can form no estimate.

Another gap of unknown interval wholly separates the cave-men from the men of the later stone (neolithic) age, who at their first appearance, as has been already recounted, are found to be an agricultural people in full possession of the most important of the cereals and of the domestic animals of the modern European farmer.

The Kelts and others, who formed the front of the first Aryan wave of emigration from Asia into Europe, doubtless joined on in time with the earlier long-skulled neolithic people. But the manner in which they must have become severed from their parent Asian stock, and differentiated from their collateral relatives, can only be accounted for by taking a large allowance of time for the previous development of the family tree. With man, as with animals, the process of evolution is now known to be ceaselessly at work, though usually slow of operation. Each individual of a generation, being the product of two factors, repeats generally by inheritance the common characteristics of its two parents, subject to variations which are due to the combination of differing elements. With an alteration in the circumstances of life, a variety so arising, better adapted than the parent form to succeed under the new conditions, while retaining its general features, will come to prevail uniformly in every community which is by any means left to its own resources shut off from foreign intermixture. In this way every offshoot from a tribe or family, especially during the earlier stages of civilization, when intercommunication is restricted and life is dominated by the external conditions of nature, seems apt, sometimes speedily, though in general slowly, to grow into a divergent branch, exhibiting differences of physical characteristics in comparison with the original type. And the change is both accelerated and augmented where the new community is formed from an intermixture of an immigrant with an indigenous race.

A like process goes on in language. The speech of each individual is generally the same as the speech of those from whom he has acquired it by imitation; this is equivalent to the rule of inheritance. At the same time it exhibits variation due to the individual himself, and the circumstances affecting him; and, on the principle of the "survival of the fittest," that variation which involves the least trouble under those circumstances consistent with clearness will in the end come to prevail with much uniformity.

In his "Introduction to the Science of Language" (vol. ii., p. 318) Prof. Sayce writes:—

"Does the science of language help us to answer the "question of the antiquity of man? The answer must "be both Yes and No. On the one side it declares as plainly "as geology or pre-historic archæology that the age of the human race far exceeds the limit of six thousand years, to which the monuments of Egypt allow us to trace back the history of civilized man; on the other side it can tell us nothing of the long periods of time that elapsed before the formation of articulate speech, or even of the number of centuries which saw the first essays at language gradually developing into the myriad tongues of the ancient and modern world. All it can do is to prove that the antiquity of man as a speaker is vast and indefinite. When we consider that the grammar of the Assyrian language, as found in inscriptions earlier than B.C. 2000, is in many respects less archaic and conservative than that of the language spoken to-day by the tribes of central Arabia,—when we consider further that the parent language which gave birth to Assyrian, Arabic, and other Semitic dialects must have passed through long periods of growth and decay, and that in all probability it was a sister of the parent tongues of Old Egyptian and Lybian, springing in their turn from a common mother-speech,—we may gain some idea of the extreme antiquity to which we must refer the earliest form we can discover of a single family of speech. And behind this form must have lain unnumbered ages of progress and development during which the half-articulate cries of the first speakers were being slowly matured into articulate and grammatical language. The length of time required by the process will be most easily conceived if we remember how stationary the Arabic of illiterate nomads has been during the last four thousand years, and that the language revealed by the oldest monuments of Egypt is already decrepit and outworn, already past the bloom of creative youth."

"An examination of the Aryan languages will tell the same
"tale, although the process of change and decay has been
"immeasurably more rapid in these than in the Semitic
"idioms. But even among the Aryan languages the gram-
"matical forms of Lithuanian are still, in many cases, but
"little altered from those used by our remote forefathers in
"their Asiatic home, and in one or two instances are more
"primitive and archaic than those of Sanskrit itself. What-
"ever may have been the rate of change, however, it is im-
"possible to bring down the epoch at which the Aryan tribes
"still lived in the same locality, and spoke practically the
"same language, to a date much later than the third millen-
"nium before the Christian era. A long interval of previous
"development divides the language of the Rig-Veda, the
"earliest hymns of which mount back, at the latest, to the
"fourteenth century B.C., and that of the oldest portions of
"the Homeric poems, and yet there was a time when the
"dialect that matured into Vedic Sanskrit and the dialect
"which matured into Homeric Greek were one and the same.

* * * * * * *

"The Ural-Altaic family of languages bears similar testi-
"mony. To find a common origin for Uralic, Turkish, and
"Mongol, we must go back to an indefinitely great antiquity.
"The Accadian of Chaldea is an old and decaying speech
"when we first discover it in inscriptions of 3000 B.C.—a
"speech, in fact, which implies a previous development at
"least as long as that of the Aryan tongues; and if we would
"include Accadian, or rather the Protomedic group of lan-
"guages to which Accadian belongs, in the Ural-Altaic family,
"we shall have to measure the age of the parent-speech

"by thousands of years. The Mongols, moreover, are
"physiologically different in race from the Ugro-Tatars, and
"it is difficult to estimate the length of time required for the
"complete displacement of the original dialects of Mongols,
"Mantchus, and Tunguses by those of a foreign stock. But
"it was at any rate considerable.

"Comparative philology thus agrees with geology, prehis-
"toric archæology, and ethnology, in showing that man as a
"speaker has existed for an enormous period; and this enor-
"mous period is of itself sufficient to explain the mixture
"and interchanges that have taken place in languages, as
"well as the disappearance of numberless groups of speech
"throughout the globe."

Thus it appears that the requirements of race-differentiation and of speech-evolution argue just as forcibly as geological considerations towards the almost inevitable conclusion, that man has had his place, and has been fighting the battle of life, in the animal world for unreckonable ages of time.

The course of ethical development (in which custom and usage has at all stages been a dominant factor of vast retarding effect), so far as it can be seized and realized, and as it has been endeavoured to be traced above, discloses therefore a history, which does no more than accord with the results of these other independent sources of testimony, and which is in no degree too protracted. The length of the period requisite for the actual progress made, and the extreme slowness of the general rate of advance, can only be rightly understood when the persistency of every social institution that has once been established is clearly apprehended. Indeed, conservatism is the primary principle of every regulated society of men. The activity of each community, and the conduct of its members, are, in all stages of culture, mainly directed and governed by custom and usage. Change means new acquisition of some sort, and commonly follows but slowly upon it.

And of all institutions among the Aryans perhaps a certain well-defined village organization, with its associated method of land-holding, has been the most widespread and has proved itself the most enduring. In the three papers which have been put together in the present small volume, an attempt has been made to describe this organization, as it is found working, at least to a partial extent, in Bengal and Ceylon at the present day, and to offer an explanation of the manner in which it may reasonably be supposed to have grown up.

The first paper, which deals with *Modern Village Life in Bengal*, was first published in the *Calcutta Review* in 1864, and embodies the results of the writer's personal observations and inquiries pursued pretty continuously for all parts of the Presidency during a residence of ten years in Calcutta.

The second and much shorter paper on *The Agricultural Community in Ceylon* is the substance of notes made by the writer while living for two years in that island from 1877 to 1879.

And the third paper was read in the interval, namely in 1872, before the *Bethune Society* of Calcutta. Its aim is to explain the growth *ab initio* of the Bengal institution, as well as the rise of the social grades and property conceptions, which are intimately connected with it, by an application of those principles of evolution and differentiation which are conspicuous in the foregoing concise review of such conclusions of modern scientific research as bear on the question, and by assuming for the purpose a great lapse of time in the development of the human race, such as the results of that research more than amply justify.

The Russian *Mir*, so fully and graphically described in Mr. Wallace's pages, is an instance of the like institution, also a living reality, in actual operation, at the present day among a third people of Aryan extraction. And there are probably few of the other Aryan nationalities in Europe which, even though they may have long lost the village organization itself, do not retain some still uneffaced impressions of the rules of landholding, and the conceptions of land rights which were incident thereto.

Moreover the manor, which has only recently ceased to have practical activity, was the English feudal form of the oriental village, or rather was the substitute for it, which was brought into existence by the superposition of a foreign dominant power. Probably, too, the Anglo-Saxon hide of land was but the equivalent of the Bengal *jot, i.e.* a one-household share of the common land, originally the extent cultivable with one yoke of oxen—a one-plough portion of land.

The landlord's absolute property in land, and the usage of hiring it out to a farmer on a cultivating contract for a money rent, which has for some time prevailed in England to the exclusion of inferior customary tenures or occupations, is the outgrowth of the *ande* or *metayer* letting, which was the first mode of tilling by deputy under the earlier village and manorial system. Mr. Caird (*Landed Interest*, p. 53) remarks, that the landlord and tenant system "is so general in the United Kingdom that we really cannot be said to know any other, and yet, with reference to almost every other country but our own, is exceptional in Europe." Even now, as the same eminent authority admits (p. 78), in Ireland the tenant "has established for himself a claim to a co-partnership in the soil itself." And this seems rather to be of the nature of a survival from an older state of things in spite of English influence to the contrary, and not to be a mere modern assertion of right on the part of the Irish farmer brought about, as Mr. Caird appears to think it has been, by reason of the landlord's neglect of his proper duties.

In England, again, and the greater part of Europe manors or villages became fused into larger administrative units—such as hundreds—and so eventually a national system of fiscal and municipal government was developed from the people upwards, and became consolidated into one homogeneous structure. In the East, on the other hand, various causes favoured the permanence of the purely village administration, and supreme political power became the prize and prerogative of the strongest arm, to be exercised through officers on the zamindari principle, with little concern for anything else but the command of the local collections.

It need hardly be added that the Turks have introduced into Europe a modification of this latter form of government, and that it is now a question of very wide interest how this can be made to work in conformity with the ideas of national welfare which have been generated insensibly under the operation of a totally different system.

With these and other circumstances of the like kind in view, it is hoped that an attempt to bring under the notice of English readers a detailed account of such village organization as is yet to be seen active among the Indian Aryans may not be altogether inopportune.

MODERN VILLAGE LIFE
IN BENGAL.

I.

INS AND OUTS OF THE VILLAGE.[1]

IN an attempt to describe for English readers a type specimen of an agricultural village as it exists in Bengal at the present day, it should be premised that the Bengal village differs as much from an English village, as two things bearing the same designation can well be conceived to differ.

There is but one form of landscape to be seen in deltaic Bengal, and that a very simple one. From the sea line of the Sunderbunds on the South, to the curve which, passing through Dacca, Pubna, Moorsheedabad, forms the lower boundary of the red land of the North, the whole country is an

[1] This with the six succeeding sections, almost as they now stand, appeared as an article in the July and October numbers of the *Calcutta Review* for 1874.

almost perfectly level alluvial plain. It exhibits generally large open spaces—sometimes very large—limited to the eye by heavy masses of foliage. These open spaces, during the height of the South-West Monsoon, are more or less covered with water; at the end of the rains by green waving swarths of rice; and in the dry season are to a large extent fallow ground, varied by plots of the different cold weather (or *rabi*) crops.

There exist almost no roads; that is to say, except a few trunk roads of communication between the capital and the district towns, there are almost none of the European sort, only irregular tracks, sometimes traversable by wheels, along the balks (or *ails*) which divide and subdivide the soil into small cultivated patches or *khēts*. The few other roads which do exist, are *kuchcha*, *i.e.*, unmetalled, and are pretty nearly useless except in the dry season.[1]

---

[1] On the relatively high land of West Bengal, which lies outside the delta and below the *ghāts*, something like roads may be seen

The function of main roads as the means of locomotion and carriage of goods is performed in a large part of Bengal by innumerable *khāls* or canals, which branching out from the great rivers Hooghly, Ganges, Pudda, Megna, &c., intersect the country in all directions. Boat travelling upon them is somewhat monotonous, inasmuch as the banks are almost uniformly of bare, greasy, mud, high enough above the water, at other times than during the rains, to shut out from view all that is not placed immediately on their upper margin. But now and then extremely pretty scenes occur, where mango topes and bamboo clumps, straggling with broken front over and along the top, partially disclose the picturesque dwellings which are clustered beneath their shade. River craft of elegant shape and quaintly loaded cargoes are drawn to the *ghāt*, as the sloping ramp is called, or are

through and about the large villages, though even these are often not fitted for wheel traffic. The description in the text is intended for the delta alone.

moored in the water way; and at the bathing hour of early noon the shallower water becomes alive with groups of men, women and children immersed to the waist, and performing their daily ablutions in truly oriental fashion.

Whether a village is thus placed on the high bank of a *khāl*, or is situated inland, it invariably stands on relatively elevated ground above reach of the waters which annually clothe the Bengal world during the period of rains, and is almost as invariably hidden, so to speak, dwelling by dwelling in the midst of jungle. In fact the masses of seemingly forest growth which appear to bound the open spaces of the ordinary landscape are commonly but villages in a pleasant disguise.

These villages can be approached on every side across the *khēts* by passing along the dividing (*ails*) balks. No trace of a street or of any order in the arrangement of the houses is to be discerned in them.

Perhaps it would be correct to say that there

are no houses in the European sense; each dwelling is a small group of huts, generally four, and is conveniently termed a homestead. This is the unit of the material, out of which every village is constructed, and therefore merits a particular description.

The site of the group is a very carefully levelled platform, raised somewhat above the general elevation of the village land, roughly square in figure, and containing say about 800 or 1,000 square yards in area. The huts of which the homestead is composed are made of bamboo and matting, or of bamboo wattled and plastered over with mud, sometimes of mud alone, the floor of the structure also of mud being again raised above the level of the platform. Each hut is one.apartment only, about twenty feet long and ten or fifteen feet wide, commonly without a window; the side walls are low, the roof is high peaked, with gracefully curved ridge, and is thatched with a jungle grass; the eaves project considerably, thus forming low verandahs on the back and front of the hut. These huts are ranged on the sides of the platform facing inwards, and though they seldom touch one another at the ends, yet they do in a manner shut in the interior space, which thus constitutes a convenient place for the performance of various household operations and may be termed the house-space; the native name for it is *uthān*. It is here that the children gambol and bask, seeds are spread to dry, the old women sit and spin; and so on.

The principal hut often has, in addition to the door which opens on this interior quadrangle or house-space, a second door and well kept verandah on the opposite side opening on the path, by which the dwelling can be best approached. This is the *baithakhāna* (sitting room), and is the place where strangers, or men not belonging to the family, are received. It is also very commonly the sleeping place of the male members of the family at night. The mud floor of the hut or verandah spread with a mat is all the accommodation needed for this purpose; though the head of the house or other favoured individual may afford himself the luxury of a *charpoy*, which is simply sacking, or a coarsely made web of tape or cord, stretched across a rude four-legged frame of wood. The hut which stands on the further side of the quadrangle, facing the *baithakhāna*, is appropriated to the women and children, one of the two others contains the *chula* or mud fireplace and serves the purpose of kitchen, and the fourth is a *gola* or store-room of grain. In one of the huts, whether in the quadrangle or outside, will be the *dhenki*, and that hut generally goes by the name of *dhenki-ghar*. The *dhenki* is an indispensable domestic utensil, a very large pestle and mortar, the main purpose of which is to husk rice. The mortar is commonly a vessel, excavated out of a log of wood, and is sunk in the ground; the pestle is the hammer head (also wood) of a horizontal lever bar which works on a low post or support, and the other arm of which is depressed by one or two women applying their weight to it; upon their relieving this arm of their weight the hammer falling pounds the *paddy* in the mortar, and by the continuance of this operation the husk of the grain is rubbed off. *Paddy*, the grain of rice, somewhat remotely resembles barley, and must be husked before it can be eaten. It is surprising how effectively the *dhenki* attains its object.

If the family is more than ordinarily well off, the house group may contain more than four huts; there will often be a hut or shed open at the sides in which the cattle are tethered, carrying on a frail loft the primitive plough and other small implements of husbandry; also in Hindu houses a *thakurbāri*, or hut in which the figure of the family deity or patron saint is preserved.

When the number of huts exceeds four in all, one or more as the bullockshed, *gola*, &c., or even the *dhenki-ghar* will commonly be situated outside the quadrangle, perhaps in front of or near to a corner.

The homestead platform is generally surrounded in an irregular manner by large trees, such as mango, pīpal, palms. In small clearings among these a few herbs and vegetables are grown for family use in the curry; and the whole area or compound which belongs to the homestead is marked off from its neighbours, generally, in some very obscure manner, by most rude metes and bounds, though very rarely a tolerably neat fence of some sort may be met with. The women of the family keep the hardened mud floor of the house-space, of the principal huts and of the verandahs scrupulously clean, and often adorn the front wall of the *baithakhāna* with grotesque figures in chalk. But as a rule, the remainder of the homestead compound is in a most neglected dirty condition, even the small vegetable plots are commonly little more than irregular scratchings in the midst of low jungle undergrowth. There is nothing resembling a well kept garden and there are no flowers. The modern Bengali has a very imperfect appreciation of neatness under any circumstances, and is absolutely incapable, unassisted, of drawing either a straight line or an evenly curved line; the traces left by his plough, the edges of his little fields, the rows of his planted paddy, &c., exhibit as little order as the marks of inked spider legs across a sheet of paper.

The ordinary agricultural village of Bengal is but a closely packed aggregate of such homesteads as that just described, differing from each other only in small particulars according to the means and occupations of their owners, and more or less concealed among the trees of their compounds. There is too, here and there, waste land in the shape of unoccupied sites for dwellings, and also tanks or ponds of water in the excavations, which furnished the earth for the construction of the homestead, platforms, &c.

These tanks are often rich in all sorts of abominations, overhung with jungle, and surface-covered with shiny pond-weed; but they are nevertheless among the most precious possessions of the village. The people bathe there, cleanse their bodycloths, get their drinking-water, and even catch fish in them. For, it should be mentioned that in Bengal every pool of water swarms with fish, small or great; the very ditches, gutters and hollows which have been dried up for months, on the first heavy downfall filling them, turn out to be complete preserves of little fish, and it is strange on such an occasion to see men, women and children on all sides with every conceivable form of net straining the waters for their scaly prey. Sometimes a fortunate or a wealthy ryot has a tank attached to his homestead all his own, to which his neighbours have no right to resort.

To find a particular dwelling among such a cluster as this is an almost impossible task for a stranger. The narrow paths which, threading deviously in and out between the scarcely distinguished compounds, passing under trees and over mounds, around the tanks and across the rare *maidān* (green), answer to the streets and lanes of an English village, but in truth they constitute a labyrinth of which none but the initiated are in possession of the clue.

The land which the cultivators of the village, *i.e.*, the bulk of the inhabitants, till, is a portion of the lower-lying plain outside and around the village. The family of a homestead which may consist of a father and sons, or of brothers or of cousins, usually cultivates from 2 to 10 acres in the whole, made up of several plots, which often lie at some distance from one another. The men go out to their work at daybreak, plough on shoulder, driving their cattle before them along the nearest village path which leads to the open; sometimes they return at noon for a meal and a bathe in the tank, and afterwards go out a second time to their work, but oftener they remain out till the afternoon, having some food brought to them about midday by

the women and children. One man and his young
son (still in his boyhood) with a plough and a pair
of oxen will cultivate as much as three acres, and
so on in proportion.[1] There is no purely agricultural labouring class as we English know it. Small
cultivators and the superfluous hands of a family
will work spare times for hire on their neigbours'
land, and in some villages, where the occupation
of a caste, say the weavers caste, has died a natural
death, the members forced to earn their livelihood
by manual labour, amongst other employments take
to labour on the land for wages. For the harvest
a somewhat peculiar arrangement is often made.
The *paddy* grown on land in one situation will
ripen somewhat later or earlier than paddy grown
under slightly different circumstances,[2] and so small
gangs of cultivators from one village or district
will go to help the cultivators of a distant village

[1] Perhaps even more, with the aid received in reaping, &c.
[2] Crops are known by designations drawn from the mouths or seasons in which they are reaped or gathered, as *Bhaduwi, Kharif, Rabi;* and these respectively depend upon the season of sowing.

to cut their paddy, this assistance being returned if needed. The remuneration received for this work is usually one bundle out of every five, or out of every seven, that are cut. The foreigners build a mat hut for themselves in the harvest field, extemporize a threshing-floor and after having completed their service, carry home their bags of grain. The large topic of agricultural cultivation and landholding will be treated of in a later page.

Perhaps the most striking feature apparent in the village community, as seen by the European eye, is the seeming uniformity in the ways and manners of the daily life of all the component classes, a uniformity which from its comprehensiveness indicates a low level of refinement. From one end to the other of the village the homestead presents scarcely any variation of particular, whether the occupant be a poor ryot or a comparatively wealthy *mahājan* or trader, and its furniture is pretty nearly as meagre in the one case as in the other. Sometimes the house of the wealthier and more influential man is *pakka* or brick-built, but it is seldom on this account superior in appearance to the thatched bamboo homestead of his neighbour. On the contrary, it is generally out of repair and partially broken down. Its plan is quadrangular, like that of the homestead, with a similar arrangement of offices, and being closed in with its own walls the house is, as a rule, very dismal and dirty on the inside. The interior courtyard by its untidyness and unkempt aspect, commonly offers a striking contrast to the wholesome cleanliness of the open homestead *uthān*. Little more is to be found in the front apartment than in the *baithakhāna* hut of the peasant, if he has one. Probably the one man will have finer and more numerous body cloths than the other, and better blankets; his cooking utensils and other domestic articles (very few in all) may be of brass instead of earthenware, his *hukhas* of metal or even silver mounted instead of a cocoanut shell—his women will wear richer and a greater quantity of ornaments than the women of his neighbour. He may have a wooden *gaddi* (*takhtaposh*), or low platform in his receiving-room, on which he and his guests or clients may sit cross-legged, slightly raised above the earthen floor. He may have a richly carved in place of a plain *sanduk*, or strong box, for the custody of his valuables, or even a plurality of them. But both households will conform to the same general habits of life, and those very primitive. The food of the two is pretty much alike, rice in some form or other and curry; and this is eaten by taking it out of the platter or off the plaintain leaf with the fingers. The appliances of a slightly advanced stage of manners such as anything in the shape of knives and forks and spoons for eating purposes, tables, chairs, &c., are almost unknown.

At home, and while at work, most men go naked, all but the *dhoti* or loin cloth, and very commonly children of both sexes up to the age of seven or eight years are absolutely naked. In Europe, as men rise above the poorer classes in means, they apply their savings in the first instance to the increase of personal comfort, convenience, the better keeping of their houses, and its incidents the garden, &c. This appears not to be the case in Bengal to any great extent. Often the foreigner's eye can detect but little distinction between the homesteads and surroundings of the almost pauper peasant and those of the retired well-to-do tradesman. The mode in which the possession of wealth is made apparent, is ordinarily by the expenditure of money at family ceremonies, such as marriage, *shraddhas* (funeral obsequies) and readings of national and religious epics, the Bhagbut, Rāmāyan, and so on. On the occasions of *shadis* and *shraddhas*, the cost is in the preparation and purchase of offerings, presents, and payments to Brahman priests, presents to, and the feeding of, Brahmans generally. For the readings, the Brahman narrator (*kathak*) is paid very highly, and both he and his audience are sometimes maintained for several days by the employer. Then certain religious festivals are kept annually by such families as can afford to do so. In particular Kalis' in Kartik (October) Laksmis' at about the same time and Saraswati's or Sri Panchamis' in Magh (end of January). And ceremonies in honour of Durga are commonly performed by well-to-do people. At these times rich families spend very large sums of money, indeed. The social respect, which is everywhere commanded by the possession of wealth, seems to be meted out in Bengal very much according to the mode or degree of magnificence with which these semi-public family duties are performed, and thus it happens that even in the most out of the way agricultural village, such small ostentation in this way as can be attained unto, is the first aim of the petty capitalist in preference to any effort at improving the conditions of his daily life. The people are still in a stage of civilization, in which the advantages of refinement and convenience in the manner of living are unfelt, and the exciting pleasures of the spectacle all powerful.

In village families, the women are almost all alike absolutely ignorant and superstitious. Their dress is a coarse cloth with rude ornaments on their arms and ankles. They do all the menial work of the household, even when the family ranks among the better classes. Their habit of going daily to the tanks to fetch water and for washing gives them opportunity for gossip and searching of reputations which is seldom lost and often produces a bitter fruit. The religious creed of both men and women is most crude and ill-formed, at best a tangled tissue of mythological fable. Such worship as is not vicarious, is fetish and deprecatory in its object. Women especially, probably from their greater ignorance and restrained condition of life, are disposed to attribute even common incidents to the agency of invisible beings. There are for them jungle spirits, and river spirits, headless spirits, six-handed goddesses, ghosts, goblins, and in some parts of Bengal witchcraft is firmly believed in. An old woman with uneven eyes is certain to be looked upon as a witch, and children are carefully prevented from appearing before such a one. Girls perform *brotos* with the purpose of averting future ills. Astrology, half science, half faith, grows out of these elements and has its professors in nearly every considerable village. Signs of prognostication are carefully sought for, and bear each an assigned importance. For instance, sneezing is generally inauspicious. The ticking sound of the lizard is a deterring omen. When certain stars rule, the women of a family will not leave the house. Women will hesitate to cross a stream of water the day before that fixed for the performance of a *shradh*. In short, their down-sittings and uprisings, walking, sleeping, eating, drinking, may be said to be subject to the arbitrary control of spiritual agencies; and a numerous body of astrologers finds employment and a not despicable means of living, in the interpretation of the phenomena, by which these supernatural governors allow their will or intention to be discovered.[1]

The plot of ground on which the homestead stands and the small surrounding compound which goes with it, is hired of a superior holder. A common rent is Re. 1, 1-4 1-8 per annum for the homestead plot, and somewhat less for the attached piece. The buildings, however, which constitute the homestead, are usually constructed by the tenant and belong to him. Should he move to another place, he may take away the materials or sell them. This is one reason why mud, mat, and bamboo dwellings are the rule, and *pakka* (brick-built) houses the exception. The largest mat hut of a homestead will cost from Rs. 30 to 50 to build entirely anew. The *chulha*, or cooking-stove, is made by the women, of mud. The *dao*, or bill-hook, which as a tool is the Bengali's very jack-of-all trades, is got from the village blacksmith for a

---

[1] To make a pilgrimage to some one of certain very holy places, and if possible to spend the last days of life there, or at least to die on the banks of holy Ganges, is the cherished desire of every one, male or female, rich or poor.

few annas. The plough-handle of the cultivator is prepared almost for nothing by the ryot himself, perhaps with the assistance of the village carpenter, and its toe is shod with iron by the village blacksmith for one rupee.[1] An average pair of bullocks may be obtained for Rs. 20, and the price of the few earthen pots and pans of various sorts, which constitute the necessary utensils for household purposes, may be reckoned in pice.

From such facts as these an idea may be formed of the exceedingly scanty dimensions of the ordinary villager's accumulated capital; and too often of this even a large proportion merely represents a debt due to the *mahájan*.[2] The extreme poverty of, by far

---

[1] The plough is a most simple wooden tool without any iron about it except the pointed ferule at the toe. In shape it closely resembles a thin anchor; one claw goes into the ground at such an inclination that the other is nearly vertical and serves as a handle for the ploughman; the shank is the plough-beam to which the bullocks are attached. There is no share coulter, or breast; the pointed end only stirs the earth, it does not turn it. The whole is so light that a man easily carries it over his shoulder.

[2] See note (A) in the Appendix.

the largest portion, *i.e.*, the bulk of the population in Bengal (the richest part of India) is seldom rightly apprehended by English people, who have not had intimate eye experience of it. It is the tropical climate and the tropical facility of producing rice which admits of life, and a certain low type of health being maintained on a minimum of means. Seven rupees a month is a sufficient income wherewith to support a whole family. Food is the principal item of expense, and probably one rupee eight annas a month will, in most parts of Bengal, suffice to feed an adult man and twelve annas a woman, even in a well to do establishment. Such of the villagers as are cultivators generally have sufficient rice of their own growth for the house consumption; the little cash which they require is the produce of the sale of the *rabi* (cold weather) crops. The other villagers buy their rice unhusked (*paddy*) from time to time in small quantities, and all alike get their salt, tobacco (if they do not grow this), *gurh*, oil, *masala*, almost daily at the general dealer's (*modi*) shop.

Purchases in money value so small as these, namely, the daily purchases of the curry spices needed by one whose sole subsistence for a month is covered by one rupee eight annas, obviously calls for a diminutive coin. The pice, or quarter part of an anna, which is the lowest piece struck by the mint, is not sufficiently small, and cowries at the rate of about 5,120 to the rupee, are universally employed to supplement the currency.

The *modi's* shop is a conspicuous feature in the village. In a large village there will be three or four of them, each placed in a more or less advantageous position, relative to the village paths, such as at a point where two or more thoroughfares meet, in a comparatively open situation, or in the neighbourhood of the place where the weekly or bi-weekly *hāt* is held. The shop in eastern Bengal is most commonly a bamboo and mat hut, sometimes the front one so to speak of the homestead group, sometimes standing singly. To open shop the mat side next the path or roadway is either removed altogether or swung up round its upper edge as a hinge, and supported on a bamboo post, pent house fashion. The wares then stand exhibited according to their character, seeds and spices in earthen or wooden platters on the front edge of the low counter which the raised floor presents, caked palm sugar (*gurh*), mustard and other oils, salt, rice in various stages of preparation in somewhat large open-mouthed vessels set a little further behind, and quite in the rear broad sacks of unhusked rice or *paddy* (*dāna*); on the side walls are hung the tiny paper kites which the Bengali, child and man alike, is so fond of flying, all sizes of kite reels, coarse twines, rude and primitive pictures, charms, &c., while the vendor himself squats cross-legged in the midst of his stores, or sits on a *morhā* outside. The liquid articles are served out with a ladle, the bowl of which is a piece of cocoanut shell, and the handle a small-sized bamboo spline, and are meted out by the aid of a measure which is made by cutting off a piece of bamboo cane above a knot. The seeds, and so on, are taken out with the hand or bamboo spoon, and weighed in very rude wooden scales. Occasionally, when the *modi* does business in a large way, the hut which constitutes his shop may be big enough to admit the purchaser, and then the articles will be piled on roughly formed tables or benches. If the sale of cloths—piece-goods—be added to the usual *modi's* business, a separate side of the hut, furnished with a low *takhtaposh*, is generally set apart for this purpose. The *modi* then becomes more properly a *mahājan*, and the bamboo hut will usually be replaced by a *pakka*, brick-built room.

A market or *hāt* is held in most villages twice a week. The market place is nothing more than a tolerably open part of the village site. If one or two large *pīpal* trees overshadow it so much the better, but it is rare that any artificial structures in the way of stalls exist for the protection of the sellers and their goods; when they do so they are simply long narrow lines of low shed roofs covering a raised floor, and supported on bamboo posts, without side walls of any kind.

The *hāt* is a most important ingredient in the village life system. Here the producer brings his spare paddy, his mustard-seed, his betelnuts, his sugar-cane, his *gurh* treacle, his chillies, gourds, yams; the fisherman brings his fish, the seedcrusher his oils, the old widow her mats and other handy work, the potter his *gharas* and *gamlahs*, the hawker his piece-goods, bangles, and so on; the town trader's agents and the local *modis* come to increase their stocks, the rural folks come to supply their petty wants, all alike assemble to exchange with one another the gossip and news of the day; and not a few stay to drink, for it must be known that this is an accomplishment which is by no means rare in India.[1] Each vendor sits cross-legged on the ground with his wares set out around him, and for the privilege of this primitive stall he pays a certain small sum or

---

[1] See a paper of Rajendra Lala Mittra, Rai Bahadur, LL.D., C.I.E., in the *Journal of the Asiatic Society of Bengal* for 1873, Part I. No. 1.

contribution in kind to the owner of the *hāt*, who is generally the proprietor, in the peculiarly Indian sense of *zamīndār*, of the rest of the village land. The profits thus derived from a popular *hāt* are sufficiently considerable relative to ordinary rent to induce a singular competition in the matter on the part of neighbouring *zamīndārs;* each will set up a *hāt*, and forbid his ryots (which may be *sub modo* translated tenants) to go to the *hāt* of his rival. If orders to this effect fail of success, resort is sometimes had to force, and so it happens that the holding of *hāts* has become fraught with danger to the Queen's peace, and the legislature has found it necessary to give extraordinary preventive powers to the magistrate.

If the village, or any substantial portion of it, is inhabited by Mussulmans, there will be a *masjīd* (or mosque) in it. This may be a *pakka* (brick) building, if the community has at any time possessed a member zealous and rich enough to defray the cost of erecting it. More commonly it is of mat and bamboo. Almost always, of whatever material constructed, it exhibits one typical form, namely, a long narrow room (often in three or more or less distinctly marked divisions) closed at each end and on one side, and having the other side entirely open to a sort of rectangular courtyard or inclosure.[1] The *mulla* who officiates there may be a tradesman, or *modi*, gifted with a smattering of Arabic sufficient to enable him to read the Korān. He is in theory chosen by the *mahalla* (Muhammadan quarter), but practically the office is hereditary and is remunerated by small money payments made on occasions of marriages and other ceremonies.

[1] The characteristic of Muhammadan architecture in India is the hemispherical domed roof. This requires a base of equal dimensions as to length and breadth; and therefore whenever an oblong span has to be roofed over the length of the oblong is made some multiple of its breadth, and is divided into the corresponding number of squares by transverse rows of pillars and arches. The whole roof is then constructed of a succession of domes. In this way the long interior of a mosque becomes a series of compartments, commonly three, open to each other between the pillars or under arches; and the village mat room, which is to serve as a mosque, is made to imitate this arrangement without independent purpose.

In passing along a village path one may come upon a group of ten or twenty almost naked children, squatting under a *pīpal* tree near a homestead, or even under a thatched verandah appurtenant thereto, and engaged in marking letters on a plantain or palm leaf, or in doing sums on a broken piece of foreign slate, or even on the smoothed ground before them. This is a *patshāla* or hedge school, the almost sole indigenous means of educating the rising generation; and by Government aid and otherwise this has under the English rule been developed into a most potent instrument for the spread of primary instruction. It still in its original meagreness exists in most country villages, serving in an infinitesimal degree to meet the needs of an enormous class which the more efficient Europeanized schools as yet fail to reach.[1] The instruction in these *patshālas* is given gratis, for it is contrary to an oriental's social and religious feelings of propriety that learning of any sort should be

---

[1] This was written in 1874.

directly paid for. It is a heavenly gift to be communicated by God's chosen people, the Brahmans, originally to Brahmans and other twice-born classes only, but in these later days, with an extension of liberality not quite accounted for, to outside castes also, so far as regards reading and writing the vernacular, arithmetic, and other small elements of secular knowledge sufficient for the purposes of zamindari accounts. The instructor in a typical *patshāla* is an elderly Brahman dignified with the designation *Guru Mahasoy;* occasionally, however, he is a *modi* or small tradesman who manage concurrently with his business to keep his eye on the group of urchins squatting under the eaves of his shop hut. Although there is no regular pay for the duty, the instructor does not any more than other folks do his small work for nothing; on the occurrence of special events in his family the parents of his pupils make him a small present of rice or *dāl*, or even a piece of cloth, and when a child achieves a marked stage in its progress, say the end of the alphabet, words of one syllable, &c., a similar recognition of the occasion is made. A Brahman *guru* will in addition get his share of the gifts to Brahmans which form so serious an item of expense in the celebration of the many festivals and ceremonies obligatory on a well-to-do Bengali.

In parts of Bengal noted for the cultivation of Sanscrit learning, such as Vikrampur and Nuddea, something answering very remotely to an old-fashioned English Grammar School may now and then be met with. A turn of the village path will bring you to a Tol; there within a half open mat shed sit cross-legged on the raised mud floor ten or a dozen Brahman youths decently clothed, with Sanscrit manuscripts on their laps. They are learning grammar from the wonderful work of that chief of all grammarians, Panini, or more probably from Bopa Deva's book, or are transcribing sacred rolls. Each remains some two or three or even more years at this very monotonous employment, until he is able to pass on to the home of deepest learning,

Nobodweep. A rude shelf of bamboo laths carries a few rolls of Sanscrit manuscripts, and this is all the furniture of the Tol. The master of the Tol is a Brahman Pundit who in obedience to the Hindu principle not only teaches but maintains his scholars. He is sometimes, though not often, a very learned man, if learning means knowledge of the Sanscrit language and of the peculiar philosophy enshrined in it: and he is always personally poor. His means of maintaining himself and his disciples are supplied in like manner as, though with fuller measure than, is the case with *Guru Mahasoy*. The Pandit who keeps a successful school, gets a Benjamin's share of presents at all ceremonies and feasts; and all the richer Hindus of the neighbourhood contribute to his needs. He spends the vacations, say about two months of the year, in travelling from house to house (of those worth a visit), throughout an extensive area; and though he seldom actually begs, his purpose is known and he never leaves a roof without a honorarium of Re. 1.

and Rs. 2, or even Rs. 20, according to the wealth of his host.

One poor homestead in a village may be occupied by two or three lone widows, who have been left desolate in their generation, without a member of their family to support them, and who have joined their lots together in order the better to eke out a miserable subsistence, and wretched creatures they are to the European eye, emaciated and haggard, with but little that can be called clothing. Yet, somewhat coarsely garrulous, they seem contented enough and certainly manage by mat-weaving and such like handy work, or when occasion offers by menial service, or perhaps oftener still by the aid of kindly gifts from neighbours, to gain a not altogether precarious subsistence.

And very few villages are without one or more specimens of the Byragi, and his female companion, coarse licensed mendicants of a religious order, in whose homestead one of the huts will be a *thakurbāri* of Krishna (an incarnation of Vishnu), whereat the members of the very numerous sect of Boistubs or Vaisnabas (Vishnubites) on certain festivals lay their offerings. The Byragi, who may be termed the religious minister of one of the sects which owe their origin to the great reformer Chaitanya a little more than three hundred years ago, or perhaps more correctly a member of an ascetic religious order, has very commonly the reputation of leading a grossly sensual life, and his appearance does not always belie his reputation. This is an unfortunate outcome of the noble latitudinarianism, which first taught in modern India that all men without distinction of race, creed, sex, or caste, are equal before God.

The homestead of the *goāla*, or cowman, of which there will be several in a village, is precisely of the same type as are those of his neighbours: and he is also a cultivator as most of them are. Probably the cowshed will be actually brought up to the *uthān* and fill one of the sides. The cows are tiny little animals often not more than three feet high and miserably thin. They are kept tethered close, side by side of each other in the open shed, and there fed with dried grass, wetted straw, and such like fare, except when under the care of a boy they are allowed to pick up what they can on the waste places about the village, and on the fallow *khēts*. The cowman and his cows are very important members of the village community, for all Hindus consume milk when they can afford to do so. After rice and pulse (*dāl bhāt*) it is the staple food of the people. Neither butter as it exists in Europe nor cheese seem to be known to the natives generally, although the art of making the latter was introduced by the Dutch, at their settlements such as Dacca, Bandel (Chinsurah) and is still practised there for the European market, and a crude form of butter, or as near an approximation thereto as the climate admits of, is also largely made for the richer natives and Europeans. This is commonly effected by first curdling the milk with an acid and then churning the curds. It is the business, however, of the *goāla* not merely to sell milk in the raw state, but also to compound various preparations of it, thickened. One such preparation, *dahi*, is in consistency not very unlike a mass of thick clotted cream, as it may sometimes be got in the west of England, with all the fluid portion omitted or strained from it, and is pleasant enough to the European taste. This appears to be a universal favourite, and is daily hawked about from homestead to homestead by the *goālas* in earthen *gharas*, which are carried scale-fashion, or *bahangi*, suspended from the two extremities of a bamboo across the shoulder.

The blacksmith's shop is a curious place of its kind, simply a thatched shed, with old iron and new of small dimensions lying about in hopeless confusion. In the centre of the mud floor is a very small narrow anvil, close to the fireplace, which latter is nothing but a hole sunk in the ground. The nozzle of the bellows (an instrument of very primitive construction) is also let into the ground. The headsmith, sitting on a low stool or on his heels, works the bellows by pulling a string with one hand while with a tongs in the other he manipulates the iron in the fire, and then, still keeping his seat, turns to the anvil whereon with a small hammer in his right hand he performs the guiding part in fashioning the metal, and an assistant also squatting on his heels follows his lead with a larger hammer. The hammer heads are long, on one side only of the haft, and unbalanced by any make-weight, and the anvil is exceedingly narrow; yet the blows are struck by both workmen with unerring precision. The villagers require but little in the shape of iron work. A few nails, the toes of the ploughs, *kudalis* (cultivating hoes) *daos*, answering to bill-hooks, the *bonti* of domestic and other use (fixed curved blade) constitute pretty nearly all their necessaries in the way of iron articles. These are mostly made or repaired by the village blacksmith. His stock of iron is principally English hoop-iron, which is bought at the nearest town by him, or for him, and which has come out to India in the shape of bands round the imported piecegoods bales.

The professions are not altogether unrepresented in a Bengal village, for you may not seldom meet the *kabiraj* or native doctor, a respectable looking gentleman of the Vaidya caste, proceeding with a gravity of demeanour befitting his vocation, to some patient's homestead. If you can persuade him to open his stores to you, you will probably find him carrying wrapt up, as a tolerably large bundle (cover within cover) in the end of his *chadr*, a very great number of paper packets, resembling packets of flower seeds each carefully numbered and labelled. These are his medicines, almost all in the shape of pills compounded after receipts of antiquity; many are excellent as specifics, and there seems reason to think that English medical men in India might with advantage resort more than they do to the native pharmacopœia. The *kabiraj* does not charge by fees in the manner of European doctors, but makes a bargain beforehand in each case for the payment which he is to receive for specified treatment; for example Re. 1 or Rs. 2 for the ordinary medicine with two or three visits in an obstinate case of malarious fever. In the event of a cure, the patient often testifies his gratitude by making a present to his doctor.

The astrologer too ought perhaps to be ranked in the professional class; and he will be found in nearly every principal village. He is an Acharjee (Lugu Acharjee), but of a somewhat low class of Brahman, whose business is to paint the *thakurs* (idols) and the various traditional representations of the deities; also to tell fortunes and to interpret omens and signs of luck, or of interposition of providence; to prepare horoscopes, and so on Those who do not succeed sufficiently in these higher branches of their craft take to painting pictures in water colours for use, in the way of decorative purpose, on occasions of the great ceremonies which are performed in the richer families.

The Hindu artist does not appear to have obtained a knowledge of perspective, and in these pictures it is seldom that any attempt is apparent to realise its effects. But outline and colour are remarkably well depicted on the flat. These men can be got to work many together on a given subject for a monthly pay of Rs. 20 or Rs. 30 according to the efficiency of the painter. But most commonly each prepares his pictures at leisure in his own house and presents them when finished to some rich person in the generally well-founded expectation of receiving ample remuneration for his labour.

The worship of God which obtains among Muhammadans, may be designated congregational and personal, while that among Hindus is domestic and vicarious. With the former, the masjid, public preaching, united prayer and adoration offered by individuals collected in heterogeneous assemblages or congregations, are its characteristic features. With the latter, the family idol (or representation of the deity), the daily service and worship of this idol performed by a priest for the family, and the periodic celebration of ceremonies in honour of that manifestation of the deity which the family adopts, as well as those for the benefit of deceased ancestors' souls, constitute its principal ingredients. Among wealthy Hindus the hereditary spiritual guide, the hereditary *purohit* and the service of the jewelled *thakur* form, so to speak, the keystone of the joint family structure: and the poor folks of a country village make the best shift they can to worship God under the like family system. Every respectable household that can afford the small expense has a rude *thakur,* or image of its patron deity placed in a separate hut of the homestead, and a Brahman comes daily to perform its worship and service. As might be supposed, it is not worth the while of any but the lower caste of, and imperfectly educated, Brahmans to pursue this vocation; so it generally happens that the village *purohits* are an extremely ignorant set of men. In some districts they are mostly foreign to the village, coming there from a distance; they reside in it only for a few years, then return home for an interval, providing a substitute or vicar during the period of their absence. These ministers of religion get their remuneration in the shape of offerings and small fees, and manage on the whole to earn a tolerably good livelihood by serving several families at a time. With other Brahmans they also come in for a share of the gifts which are distributed by wealthy men on the occasions of family ceremonies and festivals. In great measure the office of *purohit* is hereditary, and indeed strictly so in the case of families of social distinction and importance, who, as a rule, have more than one spiritual guide exclusively to themselves. For there is the *guru* or spiritual instructor of the individual who gives him the *mantra*, and the higher class *purohit* who is the Acharjee and conducts the periodic *puja* festivals of the family, in addition to the ordinary *purohit* who performs the daily service of the *thakur*. Over and above the regular service of the *thakur* performed by the priest, there is also among Brahmans a manifestation of personal devotion on the part of the individual members of the family. It is right in Brahman families that each individual should once or oftener in the day come before the image and say a Sanscrit prayer or recite a *mantra*.

The mass of the ryots who form the population of the village are too poor to have a family deity. They are forced to be content with the opportunities they have of forming part of the audience on the occasions of religious festivals celebrated by their richer neighbours, and the annual *pujas* performed at the village *mandap* on behalf of the community.

II.

ZAMINDAR AND MAHĀJAN.

MANY other members of the village society than those already mentioned deserve description, such as the carpenter, the potter, the weaver, the fisherman, and the like. It might be told, too, how a woman, or an old man incapable of laborious exertion, will venture a rupee in the purchase from the *jalkarwala* of a basket of fish, from the ryot of a bundle of chillies, &c., with the hope of earning a few pice by carrying this to the *hāt* and there selling in retail; how the pith-worker plies his occupation, or how the widow makes her mats. And the *mandal*, the *chaukidar*, the barber, the washerman will probably hereafter have their respective places in the village economy pointed out. The general texture of the village material has, however, even thus far, been sufficiently represented, and to complete the outline of the little community it only remains to sketch in the two most influential of its constituents, namely, the *zamindar* and the *mahājan*.

Preliminary to describing the status of these persons a few words more as to externals are necessary. It has already been said that the site of the loose aggregate of homesteads which forms the Bengali village is somewhat elevated above the general level of the cultivated plain, and presents, when viewed from the outside, a more or less wooded appearance by reason of the pipal, mango, tamarind, and other forest trees which usually shut in the several dwellings. This wooded dwelling area, so to call it, is skirted by waste or common land of very irregular breadth, and beyond this again comes the cultivated land of the open plain (*māth*). Up to a certain boundary line (of immemorial origin but ordinarily well ascertained) all the land both waste and cultivated, reckoned outwards from the village, belongs to the village in a sense which will be hereinafter explained. On the other side of the line the land in like manner belongs to some other village. In parts of Bengal where portions of the country are in a state of nature the limits of the village territory will include jungle and otherwise unappropriated land.

The village and its land (the entirety is termed a *mauzah*) in some respects affords considerable resemblance to an English parish, and possibly the two may have had a certain community of origin, but there are differences enough in their present respective conditions to render it impossible to pass by analogy from the one to the other. Of course, both in the English parish and in the Indian *mauzah* the principal business of the people is agriculture. But in England, now-a-days, the cultivation of the soil is not carried on under parochial rights, or in any degree subject to communistic principles. Every portion of the cultivatable area of the parish is cultivated by some one who either owns it himself as his property in the same sense as all other subjects of property are owned, or who hires it for cultivation from such an owner. In India, on the other hand, the land of the *mauzah* is cultivated in small patches by the resident ryots (or cultivators) of the village on payments of dues, according to the nature of the soil, and the purpose of the cultivation, to a person who, relatively to the ryot, is termed the zamindar, viz., the landholder (not accurately landlord) of the *mauzah*. These dues are at this day universally denominated rent; but although they are most commonly variable and capable of adjustment from time to time, between the zamindar and the ryot, they do not correspond in all aspects to rent, and some confusion of idea is occasionally perceived to arise from careless use of this word.

To the English observer it is very remarkable at first to find that the land belonging to the village is, with extreme minuteness of discrimination, classified according to characters attached to it by custom, and having relation to data which are not all concrete in kind, such as the prevailing water-level of the rainy season, the nature of the rent payable for it, the purpose to which it is put, the class of persons who may by custom occupy it, and so on. Thus we meet with :—

Sali—land wholly submerged during the period of the rains—of different grades.

Suna—not so—also of different grades.

Nakdi—land for which rent is paid in cash per bigah.

Bhaoli—land for which rent is paid in kind—part of the produce.

———land for which rent is paid in cash per crop per bigah.

Bhiti—raised house-site land.

Khudkasht—land which the residents of the village are entitled to cultivate.

Pahikasht—land which outsiders may cultivate.

These characters or qualities adhere almost permanently to the same land, and there is for each village a recognised rate of rent (or *nirkh*) properly payable according to them. Also, when the occupation of the land is, as commonly happens with the Sunaland, on an *utbandi jama*, and the cultivation is by alternation of cropping and fallow, the ryot or cultivator only pays for so much of each sort of land as he actually tills for the year. It is apparent, then, that generally speaking, the precise amount of payment to be made by the ryot to the zamindar in each year is a matter of some complexity of calculation.

Perhaps it should be here remarked that in most villages by far the larger portion of the land is Khudkasht.

The ordinary state of things, then, is shortly

this:—The open lands of the village are divided up among the resident ryots in small allotments (so to speak), an allotment often consisting of several scattered pieces, and generally comprehending land of various qualities as above defined —it rarely exceeds ten acres in the whole and is often much less—and the payment of rent by each ryot to the zamindar is made on a shifting scale, depending upon more or less of the elements just mentioned. An abbreviated example of the year's account between the ryot and zamindar are given in the Appendix.[1]

Putting aside all questions of right on the part of the cultivator to occupy and till the land of the village, we have it as a matter of fact that the Bengal ryot is little disposed to move, and that for generation after generation, from father to son, the same plots of land (or approximately so) remain in the hands of the same family.

After this preface, part of it in some degree

[1] See note (B) in the Appendix.

repetition, we are in a situation to take a view of the zamindar, considered as a personage of the village. It will be convenient to speak as if there were but one such person for a whole village. This is not strictly true as regards the ryot, or rent payer, and will be qualified by explanation hereafter. But it is the simplest form of the actual case and the normal idea of a zamindar is best arrived at by conceiving that a *mauzah* is the smallest unit in his holding—that the zamindari is an aggregate of many entire *mauzahs*.

Now when it is remembered how small is the quantity of land tilled by each ryot, that he pays for different portions of this at different rates, that the quantity of the land of each sort or the nature of the crop, according to which he pays, varies from year to year, and that the total year's rent is generally paid in three or four *kists*, or instalments, it will be seen, that the business of collecting the rents of a Bengal *mauzah* is a very different thing from the work which is done by a landlord's agent in England, and that it can only be carried on through the means of an organized staff. This staff is commonly called, both individually and collectively, the zamindar's, or *zamindari amla*. It usually consists of a *Tehsildar*, *Patwari*, *Gumashta*, and *peons*, or similar officers under different names, varying with the district.

The *Tehsildar* is the collector of the rents, and if the *zamindari* is large, one *Tehsildar* will collect from three or four *mauzahs*.

There is generally a *Tehsildar's kachahri* in each *mauzah* or village—it is the office where the *zamindari* books and papers relative to the village collections are made up and kept; sometimes a verandah-shed or hut of mat and bamboo serves the purpose of the *kachahri*, sometimes it is a *pakka* house of brick with sufficient accommodation to enable even the zamindar to pass a few days there when he resides elsewhere than in the village and is minded to visit it. Book-keeping is an art, which Hindus seem to carry almost to an absurd extent of detail, and it would be tedious to describe all the books which are kept in due course of the *kachahri* business. It will be sufficient to mention the principal among them; these are, first, three or four books bearing the denomination of the *chittha*, which amount in effect to a numbered register in various ways and in minute detail of all the small *dags*, or plots into which the village lands are divided, the measurement of each, its situation, the quality of the land, the ryot who cultivates it, and so on, the last of them being the *khatiyan*, or ledger, which gives under each man's name all the different portions of land held by him, with their respective characteristics. The *jama bandi* is a sort of assessment paper made up for each year, with the view of showing for every ryot, as against each portion of the land held by him, the rate at which it is held, according to quality or crop, and also to exhibiting the total amount which in this way becomes due from him, and the *kists* in which it is to be paid; and the *jama-*

wasil-baki is an account prepared after the expiration of the year, repeating the principal statements of the *jama bandi*, as to the amounts which had become due, and then giving the payments which had actually been made, together with the arrears.

A Bengali account book is formed by sewing together with a cord any number of very long narrow loose sheets at one of their ends, and when it is closed the free ends of the sheets are folded back upon the ends which are thus bound. When it is open the bound end rests upon the reader's arm, the upper leaves are thrown back and the writing then runs from the free end of one page down through the cincture, to the free end of the next. In this way a total page of portentous length is possible and some *jama bandis* take advantage of this property to the utmost.

The *Gumashta* and *Patwari*, or similar officers, by whatever name they may be called in the different districts, are charged with the duty of keeping up the *kachahri*-books according to the varying circumstances of the ryots' holdings; and for this purpose have to keep a sharp eye throughout the year upon the ryots' doings. It will be seen at once that persons charged with the functions of these *zamindari amla* have much temptation to use the opportunities of their situation to their own advantage. As a rule they are of the same class as the village ryots, and are themselves cultivators. It is not therefore matter of surprise when it happens, as it often does, that the plots which are in their hands are the best in the village. Their proper work prevents them from actually labouring in the fields, and they are supposed to pay those of the other ryots who till the soil for them, but it is too frequently the case that they manage somehow to get this done gratis. And they are by no means ignorant of the art of obtaining the offer of gratifications when they require them. The office is in a sense hereditary, *viz.*, the son generally succeeds the father in it. But this is almost a necessity, for it is seldom the case that more than one or two others in the village possess the small knowledge of reading, writing, and account-keeping, which is needed for the work.

Indeed the ryots are universally uneducated and ignorant, and in an extreme degree susceptible to the influence of authority. The relation between them and the zamindar is quasi-feudal in its character. He is their superior lord and they are his subjects (ryots), both by habit and by feeling "*adscripti glebæ.*" They would be entirely at the mercy of the zamindar and his *amla* were it not for another most remarkable village institution, namely, the *mandal*[1]; this is the village head man, the mouthpiece and representative of the ryots of the village in all matters between them and the zamindar or his officers. The mandal is a cultivator like the rest of the ryots, and by no means necessarily the richest among them. He holds his position in some supposed manner dependent upon

---

[1] This is his most common designation. The name, however, varies with districts.

their suffrages, but the office in fact almost invariably passes from father to son, and so is hereditary for the same reason that all occupations and employments in India are hereditary. His qualifications are, sufficient knowledge of reading, writing, and *zamindari* accounts, and thorough acquaintance with the customary rights of the villagers. He receives no emolument directly, but the other ryots will generally from time to time help him gratuitously in his cultivation, and it is not unfrequently the case that he pays a less rate of rent for his land than the ordinary occupying ryot does. It is impossible thoroughly to describe the *mandal's* functions in a few sentences. He is so completely recognised as the spokesman of the ryots, one and all, on every occasion, that it is often exceedingly difficult to extract, in his absence, from an individual ryot information upon even the commonest and most indifferent matter. The *mandal* and a few of the elder men constitute the village *panchayat*, by whom most of the ordinary disputes and quarrels are adjusted. In more obstinate cases the *mandal* and the parties go to the zamindar, or his representative the *naib* or *gumashta*, for discussion and arbitration. Thus very much of the administration of justice in the rural districts of Bengal is effected without the need of recourse to the formal and expensive machinery of the public courts.

When the village is one in which the zamindar resides, it will often be the case that the barber who shaves the members of his family, the *dhobi* who washes for them, the head *darwan* (or porter) and other principal servants all hereditary, hold their portion of the village land, at relatively low rents or even rent free, in consideration of their services. In addition to this the *dhobi* and the barber, for instance, have the right to be employed at customary rates of pay by all the ryots. Sometimes the carpenter and the blacksmith are in the like situation. There is also a hereditary village *chaukidar* (or watchman) who gets his land rent free. And the Brahman priest, whether of the zamindar's family, or maintained for the village *pujas*, &c., is supported in the same mode.

We have thus before us, in the Bengal village community, a social structure which, for want of a better term, may in a certain qualified sense be called feudal. The principal features can be summed up as follows :—At the bottom is the great mass of hereditary cultivators of the village lands (ryots); at the top the superior lord entitled to rents and dues from these cultivators (zamindar); next to him, and connected with his interests, come those who constitute his fiscal organisation *(amla)* and his privileged servants; on the other side, again, are the representatives and officers of the village, and by the union of both elements, so to speak, is formed a court leet which when occasion requires disposes of any topics of internal friction by the authoritative declaration of custom and usage.

Outside this system, with no recognised place in in it, yet nevertheless the motive power by which it is kept working, is the *mahājan*, or village capitalist. The Bengal ryot, except only a fraction of the whole class, has no accumulated wealth—no pecuniary means other than that which his own labour on the land can earn for him. He carries on a business, however, which from time to time and periodically, requires outlay of money. There is a hut of the homestead to be new built or repaired, a plough or other implement to be made, a pair of bullocks to be bought, seed for sowing to be procured, above all rice to be got for the food of himself and his family, and also several *kists* of his rent to be paid before all his crops can be secured and realised. Alone and unaided, he is almost invariably unable to meet all these current demands. In the western part of the Delta his savings are seldom sufficient to tide him wholly over the time which must elapse before the year's production comes in. To the *mahājan*, therefore, he is obliged to go for money and for *paddy* as he wants them. The commonest course of dealings between the parties is as follows:—The *paddy* for sowing and for food, and also other seed, is provided upon the terms that it is to be returned together with a surplus of fifty per cent. in quantity at the time of harvest; and the money is advanced upon condition of being repaid, also at harvest time, with two per cent. per mensem interest either in the shape of an equivalent of *paddy*, reckoned at bazaar prices, or in cash at the option of the lender. As security for the due carrying out of this arrangement, the *mahājan* frequently takes an hypothecation of the ryot's future crop, and helps himself to the stipulated amount on the very threshing floor, in the open field.

The actual result of this state of things is, at least, curious to the eye of the European observer. The zamindar, who at first sight appears to fill the place of an English landlord, is merely a rent charger; the ryot, who seems to have a beneficial interest of a more or less permanent nature in his allotments, is scarcely more than a field labourer, living from hand to mouth; and the *mahājan*, who in effect furnishes the farming capital, pays the labour and takes all the profits, is a stranger, having no proprietary interest in the land. He is a creditor only, whose sole object is to realise his money as advantageously as possible. After setting aside in his *golas*, as much of the produce come to his hands, as he is likely to need for his next year's business advances in kind, he deals with the rest simply as a cornfactor, sending it to the most remunerative market. A thriving *mahājan* may have a whole *mauzah*, or even more under his hand, and yet he has no legitimate proprietary status in the community, while those who have, namely, the ryot on one hand and the zamindar on the other, for different reasons are apparently powerless. The consequent unprogressive character of an agricultural village cannot be more graphically described than by the words of an intelligent young zamindar.[1]

"A husbandman of the present day is the

---

[1] Babu Peary Chund Mookerjee, *Beng. Soc. Sci. Trans.* vol. iv. sec. 4, p. 1.

primitive being he always has been. With a piece of rag round his loins for his clothing, bare feet, a miserable hut to live in, and a daily fare of the coarsest description, he lives a life which, however disturbed it may be by other causes, is unruffled by ambition. If he gets his two meals and plain clothing he is content with his lot, and if he can spare a few rupees for purchasing jewellery for his wife and children, and a few rupees more for religious ceremonies, he will consider himself as happy as he can wish to be. He is the greatest enemy of social reform, and never dreams of throwing off any of the trammels which time or superstition has spun around him. He will not send his son to school for fear of being deprived of his manual assistance in the field ; he will not drink the water of a good tank because he has been accustomed to use the water of the one nearer his house; he will not sow a crop of potatoes or sugarcane because his forefathers never did it; he will allow himself to be unmercifully fleeced by his hereditary priest to secure the hope of utter annihilation after death, but he will not listen to any proposal which would place within his reach a few of the conveniences or comforts of life. There are agricultural villages in which the existence of a school or of a dispensary, and the condition of the houses, roads, and tanks show a happier state of things, but it will be found that in almost all such cases the improvements have been made not by the ryots but by a rich trader, employer, or landholder, who resides in the village, or takes an interest in its welfare. The ryots themselves are too poor, too ignorant, too disunited among themselves to effect any such improvement."

III.

DOMESTIC LIFE.

AND more than one cause occurs to limit the activity of zamindars in this matter to very few instances. It is sufficient for the moment to say that wealthy enterprising zamindars are very rare in the Mofussil. The Hindu gentleman of the Bengali village, the landed proprietor, so to speak, of the locality, may have an income of some Rs. 200 or Rs. 300 per annum at most. He may not always have even a *pakka* house. His property is probably a share of the village, or of several villages together, held on some tenure, the general nature of which will be hereafter described, and his net income is that which remains of the collections made from the ryots after he has paid the *jama* of his tenure to the superior holder, or to the Government, as the case may be. His life is a very quiet one, unmarked by the characteristics of either a very active or a very refined form of civilization. His daily routine may be sufficiently described without much difficulty. He gets up before sunrise, and if he be an orthodox Hindu, as he sits upon his bed he utters, in the place of a formal prayer, the name of "Dúrga" several times in succession. Then he performs some slight ablutions. At this point the habits of Brahmans vary from those of other Hindus. The Brahman goes at once after these ablutions to bathe in the river, if there is one, near at hand; if not, to the tank attached to his house, or to the village tank. As he stands in the water, and when he comes out, he repeats, by way of prayer, Sanskrit *mantras* which he does not understand. In any village situated on the bank of a river may be seen, very early in the morning, men of the most respectable class and position returning home after bathing and muttering these *mantras* as they go. Men of respectability (*bhadralog*), however, who are not Brahmans, do not think it necessary to bathe so early, or to say anything in the shape of prayer, beyond the utterance of the name of Dúrga two or three times on rising from bed.

It used to be the practice for pious Hindus, in addition to this, to write the name of Dúrga on a plaintain leaf as many as two hundred or three hundred times every morning after the first washing, but this old custom has died out, except in perhaps a few excessively conservative families of Eastern Bengal, and now-a-days, the ordinary village proprietor of the higher class, after his early ablutions, without further preliminary, takes his seat in his *baithakhana* upon the *takhtaposh* (if, as is usually the case, there is one), which is generally covered with a white *chadr*. There he receives all whom business, or desire for gossip, may bring to see him. His ryots who come sit at a little distance on the floor, while visitors of the *bhadralog* sit on the *takhtaposh* with the master of the house. *Hukhas* for smoking are offered to each one in turn, and for this purpose two *hukhas* are generally kept ready, one for Brahmans, the other for kyasths, &c., that for the use of Brahmans being distinguished by a cowrie hanging pendent from it by a string. Not to give a visitor the offer of a smoke would be considered as very uncourteous and rude.

The Bengal village gentleman generally transacts all his business in the morning, sitting in the way just described in his *baithakhana*, while his wife is simultaneously engaged in the kitchen. He will not take food before bathing, for to do so would be considered very wrong. He remains in his *baithakhana* usually until 11 or about 11.30 A.M., sometimes even later. Then when all his visitants are gone he causes his servant to bring oil and this he rubs all over his body and head as a preliminary to going to bathe.

When he returns from bathing, which will

generally be about noon, he goes to the inner apartments (*andar mahāl*) of the house, *i.e.*, to the portion of the house or homestead which is allotted to the female members of the family, and which strangers and non-privileged males are not allowed to enter. There, if he is orthodox and has "taken the *mantra*" from his family priest, he first performs *pūjā*, and then has his breakfast brought. The servant of the house or the women of the family sweep the floor of the room or verandah where he usually takes his meals, and spread a square piece of carpet (*ashan*) or place a square wooden board for him to sit (cross-legged) upon. His food is served in a *thāl*[1] or on a stone platter by his wife, his children sit round him, and his mother comes and sits in front of him to see that everything is done as it should be; if the wife is young she seldom speaks to him in the presence of the mother, and if he has to ask for anything he does so generally through the mother. The breakfast

---

[1] A "thāl" is a metal plate or dish.

commonly consists of rice as a principal item and in considerable quantity, some kind of *dāl* (split pulse), a few vegetables separately prepared, one fish curry, sometimes also an acid curry taken after the ordinary curry, and lastly milk and sugar. The food is mostly conveyed from the platter to the mouth with the fingers of the right hand; the right hand alone can be used for this purpose, and no food may be touched with the left. Having finished eating, the master of the house washes his right hand and his mouth, receives a *pān* (betel leaf) prepared with spices by the women of the family for chewing, returns to his *baithakhana*, smokes his *hukha* and lies down to sleep for an hour or two during the hottest part of the day, namely, from about 1 P.M. to 3 P.M.

About 3 P.M. his siesta over, he does whatever work of the morning he may have left unfinished, or goes out to see his neighbours or his ryots, returning shortly after dusk, when he takes some refreshment (*tiffin*) or lunch in the shape of sweetmeats. For the rest of the evening he sits in his *baithakhana* conversing with friends and neighbours who may have come in, or plays games with cards or dice, or plays chess. In this manner he amuses himself and passes his time till dinner, or the last meal of the day is announced about 10 P.M., a female servant comes and says "rice is ready," and he goes for his dinner to the same place where he took his breakfast, and eats it in the same fashion. In fact, there is scarcely any difference between the morning meal, either in regard to the food or to any other particular. The second is essentially a repetition of the first.

The women of the house always take their meals after the men have finished theirs; and all the members of the family retire to their sleeping quarters immediately after the night meal.

The foregoing is a brief outline of the every-day life of a Bengali village proprietor belonging to the gentleman class who lives on an income of say from Rs. 200 to Rs. 500 a year derived from land.

It should be added that the women of the family do a great deal of domestic work, such as cooking, pounding rice, fetching water, &c. Early in the morning they sprinkle water over the *uthan*, and proceed to clean the *thāls* and the cups used the previous evening. Of such a family as that just described, the female members are not so secluded as the women of a similar family would be in a large town. In a Bengali village all the neighbours are allowed to see and speak with the women of the family (except the newly-married *baus*, not belonging to the village) unless they are prevented by village relationship.

Domestic life in a cultivator's family is, of course, very different from that of the *bhadralog* just described. The exigencies of field labour, cattle tending, and poverty introduce very considerable disturbing causes. Still there are generic features of resemblance between the two. The women prepare the meals for the men, and these are eaten in the more private part of the homestead which answers to the inner apartments of the gentlemen's *bāri,* also the women take their meals after the men have eaten. The food is almost exclusively rice, *dāl* and vegetable curries. Now and then fish is an ingredient in it, and occasionally milk. The front verandah of the principal hut of the homestead is the ryot's *baithakhana,* and there, after his day's work is done, he will spread a mat for his neighbour and share with him his hubble-bubble. Or a village group will form under a convenient *pīpal* tree, and gossip and smoke away the affairs of the *mauzah.*

It is the universal habit in Bengal prevalent in all classes for the members of a family to live joint and to enjoy the profits of property jointly. What this amounts to is by no means easy to describe in few sentences. To take the instance of a ryot's family, it grows joint somewhat in this fashion; namely, on the death of the father, his sons, who before were dependent members of the family living in the same homestead and assisting him in the cultivation of his *jot*, henceforward continue still in the same homestead, cultivating the same *jot*, but now in the capacity of owners. Sometimes they get their own names collectively substituted for that of their father in the books of the zamindar's *kachahri;* and sometimes the dead man's name is allowed to remain there unaltered. While thus situated each brother with his wife and children, if possible, occupies a separate hut in the homestead, and as often as is necessary for this purpose, or when it can be afforded, an additional hut is added to the group.

Also in this state of things, the brothers are by law entitled to equal shares by inheritance in the whole of any heritable property which they have thus taken in common from their deceased father, and each has a right at any time to compel a partition. In the event of one of the brothers dying, his sons, if he has any, if not, his widow, step into his place and represent him in all respects.

This sort of process carried on for several

generations obviously would bring about a very complex distribution of undivided shares; but in the case of ryots it very speedily comes to an end by reason of the smallness of the original subject rendering the aliquot parts insignificant. Before that stage is reached the younger members of the family give up or sell their shares to the others and find occupation elsewhere as best they can. When the *jot* is inheritable in its nature the members of the family while living in the same homestead will actually divide the land among themselves according to their shares and cultivate separately. In this way the land in some villages has come to be subdivided into absurdly small plots, and this evil has a natural tendency to increase rather than diminish.

When the family is well off and has considerable possessions as well, it may be, in the way of trade as in the shape of zamindaries and other landed tenures, the state of "jointhood" commonly long remains. The whole property is managed by one member of the family who is called the "karta" and who is usually the eldest individual of the eldest branch. He is theoretically responsible in a certain vague way to the entire body of joint co-sharers, each of whom can, if he likes, see the family books of accounts and papers which are regularly kept in a sort of office (or *daftarkhāna*) by the family servants; but as a matter of fact it is seldom that any one interferes until some occasion of quarrel arises and is fought out with acrimony, a partition effected and accounts insisted upon. Events of this kind happen from time to time, with ultimate wholesome effect, but as a rule the co-sharers are only too willing to let well alone, content to be supported in the family house, out of the family funds, without asking any questions, each getting, as he wants, sufficient small sums of money for ordinary personal expenses. This constitutes the enjoyment of the joint family property by a joint family. Whatever money is saved, after the disbursement of the general family and proprietary expenses, is invested by the *karta* in the purchase of some addition to the joint property; and whatever money is required for the performance of extraordinary family ceremonies or religious performances is commonly raised by the *karta* in the form of a loan charged on the joint property. The family proprietary body is thus a sort of corporation the ostensible head of which is the *karta*, and in which the individual members have acquired no proprietary rights as distinct from those of the whole body, except the right on the part of each co-sharer to separate at any moment and have his aliquot share of the common property divided off and given to him.

The domestic community which in this system of living grows up under, so to speak, the same roof-tree is curiously heterogeneous and sometimes very numerous. There are first the co-sharers; these are brothers, nephews, and male cousins whose fathers' shares have devolved upon them and the widows or daughters of co-sharers, who have died without leaving sons or grandsons; and secondly, there is the mixed class of dependent members made up of the wives and children of existing co-sharers, the wives and daughters of former co-sharers (whose shares went to sons) and individuals labouring under any such infirmity as disqualifies them from inheriting. Instances occur in Calcutta and even in the Mofussil, of families comprehending as many as 300 or 400 individuals including servants living in one house; and it is probably usual for a family to amount to something between 50 and 100.

The Bengali's house is everywhere, whether in town or in the country village, and whether large or small, of one typical form, especially adapted to the needs of joint family life; its principal elements are apparent even in the homestead of the smallest ryot. That of an old family may be described as follows:—The building is of brick, and two-storied, that is, it has a ground floor and a first floor; the term "upper-roomed house" always designates a house which ranks above the ordinary run of respectability. The front is generally long, exhibiting

G

a pillared verandah or a row of French casement and jillmilled windows on the first floor. The entrance is by an archway, or large square-headed door in the centre of the front; and in the entrance passage, often on both sides of it, is a raised floor with one or two open cells in which the *darwans* (or door-keepers) sit, lie, and sleep—in fact dwell. This is the *deorhi* and answers to the *conciergerie* of French houses. The entrance passage on the inside opens upon a quadrangle which may or may not be complete. On the quadrangle side the house is generally faced all round by a two-storied pillared verandah which serves as a passage or corridor for each floor, and gives access to the different rooms; the upper verandah is reached from the lower by a narrow winding staircase of steep brick-built steps usually situated at the corners and very closely resembling turret stairs of an English country church. From outside to inside the breadth of the house is always very narrow, and as the rooms are less than the full width by the width of the verandah, they are also necessarily narrow; sometimes, however, they are found of considerable length. On one side of the quadrangle is the *puja dalan*. This may be described to be the verandah of the other sides very much enlarged and deepened. It is approached from the central area by a flight of steps, which in its breadth occupies nearly the whole length of the side, and its lofty ceiling is supported by inner pillars additional to those which stand in the place of the ordinary verandah pillars. Its chief purpose is to serve as a stage for the performance of religious and domestic ceremonies on special occasions, the quadrangular area then affording convenient space for the general audience of dependents and invited guests; and the women of the house, themselves unseen, finding gazing places in the upper windows and verandah. At these times the quadrangle is commonly covered in by a *shamiana* stretched across the top from side to side. In this manner a magnificent reception hall or theatre can be constructed in almost every native gentleman's house at the shortest notice.

Besides this first quadrangle, there is often in large houses a second or a third quadrangle, and even more, the one behind or annexed to the other, much as is the case in our colleges at Oxford or Cambridge. Then, too, there is the *thakurbāri* or chamber, where the figure of the family deity resides and where the daily service or worship of the *thakur* is performed by the inferior family priest. Among Brahmans, and also *kulin kaists*, who are now-a-days privileged to receive the *mantra*, the father and mother of any branch of the family may for some purposes each have his or her private personal *thakur* quite apart from the family *thakur*. But neither a *kaist* nor even a Brahman woman can themselves worship the family idol or any visible *thakur*, except the clay figure of Siva which is made for every-day worship. They must make their daily *puja* and utter *mantras* apart from any idol.[1]

---

[1] The Shastras forbid to women and Sudras all knowledge and use of sacred texts.

It is by no means easy to describe the mode in which a large family distributes itself over a house such as that just now sketched. If the stage which the family has reached is three or four generations removed from the common ancestor there will be several heads of branches; and these branches will settle themselves per stirpes, so to speak, in separate parts of the house under their own heads, more or less separate from the rest. Sometimes this separation is so complete that the portion of the house allotted to each branch is parted off from the remainder of the house by such blocking up of doors as may be necessary for the purpose and by the opening of a separate entrance. Each group as a rule messes by itself, and every adult member of it has a room to himself in which he lives, all the female members together finding accommodation of some sort in the *inner apartments*, *i.e.* the portion of the dwelling house which is allotted to the females, and commonly among Europeans called the zenana. All the branches usually keep joint with regard to the worship of the family deity. And even when the different branches have gone so far as to sever in everything, *i.e.* in food, worship, and estate, as the phrase is, the same family deity is commonly retained by all, and the worship of it conducted by the different separated branches in turn, each turn proportionate in duration to the owner's share in the joint property. For instance, if the family in its divided state is represented by four heads, namely, two brothers and their two nephews, sons of a third brother deceased, the turns or pallas of worship would be respectively four months, four months, two months, and two months or equimultiples of these.

It is, of course, only in Calcutta or other very large towns that the family swarm continues in the family hive at such dimensions as those just mentioned. But in the few country villages, where the zamindar's family has been fortunate enough to maintain itself for many generations, much about the same thing occurs. There will be the brick-built, quadrangled house with imposing front, sheltering under one connected roof many families of cousins who bear to each other varying degrees of relationship and constitute in the whole a joint family, all the adult independent members of which have their own joint (but separable) coparcenary interest in the property of the family whatever that be. The *karta* of this family (generally by the nature of the case the senior member) is in most respects the ostensible head, and although in the village all of the others are "the babus," yet he is especially "*the* babu" to whose activity such good work, when it is done, as the maintenance of a dispensary, the support of the *mandir* and its priest, and the keeping the *mandap* in good condition, is to be attributed.

IV.

GRAVE AND GAY.

AMUSEMENTS do not appear to occupy any great space of life in a Bengali village. Although the circumstances of agricultural labour are such as to leave the ryot in comparative idleness for the larger part of the year, the truth seems to be that, for generations, the rural population has been a pauper, under-fed class, and does not possess the vigour and excess vitality, which, in the case of the Burmese, overflows in vivacious games and athletic sports. Bright, hearty, healthy play of a boisterous character is seldom or never to be met with among the children. Gymnastics, however, of undoubted indigenous origin, is, in some places, a great favourite and very successfully pursued, and there are parts of Bengal in which the boys have even laid hold of cricket. Nevertheless, all Bengalis are possessed with an inordinate love of spectacles and shows of every kind. The Hindus flock as readily to the public religious processions and displays of the Muhammadans as to their own, and *vice versâ*. The Muhammadans find occasions for these at the Muharram and some other periodic commemorations of events in the lives of the Prophet and his chief apostles. And the Hindus have their village *pújas*, which are celebrated with more or less show and magnificence according to the wealth and public spiritedness of the local zamindar. Then there are from time to time family festivals and ceremonies already spoken of at the houses of the better-to-do folks, such as marriages, shraddas, readings of the Rāmāyana, &c.

The Bengali ryot is not often in a hurry. He dearly loves an opportunity for a bit of gossip and the hubble-bubble, and the evening groups under the *pīpal* tree are usually the wholesome substitutes for the *tarí* shop. Drinking does, however, obtain to a considerable extent among the lower castes and is said to be increasing. Native writers are fond of attributing the introduction of this vice or, at any rate, its encouragement in some way to the English, but there can be no real doubt that it is a natural product of the country itself.[1] In a portion of the Veds the delights of intoxication are dwelt upon, and some of the *tantric* writings are devoted to the encouragement of drink. The habit of drinking appears to have been so mischievously prevalent in the best days of the Muhammadan rule as to have called for repeated prohibitive legislation. And, indeed, the spirit which is everywhere drunk, namely *tarí*, is evidently of purely home origin, and is made largely in every village by crude native methods from many sorts of saccharine juices, especially from the juice of the *tarí* palm.

Gambling has great charms to the Bengali of all

[1] *Journal of Asiatic Society* for 1873, Part I. No. 1.

ranks, and some very amusing modes of applying the element of chance are in vogue. But gambling with cards and dice is the common form prevalent with the middle classes.

To describe fully the religious aspect of a Bengal village community would be a very long and difficult task—a task, indeed, which a foreigner could hardly carry through with success. A few of its more conspicuous features may, however, be pointed out without much risk of error. The Muhammadans exhibit two very distinct sects in Bengal, namely, the Sunnís and the Shias. Both seem to be a good deal given to observances and practices of Hinduism; and it is pretty clear that the Bengali Musalman is nothing but a roughly converted Hindu. He is quite undistinguishable from the ordinary Hindu in all race characteristics, and retains very marked caste notions and habits. In the best and most fertile parts of the delta the Muhammadan element exceeds 60 per cent. of the population, and in the rest of Bengal Proper it rises as high as 30 or 40 per cent. In some districts the agricultural villages are either wholly Muhammadan or wholly Hindu, but more commonly each village has its Muhammadan quarter and its Hindu quarter.

Hinduism also has its sects quite apart from its castes, though a marked distinction of sect is apt in the end to become synonymous with distinction of caste. The peculiarity of Hinduism, which has been already spoken of, namely, its want of the congregational element, seems to favour the growth of sects. At any rate, no one appears to care much what particular form of faith his neighbour professes, as long as it is not of an aggressive character. It may look like making an exception to say that Christians are a good deal objected to in an agricultural village; but this is mainly for two reasons, *i.e.*—1*st*, because it is generally supposed to be of the essence of Christianity to work actively towards the subversion of Hinduism; 2*ndly*, because Christian ryots backed by the support (by no means always judiciously given) which they obtain from European missionaries are apt to be a very contumacious, unaccommodating set of people.

We find pretty universally in the rural villages, Boistobs, Saktas, Sivas, Ganapatyas, &c. Of Boistobs there are an immense number of varieties or sub-divisions. Their chief distinguishing tenet seems to be that Vishnu is the Brahma : that he existed before all worlds, and was the cause and creator of all. They endue him with the highest moral attributes, and they believe that, besides his more exalted form as creator of all things, he has at different times and for the benefit of his creatures assumed particular forms and appearances. The best known and most celebrated of these is Krishna ; whose bright and frolicsome, and, indeed, somewhat sensual career of adventure on earth is a very fascinating topic of contemplation to his votaries.[1]

[1] It is perhaps noteworthy that a great many educated Bengalis have the notion that our Christ is none other than their Krishna.

The chief development of the Boistobs originated with Chaitanya, who preached purity, meditation, and the equality of all men, without distinction of sect or caste, before God. He threw aside all ceremonies and outward symbols. And a certain freedom from caste trammels and disregard of religious observances, with an appreciation of the importance of conduct, still seem to characterise the sect. The Boistobs have been, and even now are being, recruited from all castes, but taken together in all their varieties they are commonly reckoned as a sort of caste by themselves. Their especially ascetic members go by the designation of Bairagi (amongst others), and live a life of mendicancy and freedom which, as has been already mentioned, is not always altogether reputable.

The Saktas, perhaps, constitute the majority of the inhabitants of the villages. They have come to be, in a great degree, united with the Saivas. These latter look upon Siva (the destroyer) as the primary and more exalted form of Brahma, and the Saktas especially contemplate and worship the divine nature in its activity, in other words, the female forms of the supreme deity, as Dúrga or Kalí. The Sivaite and Sakta worship is in a marked degree a worship of dogma, of gorgeous ceremony, and bloody sacrifices. The Sakta consider themselves conservative of the purer and Puranic type of religion. Like the Pharisees of Judea, they are strict in small observances with regard to food, meals, &c., perhaps even to the neglect of the larger precepts of the law. It was against this system and its abuses that Chaitanya lifted up his voice, and that the Boistobs are the protestants; but the older faith still appeals the most successfully to the passions of men, and with its vicarious helps to acceptance with God still holds sway with the masses of the people.

The Ganapatyas hardly, perhaps, deserve to be called a distinct sect. They particularly seek the protection of Ganesa, and devote themselves to his worship, but apart from this they may belong to almost any sect of Hinduism.

The mention of these different sects of Hinduism leads naturally up to a description of a very remarkable institution, which although it does not by any means find illustration in every village of Bengal, yet is very common in certain parts of the presidency. In most of the sects there is (as it may be termed) a clerical class, which is itself separated into two orders, namely, to use European designations, the monastic (or ascetic) and the secular. The monastic order is celibate and in a great degree erratic and mendicant, but has anchorage places and headquarters in the *maths*. The original meaning of the word *math* seems to be cell or chamber, as of a hermit.[1] Now-a-days the typical *math* consists of an endowed temple or shrine, with a dwelling-place for a superior (the Mohant) and his disciples (*chelas*). The endowment of a *math* is either the result of private dedication, or it is the subject of a grant

[1] For the root of the word see Thomas's *Jainism*, note, p. 3.

made by an already existing wealthy *math*. In the latter case the new institution becomes an off-shoot of the old, and remains allied with it in some sort of subordination. The extent or amount of the property is not generally very large; though in exceptional cases it is so, and in some *maths* the Mohants, either by decline from the strict path of sanctity originally marked out for them, or even in prosecution of the founder's purpose, make the acquirement of wealth by trade their great object. Instances of this are most plentiful in the north-western parts of the Bengal presidency, where numerous trader Mohants of great wealth and influence are to be found.

As a rule, the Mohant, when he devoted himself to the ascetic form of religious life, *ipso facto*, severed himself from all such worldly possessions as he might otherwise have been entitled to as an ordinary member of society. He became theoretically dead to the world, and incapable of holding or inheriting property generally. But with regard to the property of the *math* or Mohantship it is different. The Hindu law recognises a special devolution of the property belonging to a *math* upon the occurrence of the death of the Mohant. A certain precept[1] in the writings of the sages to the effect that the virtuous pupil takes the property, is the foundation of the different rules observed in different cases. The variation is in the manner in which the virtuous pupil is ascertained. There are instances of *maths* in which the Mohantship descends to a personal heir of the deceased; and others in which the existing Mohant appoints his successor. But the ordinary rule is, that the *maths* of the same sect in a district are associated together, the Mohants of these acknowledging one of their number, who is for some cause pre-eminent, as their head; and on the occasion of the death of one, the others of the associated body assemble to elect a successor out of the *chelas* (or disciples) of the deceased, if possible; or, if there be none of them qualified,

[1] *Mitak.* chap. 2, sec. 8, sl. 1—6.

then from the *chelas* of another Mohant. After the election the chosen disciple is installed on the *gaddi* of his predecessor with much ceremony. Sometimes most unseemly struggles for the succession take place. It has happened that two rivals, each backed by a section of neighbouring Mohants and other partizans, though neither, perhaps, very regularly, a *chela* of the deceased, have started up to make title to the vacant Mohantship. Both accompanied the dead body a long distance to the sacred river and put fire into the mouth, as the corpse was launched into the Ganges. Both returned to be formally elected by their respective adherents in two separate *majlís* held within the same compound of the *math*. Both were carried in a grand procession with elephants and horses and flags and drums and a crowd of followers round the village; and, finally, both came into a court of law to establish, by prolonged litigation reaching even to the Privy Council, rights which probably neither of them was strictly entitled to.

The *mandir* (or temple) of the *math*, if there is one in the village, is generally a conspicuous object. It has usually only one chamber, in which the *thakur* or image of the deity resides, and its ground section is a square of no great dimensions; but it is often carried up to a considerable height, and terminates in various, more or less, conoidal forms. In some districts it is acutely pointed, and presents very much the appearance of an English church-spire, as it is seen from a distance piercing the village mass of foliage.

There are also very frequently to be seen, in or about a village, *mandirs* which do not belong to any *math;* these commonly owe their origin to private dedication. There is seldom, however, any endowment attached to them, or, perhaps, just sufficient lakheraj land to maintain the attendant Brahman who performs the daily worship and keeps the place in order. More often the Brahman gets his living out of the offerings made to the *thakur* and the contribution of the orthodox, or is supported by the zamindar.

A shrine (*dargah*) or tomb of some holy Muhammadan *fakir* is often to be met with on the wayside, with the hut or homestead of its keeper near at hand. Passers-by of all creeds and denominations throw in their cowries and pice. And if the sanctity of the deceased be much out of the common, the tomb may even be a valuable source of revenue. In that case it is treated as a subject of property which passes by inheritance from owner to owner, and the keeper is paid by salary from the person entitled to it. Generally, however, the keeper of the place alone is interested in it, and transmits his humble effects to his heirs.

In a large village there will be a *mandap, i.e.* a spacious open-sided covered-in room, in a sense, a vestry-room, where the village *púja* festivals are celebrated and other village gatherings occur. Sometimes the *mandap* is a *pakka* structure, the roof being supported on brick-built pillars. But more often it is of bamboo and thatch. It is usually kept up by the zamindar.

V.

RURAL CRIME.

Rural crime does not assume any very varied forms. One of the commonest is dacoity (*dakaiti*), *i.e.* gang robbery. The *badmashes* or bad characters of two or three adjoining villages are, to a certain extent, associated together. They are ostensibly ryots, or sons of ryots, and like everyone else about them are more or less dependent upon agricultural labour for their livelihood. Though it generally happens that they become to their neighbours the objects of a somewhat undefined suspicion, still, as a rule, they manage to maintain their social position whatever that may be. Their method of operation is very simple. Some one whose reputation for accumulated wealth makes him worth attacking is selected. A dark or stormy night is taken for the purpose, and then the band assembles under a *pīpal* tree, or at some other convenient place of assignation. Each man wears a mask or is in some other manner disguised, and carries some weapon : *lāttees* are the most common, but sometimes quaint old swords of an almost forgotten shape make their appearance; and instruments specially contrived for cutting open mat walls and probing thatch are brought out. From the place of assembling the gang proceeds to the victim's homestead, and surrounds it; next, at a signal, when all is ready, the more daring rush forward and break into the homestead by cutting through the matting, or forcing down a door, or climbing over the roof. The males who may be sleeping in the outside verandah are immediately seized and bound. Those who are inside are not always so easily disposed of, because they will probably have been aroused by the uproar before their assailants reach them. In a very few seconds, however, as the attacking party is invariably greatly superior in force, and by no means scrupulous in the use of their weapons, these too succumb and are bound hand and foot or are otherwise secured.

Then commences the looting, which must be effected very hurriedly, for a little delay might suffice to bring the whole village down upon the robbers. A torch or two is lighted, *pitaras* forced open, every likely corner is searched. The floor of the huts is hastily probed or is dug up to discover the buried pot, which is a favourite form of safe for the custody of jewels or of spare cash when it happens that the ryot has any. Or perhaps the owner of the homestead is compelled by torture to reveal the place of his valuables: for instance he is rolled naked backwards and forwards over hot ashes, or a burning torch is held under his armpits, &c. All the booty which can in these modes be laid hold of is promptly carried off, each man loading himself with what he succeeds in putting his hands upon. If there is a probability of immediate pursuit, everyone will go his own way, and take care of himself, and all will meet again subsequently in some previously determined spot to divide the spoil. If there is no such danger, the *dakaits* will at once go to a place of meeting (in a jungle if possible) and settle each man's share of the stolen property.

The police are almost entirely powerless to prevent these outrages, and they cannot always be said to be successful in detecting the perpetrators of them. There can be no doubt that in some parts of Bengal the profession of a *dákait* is sufficiently lucrative to tempt idle men to brave its risks. If somewhat irregular measures were not taken to suppress it, probably it would attain unendurable dimensions. Accordingly, the police may sometimes be found waging a warfare against *dákaiti* which is very characteristic. When information of a *dákaiti* having been committed reaches the thannah, a Darogah with a few *chaukidars* goes at once to the spot. He satisfies himself by inquiries as to who are the reputed *badmashes* of the neighbourhood, and then immediately arrests some one, two, or three of them, such as he thinks will be most likely, under the circumstances of the case, to serve his purposes. Having thus got these unfortunate men into their hands, the police, by promises of pardon coupled with material inducements, which, in most cases, amount to a refined system of torture, procure them to make confessions and to implicate a great many others of the previously ascertained *badmashes*. The next step, of course, is to arrest all these, and to search their houses. At this stage of matters the complainant is in a position such as to render him a ready tool of the police. He will have a nest of hornets about his ears for some years to come, unless he succeeds in bringing a conviction home to each of the arrested men. So he seldom finds much difficulty in recognising in the searched houses articles which had been stolen from him. If, however, for any cause he cannot at first do this, the police have recourse to a very simple expedient for the purpose of assisting him. They obtain from the bazar, or elsewhere, articles similar to those which the complainant says he has lost; and, under colour of watching the prisoners' houses, manage to get these articles secreted in or about the premises according as opportunity may offer itself. About this time the Sub-Inspector or other officer charged, as it is termed, with the investigation of the case, comes upon the ground. Also the prisoners, who have all of them been separately and constantly worked upon by the police, have generally become pliable enough to confess in accordance with the story marked out for them, and sometimes even are persuaded to point out (under the guidance, of course, of the *chaukidars*) the very places where the imported articles have been concealed! These places are generally, for obvious reasons, more often outside the accused persons' homestead than inside, such as in tanks, trunks of trees, under the soil of the *khēt*, &c. But sometimes opportunity serves for placing the articles inside the very huts of the dwelling.

The Inspector on his arrival thus finds his case complete; he takes it before the Magistrate; the evidence of the witnesses is written down; the articles are produced and sworn to. It seems that they have all been found in the prisoners' possession in consequence of information or clues afforded by the prisoners themselves, and the case of the prosecution is overwhelming. But even the very last nail is riveted by the prisoners, or most of them, confessing in the most satisfactory manner possible. Thereupon they are all committed to take their trial at the Sessions in due course. On entering the prison walls the state of things changes very much. The committed prisoners are relieved from the immediate personal supervision and control of the police. They converse freely with one another and with other prisoners waiting trial; they also communicate with Mookhtars or law agents, concerning their defence. They find that whether innocent or guilty, they have made great fools of themselves by confessing at the police dictation;

and the upshot of it is, that when the trial in the Sessions Court comes on they all plead not guilty, and say that their former confessions were forced from them by the police. This, however, avails them but little. Their recorded confessions are put in against them, and the Court with the remark that prisoners always do retract when they get into jail, holds that the confessions are supported by the discovery of the articles, convicts the prisoners, and sentences them to long terms of imprisonment or transportation.

When a case of this character occurs the Sessions Judge is not usually quite unconscious of the police practices in these matters, but he is almost invariably, in the particular case before him (and often rightly), so convinced of the guilt of the persons whom he is trying that he is astute enough to find out reasons why the confessions produced in evidence were made voluntarily, and why the alleged finding of the stolen articles may be depended upon. On a comparatively recent occasion of this kind the Judge said that he could not help seeing that the police had behaved very cruelly to the prisoners, and had made them illegal promises of pardon in order to extort confessions; but still he thought that the discovery of the articles on the premises of the different prisoners (effected, by the way, in a more than ordinarily suspicious manner) entirely corroborated and rendered trustworthy the confessions which were made.[1]

[1] The mode of action on the part of the police, which is above illustrated, is a survival from former times, and is from its nature very difficult of riddance. The tendency of the Bengal policeman seems to be to force out truth rather than to find out truth. He is not apt at building up a case with independent and circumstantial materials drawn from various sources, and would certainly never willingly venture to present to the court, which has to try the case, merely the constituent materials, leaving the court itself to put them together. He feels it necessary to take care that some, if not all, of the witnesses should narrate the whole case from beginning to end. There is also extreme readiness in the lower classes of Bengalis, when under coercion or pressure, as in all whose civilization is of a servile order, to say anything even to the extent of accusing themselves, which they may be led to think will smooth their way out of immediately impending danger; and this is coupled with extraordinary quickness at perceiving the existing state of matters, comprehending what will be agreeable to those who care for their information, and making their statement consistent therewith. The police are, therefore, naturally under

Little hesitation is felt even at this day in vindicating family honour by taking life. Sometimes this is done in a most savage and brutal manner. A story constructed from the facts, slightly altered, of a case which actually occurred not long ago will serve as an illustration. An enterprising young Muhammadan, who had been in the habit of finding employment in some district remote from his native village, and who may be called Abdool, returned home on one occasion for a few weeks as he had several times done before; and while at home he stayed in his family homestead, where his mother, a brother, a

---

great temptation to avail themselves of a means of evidence which lies so near to their hands, and is so entirely adapted to their purpose. But bad as confessions of prisoners, evidence of accomplices, declarations of dying men, who have played a part in criminal occurrences, generally are in Europe, they are for the cause just mentioned greatly worse in Bengal. They cannot safely be relied upon even as against the speakers themselves, except as a sort of estoppel, unless they be corroborated. As against others they are hardly of any value at all. If the circumstances of native society were not such that suspicion commonly directs the police to the real offenders, convictions on a basis such as that exemplified in the text could not be tolerated.

cousin, and others resided. He visited his old friends and, amongst others, he seems to have been received with especial cordiality by the members of a Hindu family who may be designated as the family of one Kissori Mohun. Almost every evening he used to go to their homestead, and played cards or dice with them in the *baithakhana* up to a late hour of the night. One night, however, just as his home visit was drawing to a close, he had not done so and he was sleeping in the outside verandah of the family *bari* in company with his brother, the other members of the family being inside the huts; about midnight some stranger came up to the verandah, aroused him, spoke to him, and then the two went away together; the brother who was lying asleep near him was partially awakened by the voices, saw the two men go off in the dull light of the night, but troubled himself no more about the matter, and went to sleep again. In the morning Abdool was nowhere in the *bari*, and in fact was never after seen again. Still the members of his family did not fee any anxiety about him. They supposed that he had for some reason gone back to the place of his employment without giving them notice of his intentions, for he had on a former occasion acted precisely in this manner.

Four or five days after this disappearance of Abdool two boys who were tending cattle grazing in the *māth*, found a skull lying in a short sward of *arhar* not very far from the bank of the Ganges. The skull was entirely denuded of flesh, but was stained with recent blood, and had the teeth in the jaw. The news of the discovery soon reached the village, and Abdool's mother and brother immediately went to the spot. They suspected at once that the skull was Abdool's, and afterwards became satisfied that it was so by reason of some peculiarities in the teeth. Information was sent to the nearest police thannah. The usual kind of investigation took place. Several arrests were made and confessions obtained. Two of these could be depended upon, so far as the confessing persons were concerned, though not further; and corroborating evidence manufactured by the police was of an unusually despicable character. From these confessions it appeared that what had happened was as follows: Kissori Mohun's people had formed the notion that Abdool had become too intimate with a young married girl of their family, and they determined, before he left the village, to put him out of the way. So on the eve (so to speak) of his departure, a dependent of Kissori Mohun's was sent at night to invite him to play as usual; the attraction was great and he went. On his arrival at the *bari* he was surrounded in the darkness by half a dozen members of Kissori Mohun's family, who were prepared for the task; a cloth was twisted round his neck by which he was dragged into the *baithakhana*, all present fell upon him, and killed him by pounding him with their elbows. They then carried the body towards the Ganges, and in order to secure its rapid disappearance without identification, they stopped half way in the *math*, hacked it into small pieces with a *dao* which they had brought with them, put the pieces into a sack so carried them to the bank of the river, and there shot them out into the swift flowing current. But, unluckily for them, in the hurry, and the darkness, without noticing the fact, they left the skull in the *māth*; jackals and vultures speedily bared the bone and removed the features of the face, but enough remained to furnish the clue, which led to the discovery of the savage deed.[1]

But there is a class of purely agrarian outrage, which is, perhaps, more common than any other form of rural crime. Its root lies in the complex relations which connect the tillers of the soil with one another, and with the rent-receiver. A strong sense of vested right unprotected by the arm of the law leads in India as elsewhere to the endeavour at vindicating it by violence. Very often a ryot, taking advantage of a dispute between the zamindar and

---

[1] This was the case of the prosecution; and it was only established against one out of several persons accused.

his neighbour, will get the plots of the latter, or a portion of them (probably on higher terms) transferred to him at the *kachahri*, but will be obliged to resort to force in order to obtain or keep the actual possession of them. Or one of several co-sharers, cultivators, will pay the entire rent of a holding, and failing to obtain from one of the others the quota due from him, will forcibly prevent him from tilling his plot till he pays—a very effective mode of coercion when it can be exercised, for the sowing period of the year may be limited, and not to till then means starvation. The following true narrative is an example :—

Fakir Baksh, Somed Ali, Sabid Ali, and others, were co-sharers of a certain *jot*, or holding of land, as representing the different branches of what was originally one family. There had been a great deal of disputing about the shares, and when Fakir Baksh was about to prepare his allotment for sowing, Sabid Ali, who had paid up the full rent, or at any rate more than his share, and felt aggrieved at

Fakir Baksh's refusal to recoup him, determined to prevent him from cultivating his land until he did so. In this state of things, at sunrise one morning, Fakir Baksh and his three kinsmen, Somed Ali, Sharaf Ali, and Imdaz Ali, began ploughing with four yoke of bullocks, and almost immediately afterwards, while they were so engaged and unarmed Sabid Ali came upon them with eight or nine men at his back and attacked them with the intention of driving them off the ground. The members of Sabid's Ali's party were all armed with *lattees*, except one Taribullah, who had a gun, and they therefore expected to meet with an easy victory. Somed Ali, however, and Sharaf, who were both unusually powerful young men, left their ploughs, and boldly facing the enemy actually managed to wrench a *lattee* each from the hands of their opponents. With these they laid about them so lustily and with so much skill that Sabid Ali and his men were forced to retreat. Close in their rear was a shallow *khal* somewhat awkward to cross, and Taribullah, in desperation, raised his gun, which was loaded with small shot, fired and hit the advancing Somed Ali full in the chest, killing him on the spot. By the same discharge Sharaf Ali was seriously wounded. On the happening of this catastrophe the affray ended. Sabid Ali's party, thoroughly frightened at the results of the expedition, dispersed as best they could without having attained their object.

A story of much the same kind may be told wherein the zamindar's people figure as the aggressors. A *mauzah*, or village, had been sold in execution of a decree, and a stranger had purchased it. This new zamindar very soon took measures for enhancing the rents of his ryots. He was successful in obtaining *kabulyats* at increased rates from several ryots, but the headman of the village (*mandal*), whose example was most influential, sturdily held out and led the opposition. It was resolved that he should be coerced; so at day-break, one morning, a party of the zamindar's peons and adherents, armed with *lattees* and guns, started from the *kachahri* for the *mandal's* homestead, with the view of capturing him and carrying him off. This homestead fortunately was a substantial one, and the different huts were connected by pretty strong bamboo fencing. Thus the *bari* admitted of being defended by a relatively small force. In the *mandal's* family were four or five grown-up men, besides the women and children, and in addition to these, as it happened, two friends come from a distance had passed the previous night under their host's roof. No one had left the *bari* when the zamindar's party arrived. The latter, very largely out-numbering the men of the homestead, with threats of an abominable kind called upon the *mandal* to surrender, but these threats only nerved the *mandal* and his friends to resistance in defence of the female apartment. For a time the attacking party seemed unable to do anything, until taunted by their leader they at last made a rush, broke down the fence at one corner of the homestead, and fired a gun at the men inside, of whom two fell. The immediate effect, however, was not that which might have been anticipated, for one of the remaining defenders promptly seizing the gun which had just been fired, knocked down its owner; two of his companions laid hold each of an opponent, and the zamindar's party forthwith decamped, leaving three of their number prisoners in the hands of the *mandal* and his kinsmen. The cost of the victory was severe, for it was found that one of the two men who had been shot was dead.

In another case the *mandal* of a village had, as the ryots thought, been taking too much the side of the zamindar in certain matters, and it was therefore resolved in "committee" that he should be punished and warned. A certain number of the ryots were charged with the duty of giving him a beating at the first convenient opportunity, and the whole assembly undertook to hold them harmless as far as money might afterwards serve to do so. A few days after this, one evening, when it was dusk, these commissioned ryots managed to meet the *mandal* as he was alone driving two or three small cows home from the *khet*. They succeeded in getting into an altercation with him, and beat him, leaving him on the ground, from which he never again rose alive.

A last instance of rural crime may be given in the shape of a faction fight. As frequently happens in some parts of Bengal, the ryots and tenure-holders of a certain village and its neighbourhood were divided into two parties, the one consisting of the partizans and adherents of the Rajah, ten-anna shareholder of the *zamindari* or ten-anna zamindar, as he was termed, and the other of those of the Ghoses, the six-anna zamindars. One Asan and his brother Mānick, who lived in one homestead and held land under the Ghoses, had had a quarrel with one Kalidas, a substantial ryot on the Rajah's side, relative to the common boundary between their respective plots of ground; and some effort had been made by the Rajah's people to make Asan give up his jote to Kalidas or to enter into *amma* relations with the Rajah. Nothing, however, came of this for many months, until one morning early four or five *lathials* of the Rajah's party came to Asan's homestead on some vaguely explained errand. Most of Asan's neighbours were like himself, adherents of the Ghoses, but one or two and among these a man called Kafi Mahomed, whose *bari* was only two or three hundred yards distant from that of Asan, belonged to the Rajah's faction. The *lathials* apparently, not succeeding at once in their mission to Asan, retired for a time to the *bari* of their friend Kafi Mahomed, sending meanwhile a message to the Rajah's *kachahri*. Two or three hours passed. Asan and his brother Mānick, having taken their mid-day meal, were resting in their *bari*, when suddenly an uproar occurred—four or five men rushed in to seize Asan and Mānick, who then found some 100 or 150 men had come up to the assistance of the *lathials* of the morning, and were approaching in force from the south side to the attack of the *bari*. The brothers attempted to escape, and Mānick was fortunate enough to get away on the north; but Asan was laid hold of by the men and was carried off in triumph to the main body of the assailants, who were collected on a *banga*, running east and west on the south side of the *bari*. Mānick then came up with some of the Ghose party, whom he had hurriedly collected, and, seeing his brother a prisoner in the hands of the enemy, rushed forward to save him. He was, however, almost immediately speared by two men in succession. On this Asan got free and laid hold of one of these men, but was beaten off, receiving himself a slight spear wound in his hand. On Mānick's falling, the cry was raised that a man had been killed, and as is not unusual on such occasions, the attacking party immediately fled. Mānick died a few minutes after he was stabbed, and thus ended the conflict, as suddenly as it had begun.

VI.

ADMINISTRATION AND LAND LAW.

OF course doings such in kind as those which have been lately narrated (generally, though not always), come sooner or later under the cognizance of the police and their English superior officers. But the general peace of the village is, as a rule, preserved by the influence of the zamindar and the *panchayat*. The English official is personally seldom seen in the remoter country village. The reason for this is very plain. A zillah district in Bengal, which is sometimes roughly compared with an English county, comprises an area of from two to three thousand square miles, and has a population of say from one to two million souls, while the county of Suffolk, to take an example, has only an area of 1,454 square miles and a population of some 360,000. Now all the European officers in a whole zillah, will be one magistrate and collector, with three or four joint, assistant, and deputy magistrates, one district and sessions judge, one additional judge, one small cause court, or subordinate judge, one superintendent of police, one assistant superintendent of police, and one medical officer, say eleven or twelve in number, of whom about one-half are kept by their duties at the zillah station.

It would be impossible, in a few lines, to convey any very accurate idea of the functions of the magistrate and of the rest of the executive officers. Nor is it needful to attempt to do so here. Their administrative powers are very considerable. The magistrate and collector especially is to the people almost a king in his district. His name and authority travel into the remotest corners, though he himself in his cold weather tours can only visit comparatively few spots of it in the year. And, generally, the awe in which a magistrate or European official of any grade is held by the people is very great. It must, however, in truth be said, that the feeling of the ordinary village ryot towards these officials has not much affection in it; and this is by no means matter for surprise. It is a very exceptional thing for one of them to possess a real command of the colloquial vernacular. To acquire it in any case, many years are, as we all know, requisite under the most favourable circumstances of intercourse between the foreigner and the people; and these do not exist for many civilians. Scarcely any one thus is able to converse easily with the ordinary ranks of the people. The Englishman, moreover, is awkward, cold, reserved; his bearing becomes, in the eyes of the native, at any rate, abrupt and peremptory. He knows really next to nothing of the habits, standpoints, and modes of thought of the mass of the people, though his position and circumstances too often lead him to entertain the opposite opinion. Want of consideration flows from want of intimacy.

In ways of life and in associations which govern his conduct and opinions he is separated by an impassable gulf from the people of the country. He stands upon a platform apart and looks down upon them. Whenever he makes a movement of approach it is with a feeling of superiority which cannot be concealed. In most cases he does not care to conceal it. He is self-reliant. All persons around him have to give way to his will in the arrangements which he makes either for business or pastime. Too often, in small matters, their feelings and wishes are needlessly disregarded simply because they are misapprehended or not suspected. On the other hand, his probity and uprightness are next to never impugned. But the result is that he is certainly not loved. Rather it may be said that, to the eyes of the native, the English official is an incomprehensible being, inaccessible, selfish, overbearing, and irresistible.

However, for the causes already mentioned, the great bulk of the people in the country villages have no personal relations with the European officer of any kind. The small zamindar, who has been before described, or the naib of a larger man, is commonly the person of ruling local importance. And there are no taxgatherers even:[1] all the taxation of the country takes the form of land-revenue, stamps, customs, and excise, for the assessed taxes, on the whole, are insignificant, and certainly never reach the mofussil villages. The excise tends to make the *tari* somewhat dearer to the ryot than it otherwise would be, a result which is hardly a grievance, but it also increases the price of salt, a prime necessary of life, and this is a serious misfortune. The customs scarcely touch the ryot. Stamps, for special reasons, he has very little objection to, and the revenue is inseparable from his rent, so that, on the whole, with the agricultural population, the incidence of taxation is chiefly felt in three modes: in the payment of *rent*, in the price of *salt*, and in the *stamps*, needed for every proceeding in a court of justice or public office, or for a copy of any paper

[1] This was written before the imposition of the license tax.

filed in any court or office, or document of agreement, or receipt, &c.

Omitting the latter as being in some degree of a voluntary character, the two others remain as the two great burdens upon the ryot. It has been explained, in the foregoing pages, how extremely poor the ordinary ryot is, and how he depends upon the *mahajan* system for the means even of paying his rent. It seems impossible, then, at first sight, to devise any method by which the public revenue of the country can be increased by contributions from this class of the community. Lately an attempt has been made in this direction by the imposition of a road cess. The cess may be roughly described as a small rateable addition to the rent of each ryot which he has to pay to his rent-receiver through whom it is eventually transmitted to Government, together with a further small addition to be paid by the rent-receiver himself. There are many very grave objections to this form of increased taxation intrinsically, but the fatal objection to it is that it is capriciously unequal; it exacts more from the ryot who is already highly taxed by his rent than from him who is less so. And it is not possible, by any general rules of exception, to bring about even approximate equality in this respect.

If the amount of taxation must needs be increased, it can only be done so equitably by a contrivance which shall have the effect of apportioning the tax to the means of the payer. While the general body of ryots are miserably poor and can hardly bear the existing taxation, there are no doubt many among them who are comparatively well off, some of them being rent-receivers, in some manner or another, as well as cultivating ryots; and there are besides, in every village, well-to-do persons, petty dealers, and others, of more or less accumulated means. These all have a margin of means which may be said to be at present untaxed relative to their neighbours, the ryots, and which will fairly enough admit of being taxed if some equitable plan of making the levy could be discovered.

It might, perhaps, be imagined that something in the nature of an income-tax would answer this purpose. But the fact is that an income-tax must fail in India, even if it be only for the reason that the necessary machinery for assessing and collecting it is inevitably corrupt and oppressive. But probably the difficulty might be overcome by making an assessing body out of the village *panchayat*, who should be charged with the duty of assessing the means of every resident of the village above a certain minimum amount; and by then allotting to each village certain local burdens of a public character, which should be discharged out of rates to be levied from the persons assessed under the superintendence of local officers. In this way some of the work now done at the cost of Government for local objects out of the national funds might be better carried out than it is at present, and even additional work done by the village itself, and so the money in the hands of Government would in effect be correspondingly increased. This machinery would in particular be singularly appropriate for meeting the emergency of famines.[1]

Another very useful end would possibly be served by the creation of something in the nature of parochial administration. The general tendency to engage in litigation might be in some measure damped by providing occupation of this sort; if it be the case, as many well-informed persons believe, that the unquestionable prevalence of litigation is due to the idleness in which the ryot spends the larger portion of the year.

There are, however, much more potent causes of litigation existing in Bengal than the leisure of the ryots: and as one of them, namely, the nature of the land tenure, very greatly affects the different phases of village life, some account of it will not be out of place here.

In the foregoing pages[2] the designation "zamindar"

---

[1] This suggestion was expanded by the writer in a paper read before the East India Association in 1877.

[2] Much of the matter in the immediately following paragraphs appeared in a paper which was read at a meeting of the Social Science Association of Bengal at Calcutta in 1873.

has been given to the person who collects rents from ryots by virtue of any sort of right to enjoy the rents, and it will be presently seen that such a right may be of various kinds and denominations. The system throughout all India is, that a portion of the rent, which every cultivator of the soil pays for his plot, goes to Government as land revenue. In the whole, the Government of India receives about $20\frac{1}{2}$ millions sterling per annum in the shape of land revenue. Three very different modes of collecting this prevail in, and are characteristic of the three great Presidencies respectively. In Bengal the amount of this revenue and the method of collecting it formed the subject of the famous Permanent Settlement of 1793. Previously to the assumption of the Government of the country by the English, a land revenue, more or less defined in its characters —often spoken of as a share in the produce of the land—had from time immemorial been paid to the established Government of the day, Hindu or Muhammadan, as the case might be. The collection of the revenue and its payment to Government was effected by officers who, in later days were, in Bengal, generally called zamindars, each being responsible only for the revenue of the *zamindari*, *taluq*, or otherwise named district, of which he was certainly the fiscal head. Whether he was anything more than this, whether he was regarded by the people as the proprietor, in any degree, of the *zamindari*, or whether he himself looked upon the land of the *zamindari* as belonging to him personally, are questions which, perhaps, cannot now be satisfactorily answered. As a matter of fact the son, on the death of his father, usually succeeded to his father's functions, and it was avowedly the principal object of the legislation effected in 1793 to turn all these persons into hereditary landed proprietors, whether they were so before or not. Under the Permanent Settlement an engagement was entered into by the Government with each existing zamindar by the terms of which, on the one hand, the zamindar became bound to pay a certain *jama*, or fixed amount of money, assessed upon his *zamindari* as land revenue; and, on the other, the Government recognised him as hereditary proprietor of the land, and undertook never to alter his *jama*. At the same time the Government required the zamindar to respect the rights of the cultivator of the soil.

The results of this new arrangement will be pursued presently. For the moment it may be asserted positively that the zamindar never did before the Permanent Settlement (and that he does not to this day) stand towards the ryot in the position which the English landlord occupies relative to his tenant. The area of his *zamindari* covered large districts of country, and was reckoned not in *bighas* (the unit of land measure = one-third of an acre) but in communities of men, *mauzahs*. The money proceeds of the *zamindari* were not spoken of as rent, but as the *jamas* (collections) of the included villages. The assets of a *zamindari* made up of the *jamas* of sub-tenures, and the collections of the villages, scarcely, if at all, resembled the rental of an English estate. The zamindar himself was a superior lord enjoying personal privileges, and through officers, exercising some powers of local administration. The populations of the villages in his *zamindari* were his subjects (ryots), and it is not until you get within the *mauzah* itself that you find any one concerned with the actual land. Some comparison might be made between the feudal lord, his vassals, and serfs, on the one side, and the zamindar, his gantidars and ryots, on the other; but how little the two cases of zamindar and landlord ever have been parallel may be perceived at once from a simple illustration. When an English landed proprietor speaks of a *fine estate* he mentally refers to the extent of the acreage, the fertility of the soil, the beauty of the landscape, and so on; not at all to the tenants, the labourers, or the dwelling-houses which may be upon the land; whereas, if a Bengali zamindar makes a like remark, he has in his mind the number and importance of the villages which form the zamindari and their respective *jamas*, but he takes almost no thought at all about the physical character of the land.

Whatever was the true nature of the right by virtue of which the zamindar exercised his functions and enjoyed his privileges, he made his collections from the *zamindari*, and administered its affairs by means of an organization very simple and enduring in its character. It had its root in the village, and no doubt remains the same now in all essential particulars, as it was very many centuries ago. Probably, in the beginning, the village community itself managed the matter of the allotment of land, and the distribution among its members of the liability to pay the zamindar's dues. But in Bengal, long before the English came to the country, the zamindar had got into his hands so much, even of that business, as had not been consolidated and stereotyped by custom. The zamindar's village *kachahri* has been already described, or rather spoken of. It was an office (as it would be called in England) in each *mauzah*, with a head man, an accountant, and a field officer. The business of these men, as has before been said, was to keep a close eye on the ryots, to register in minute detail the subject of each man's occupation, the payment and cesses due from him according to shifting circumstances, and from time to time to collect the moneys so due. The system of *zamindari* accounts, which these duties entailed has been commented upon in the passage where the zamindar's position in the village was referred to. The *kachahris* of every five or six *mauzahs*, according to their size, were supervised by a superior officer (say a *tchsildar*) who had his own *kachahri*, with its books and papers, either duplicates of, or made up from those of, the *mauzah kachahris*. The collections effected by the officers of the village *kachahri* were handed over to him, and he passed them to a next higher officer.

In this manner the moneys at last arrived at the zamindar's own *kachahri;* out of them he paid the Government revenue which was due from his *zamindari* and he kept the rest for himself.

Zamindaris in different parts of the country differed very much from each other in their extent and in their circumstances. No one description could be given which should be true of them all. But the foregoing may be fairly taken to represent the type of the general system.

It is apparent almost at first sight, that the system, though simple and complete, had a natural tendency to disintegrate. Each middleman was the apex and head of a structure precisely like the principal structure in form and constitution, with this difference only that it had a smaller basis. A slight disturbing force might serve either to detach it and so leave it standing by itself, or to put it into an appendent condition.

In the event, for instance, of the Government finding difficulty in obtaining all the money which it required it might go direct to a middleman, who was willing to make terms for his quota, and so might be originated an example of a constituent portion of a zamindari being converted into a *mahal* paying revenue directly to Government. Also the zamindar himself, for motives arising from relationship, or from pecuniary or other obligation, might allow a middleman to retain and enjoy an exceptionally large proportion of the collections for his own benefit, might, in fact, leave to him the collections which centered in his hands, and be satisfied with the receipt from him of a *jama* only. Thus would arise a dependent *mahal* paying a *jama* to the zamindar which might be considered as part of the *zamindari* assets, or as revenue due to Government, only not payable directly. Again, some *zamindaris*, no doubt, as Mr. Hunter well describes in his *Orissa*, lost their coherence actually at head-quarters by reason of the head officials dividing the office management and care of the district between themselves, and so in the end coming to be recognised as the responsible heads of divisions.

In these various and other like ways, long before the period of English legislation commenced, the original simplicity of the *zamindari* system had been lost; there were *zamindaris* and *taluqs* of several orders and designations paying revenue directly to Government; within these were subordinate *taluqs* and tenures converted from the condition of being parts of a homogeneous collecting machine into semi-independence, and in that character paying a recognised *jama* directly to the superior *kachahri* instead of sending on to it in ordinary course their respective collections.

The practice of commuting collections, or allowing them to drop into *jamas*, was obviously so convenient and advantageous to the parties primarily concerned that it was certain to grow and prevail in inverse proportion to the power or opportunities of the immediate superior or principal to insist upon an account. So that every subordinate *jama*-paying *mahal* or tenure, when established, speedily became a miniature *zamindari*, in which certain *jamas* were taken in lieu of collections, and the remaining collections were made by the old machinery. Waste land grants or concessions were also the origin of *taluqs*, both dependent and independent, and so, too, *jaghir* grants for services.

Within the village itself an analogous process, for much the same reason, came into operation with regard to the occupation of the land. The principal persons of the *zamindari amla*, and the headmen of the ryots (*mandals*,) or others of influence, and privileged persons such as Brahmans, often got recognised as holding upon fixed and favourable terms larger portions of the village lands than they could or did cultivate. These, of course, they sub-let, either wholly or in part, and so arose varieties of *jots* and ryottee-tenures.

And before the legislation of 1793, the middle tenures, such as they then existed, depended for their maintenance upon usage, and the personal power and influence of the holder. The ryottee-tenures and *jots* were regulated by usage also, and by the arbitrament of the village *panchayat* and the *zamindari amla.* Sir H. Maine has pointed out (*Village Communities*, Section 3) the true nature of customary law, upon the footing of which such a system as this works, and has shown that it does not involve the idea of a personal proprietary right. Indeed, it was the absence of this element of proprietary right which caused so much embarrassment and difficulty to the first English inquirers into this subject. They could not readily comprehend a land system in which no one seemed to possess an absolute proprietary right to the soil. Still less, if possible, could they understand how the due relation of the different parts of the system could be legitimately maintained without express positive law. The ills and confusing irregularities which were the results of somewhat rude attrition between feudal power and customary local authority, were only too apparent, and the first Indian politico-economists sought to remove them by simply making the (as they supposed) already existing personal rights of property more definite, and providing facilities for their enforcement by the arm of the law.

With substantially this view the legislators of 1793 performed their task; and in order that no extensive disturbing force should remain, they took care that the amount of the Government claim upon the zamindar should be fixed in perpetuity. The authors of the Permanent Settlement thought that they had thus freed the subject of property in land from incrustations which were merely the growth of a lawless time, and reduced it to its pristine proportions; and they expected that the English arrangement of landlord and tenant, with all its simplicity and advantages, would assert itself at once.

But in truth, nothing in the world was less likely to happen than this. It could not happen until the zamindar, or tenure-holder, came to look upon himself as the owner of the soil, personally interested in, and responsible for, its physical condition,—until the cultivator ceased to regard himself as ryot, and acknowledged that he was only a contracting party. These contingencies are just as remote now as ever, and the agricultural system of Bengal consequently still presents us with the zamindar and ryot, not with landlord and tenant.[1]

Nevertheless, a very important change was brought about by the legislation of 1793. The legislature then for the first time declared that the property in the soil was vested in the zamindars, and that they might alien or burden that property at their pleasure without the previously obtained sanction of Government; and the moment this declaration was made, obviously all subordinate tenures and holdings, of whatever sort, became also personal proprietary rights in the land of greater or lesser degree, possessing each within itself, also in greater or lesser degree, powers of multiplication. When the zamindar's right had become in a certain sense an absolute right to the soil—not exclusive, because

---

[1] A very close analogy to the state of things here described may be found in some districts of Ireland.

the legislature at the same time recognised rights on the side of the ryot—with complete powers of alienation, the rights of all subordinate holders were necessarily derivative therefrom; and the ascertainment, definition, and enforcement of them immediately fell within the province of the public Courts of Justice. Sir H. Maine writes (*Village Com.*, p. 73,) "If I had to state what for the moment is the greatest change which has come over the people of India, and the change which has added most seriously to the difficulty of governing them, I should say it was the growth on all sides of the sense of individual legal right—of a right not vested in the total group, but in the particular member of it aggrieved, who has become conscious that he may call in the arm of the State to force his neighbours to obey the ascertained rule." This change was deliberately and designedly made by the legislature, as regards the zamindar; but no one at the time perceived, and very few persons since have recognised, that it also involved a like change with regard to every one, from zamindar to ryot, who had practically in any degree a beneficial interest in the land system. Even now it is not uncommon to hear fall from well-informed persons expressions of regret that the forum of the *mandals* and the zamindar's *amla* should be forsaken so much as it is for the *kachahri* of the deputy-magistrate or of the Moonsiff. And yet this result seems on reflection to be the inevitable consequence of the change effected in 1793. The first menace to any member of the land system necessarily brought him into Court to have his legal position authoritatively ascertained and asserted; and nowhere else could he afterwards go to have his proprietary right maintained.

A further most important consequence bearing a double aspect followed the change. When all intermediate (even to the very lowest) interests became rights of property in land, not only could the owner of any such interest carve it as a subject of property into other interests, by encumbering or alienating within the limits of the right; but even his ownership itself might be of that complex heterogeneous kind, which is seen in Hindu joint-parcenary, and of which some examples have been given above.

Let us look more nearly at the first side of this proposition. Remembering that a middle tenure or interest below the revenue-paying zamindar resembles the primary *zamindari* and is essentially the right, on payment of the proper *jama* to a superior holder, to make collections from the cultivators of land and to take the *jamas* from subordinate holders within a specified area, we see that as soon as the tenure is converted into a proprietary right, there must almost necessarily be a constant tendency to the creation of minor tenures. The owner of the smallest and lowest tenure is severed from the land itself by the customary occupation of the ryots and by ryottee-tenures, if there are any,—indeed the ryot holdings contain more of that which goes to constitute the English idea of land property than do the middle tenures, although it is not always easy to draw the line which separates the two. The middle tenure of every degree is thus in a great measure an account-book matter, and is very completely represented by the *jamabandi* paper. If the owner of such a property desires to benefit a child or a family connection, he can do so by making him a *mokarari* grant, in some form, of a portion of his collections. It would be no easy matter to describe fully the various shapes which such a grant is capable of taking. It may cover a part of a village only, or a whole village, or many villages (according to the circumstances of the grantor and the transaction), and may convey the right to take the rents, dues, and *jamas* within that area by entireties; or it may convey the right to take a fractional part only of them; or again, it may convey the entireties for some villages and fractional parts for others, and so on. Most frequently the tenure of the grantor himself amounts only to a right to a fractional share of the rents, &c., and then his grant will pass a fraction of a fraction, and so on. But not only may a tenure-holder make a grant of this nature to some one whom he desires to benefit, he may do the like to a stranger in consideration of a bonus or premium. Again, he may do so with the view to ensure to himself, in the shape of the rent reserved on the subject of grant, the regular receipt of money wherewith to pay his own *jama*. Or he may, by way of affording security for the repayment of a loan of money made to him, temporarily assign to the lender under a *zar-i-peshgi ticca* his tenure-right of making collections. In these or similar modes, the Bengali tenure-holder, landed proprietor, or zamindar (however he may be designated), is obliged to deal with his interest when he wants to raise money, or to confer a benefit; and it is obvious that in each instance (excepting that of out-and-out sale of the entirety of his interest, to which he rarely has recourse if he can avoid it) he creates a fresh set of proprietary rights.

And if we turn now to the second aspect of the case, we find it is the rule, all but universal, in Bengal that every subject of property, including, of course, a middle tenure or right of any kind in the laud system just described, is owned not by an individual, but by a more or less numerous group of persons jointly, each member of the group being entitled to his own share in the subject of ownership, and such share being capable of existing in any one of various, more or less complete states of separation, or division, from the rest. Thus, returning to an instance just now given, suppose a fractional, say $9\frac{1}{2}$ annas share of a village (the whole being considered as 16 annas), or of any number of villages to be the subject of a *mokarari* tenure. This may be the case in three or four different ways. It may mean that the tenure-holder has a *mokarari* right given him to the rents and dues arising out of a specified portion of the area of the village which is separated from the rest by metes and bounds, and which bears to the entirety the proportion of $9\frac{1}{2}$ to 16. Or it may mean that he has the right to collect separately by his own *amla* from the ryots throughout the *entirety* of the village $9\frac{1}{2}$ annas out of each rupee of rent. Or, again, it may mean that in certain parts of the area covered by the grant he has a sole right to the rents, and in other parts to a fractional portion only, so arranged that in the whole he gets $9\frac{1}{2}$ out of 16 annas of the entire profits of the area. And it may further be, as it usually is, that it is incidental to his right to collect the share of rents, &c., due to him in respect of the tenure by his own officers at his own *kachahri*; though it may also be that he has only the right to draw his fractional share of the net collections which have been made at a joint-*kachahri* belonging, so to speak, to several shareholders.

But in whatever way this *mokarari* tenure of $9\frac{1}{2}$ annas of property is to be possessed and enjoyed, the owner of it is usually a joint-family, or a group of persons representing an original joint-family : and all the members of the group have each his own share in the tenure, which, although existing in a state undivided from the rest, is capable of being assigned to a purchaser separately from them. Also, very often, each member of the group can, as between himself and his shareholders, insist upon having an actual partition of the subject of tenure. When this is done he becomes by himself separately entitled to a fraction, say, of the supposed $9\frac{1}{2}$ anna tenure. For illustration's sake let us take the fraction to be $\frac{1}{6}$th; then his separate share of the rents and profits accruing from the area which is covered by the tenure, subject of course to the payment of the superior rent or *jama*, is $\frac{1}{6}$th of $9\frac{1}{2}$ annas, *i.e.* 1 anna 9 pie. In this way it happens that even the village (or *mauzah*), the unit in terms of which the *zamindari* may be said to be calculated, comes to be divided into small portions; and the rent-receiver who stands to a particular ryot in the position of zamindar may be, and often is, a very small man indeed. Adhering to the instance already given, we may say that the ryot may have to pay the whole of his rent to the *patwari* of the 1 anna 7 pie shareholder, or to pay 1 anna 7 pie out of 16 annas of his rent to him, and the remainder to the other shareholders separately, or in groups; or he may only have to pay the entirety of his rent to the joint-*kachahri* from which each shareholder will get his share on division.

This system of sub-infeudation and sub-division of joint-interests, accompanied by severalty of right, prevails universally throughout Bengal. One result of this is a condition of complexity of landed interests which is probably without a parallel elsewhere. And a still more serious consequence is, that the so-called owner of the land has the least possible motive for doing anything to benefit it. It will be seen that the rent paid by the cultivator for the use of the soil does not go to one person bearing the character of an English landlord, but is distributed among a series of owners, namely, the middle tenure-holders with the revenue-paying zamindar at their head, each independent of the others, and each probably consisting of several persons with independent rights among themselves. Why should one shareholder out of this lot advance money for improvement, the advantage of which, if any, will be shared in by many others over whom he has no control or influence, to a greater extent than by himself? Furthermore, under this system, the locally resident zamindars are very generally small shareholders of subordinate tenures, whose means are not greatly superior to those of the well-to-do ryots, and who cannot be possessed of any amount of education or culture.

So much for the situation and circumstances of the rent-receivers: that of the rent-payers, *i.e.* of the cultivators of the soil, deserves some notice. The lands of a village may be broadly distinguished into two sets, namely, the ryottee lands, on the one hand, and the zamindar's *ziraat, khamar, nij-*

jot, or *sir*-lands, or whatever they may be termed, on the other. The ryottee-lands constitute the bulk of the village area. They are in a certain sense emphatically village lands; the right to occupy and cultivate the soil thereof rests upon a basis of custom, and is in no degree derived from the zamindar. Sometimes the resident ryots of the village have a preferential claim, more or less openly acknowledged, to any portion of them which may for any cause have become vacant. In others, the zamindar is practically unfettered in the selection of a new occupant. But in all cases alike the occupier's interest is looked upon as bottomed on something quite independent of the zamindar. In Bengal, it is commonly termed the ryot's *jot*. Even when the actual possession of a plot of land comes, as it may come, into the hands of the zamindar himself, by reason of abandonment by the ryot, it is more than doubtful whether the *jot* interest disappears, or its character changes. In short, on the ryottee lands the occupying ryot holds his *jot*, *i.e.* occupies the soil, by a customary right, to which he has personally succeeded, either by inheritance from an ancestor or by transfer from a predecessor, or by admission through the zamindar. He may sub-let; but it seems that, if he does so his lessees never get any better position than that of being his tenants, deriving everything from him and going out of possession with him whenever he goes.

This right to occupy and till the land may be of several kinds: it may be personal only, or may be inheritable, or it may by custom involve, as incident to it, a power of alienation; or again, the zamindar may, if he chooses, create in favour of a ryot a perpetual inheritable right of occupation with power of alienation. By legislative enactment, actual occupation of the same land for a period of 12 years confers upon the ryot (if he has it not otherwise), a personal right of occupation on payment of a fair and reasonable rent; and occupation for 20 years at a *uniform* rate of rent generally confers a right of occupation at that rate. A very large number of ryots in Bengal have in one way or another acquired permanent rights of occupancy in the land which they cultivate, but the remainder, a larger number, merely occupy, on payment of the rents and dues which have usually been paid to the zamindar's *kachahri* in respect of their land. These are commonly much less in rate than rents paid by agricultural tenants in England. Theoretically, the zamindar is entitled to ask what he thinks fit before the commencement of every year, and perhaps turn this class of ryot out, if he does not agree, but the zamindar seldom does so.

On *ziraat*, *khamar*, *nij-jot*, or *sir*-lands, in contradistinction to ryottee lands, the zamindar may cultivate the soil on his own account, if he chooses, or put in cultivators on any terms which they may agree to accept. In truth, there the cultivators are tenants, and the zamindar is their landlord in the ordinary sense of the word. The ownership of the zamindar is unqualified by the right of any one else to the use of the soil.

In the conception of the agricultural community, the distinction between the two classes of land is substantially this, namely, in the ryottee-lands, the use of the soil belongs to the ryots; in the other, the zamindar may regulate and dispose of it as he likes.

In an early part of this description it was mentioned that the holdings of the village ryots were commonly very small. In some parts of the country, however, *jots* or ryottee interests in considerable tracts of unreclaimed jungle, or otherwise waste land, have at times been granted, of a perpetual character, upon insignificant rents. The land, which is the subject of these grants, has afterwards come to be sub-let to cultivators. Under circumstances such as these, it seems almost impossible to distinguish between the *jot-dar*, and an ordinary middle tenure-holder.

VII.

WAYS AND MEANS.

In the foregoing pages an attempt has been made to describe a type specimen of a Bengali village, and the principal conditions of the life led by its inhabitants. By imagining the specimen sufficiently multiplied an approximately correct idea of the entire province, or at any rate of the deltaic portion of it, may be reached. We should thus have before us a very large area of exceedingly fertile agricultural country, covered by a dense population and possessing most imperfect means of intercommunication between its parts: the whole divided into petty communities, each of which in the ordinary course of things may as a rule be said to be self sustaining, and to manage its own affairs without much thought of an external force. There is, at the same time, throughout the population an all-pervading consciousness of a great superior power which may at any time become specially active, and which is remorseless when it interferes or is invoked through its courts, in matters relating to revenue or to land.

The imperfection of the means of intercommunication between village and village, and between one portion of a rural district and another, is sometimes laid as an inexcusable fault at the doors of the English administrators of this country. But it is not really so; although, no doubt, the Government might with proper diligence have done more in this matter during the last seventy years than it has. The magnitude of the task of creating a sufficiency of roads in Bengal, according to an English standard of requirement, may be conceived by imagining the whole of England, except the neighbourhood of large towns, entirely without roads other than two or three trunk lines, and a few unmetalled "hundred lanes" in the different manors, coupled with an absence of desire on the part of the people for anything better. What could the efforts of the executive Government do in a case like this? And in order to make this picture approach a Bengal reality, it must be added, that there is not a stone, or anything harder than clay, to be found in the soil of the delta; and that the floods of the rainy season break down, and sometimes almost obliterate, such roadways as have not been expensively constructed by skilled engineers. To create in deltaic Bengal such a network of permanent roads as an Englishman expects to find in a civilised country would be entirely beyond the strength of any Government whatever. Any considerable advance in this matter can only proceed from the exertions of the landholders and the cultivators themselves; and as long as the complexity of tenures, which has already been pointed out, and the condition of the people, remains substantially that which it is at present, it will be useless to look for any effort of the kind.

And indeed the ordinary needs of the people in this respect are met by the existing state of things. The vehicles in use for the carriage of goods are boats, the heads of men and women, little tiny bullocks, and bambu carts of very rude construction; and if well-to-do folks travel they are carried in palkis and doolies, or go by boat. In the dry season the men, the bullocks, and the carts can and do go almost anywhere. And the local traffic, such as it is, usually takes place in detail of very small quantities. The *dana* or other seed is trodden out [1] by the bullocks at the *khaliān* almost on the plot where it is grown; and both the grain and the straw are very easily carried to the homestead on the heads of the various members of the ryot's family. The surplus produce, if any, of the ryot which does not go to his *mahajan* passes in little items to the nearer

---

[1] In some districts, as in Chota Nagpore, a rude handflail is used for thrashing grain.

hāts, and so becomes diffused over the neighbouring *mauzahs,* or is carried on further to the larger *hāts,* the *mahajan* and the *modi* affording the only village depôts. The larger *hāts* again, or local centres of country produce trade, are commonly situated on roads or *khals.* The produce trader here, by his agents, gathers in the result of his scattered purchases, and sends it away in carts or boats; and thus the out-flow takes place very evenly, without the thought, probably, having occurred to any one, that the means of carriage admitted of improvement.

It is often said, on occasions of scarcity or famine, that the stream will not reverse itself when necessary. But this appears to be erroneous. Manchester piece-goods find their way regularly by these very same channels to the remotest Bengal village. In some districts, too, there is in the normal state of things an actual importation and distribution of grain in this way every year to a considerable extent, and there cannot be the least doubt that, as long as the ryots are able to pay the requisite retail price, the village *mahajans* and *modis* will succeed in keeping up their stocks, whatever the local deficiency of crop. It usually happens, unquestionably, when a season of scarcity is seen to be closely approaching, that both the *mahajans* and *modis* are inactive. They know very accurately the extent of their clients' and customers' means. The *mahajan*, although he does not, as some think, hold back for starvation prices the stock which is actually in his *golas*, naturally enough declines to increase that stock at great cost to himself, when his clients are already hopelessly involved in debt to him; and the village *modi* for like reason will not lay in a stock at abnormal prices to retail it to those who cannot pay for what they purchase. This state of things would be completely changed if neither the *mahajan* nor the village dealer had reason to doubt the ability of the ryot to pay a remunerating price for imported food. Grain would then come in, by the routes through which it ordinarily flows out, smoothly and imperceptibly, in obedience to the attractive force of price; and probably no one but a most attentive observer would be aware that anything extraordinary was taking place. It is the occurrence of pauperism in the ryots, when a certain price of food-stuffs is reached, which throws the ordinary machinery out of gear; and it seems to be obvious that this would be remedied, if by any external means the purchasing power were maintained to them. It is not the purpose of these pages to discuss a question of political economy. But it may here be added that in times of scarcity the action of Government does not always appear to have been directed immediately to this object. The institution of relief works on a large scale, where great numbers of people, drawn from their homes, are massed together within limited areas, and the transportation of grain in considerable quantities from the outside to certain local centres, for the support of those engaged on these works and for distribution so far as practicable by the hands of local committees in the pauperized districts, are the principal measures adopted by Government in emergencies of this sort. Whatever may be the amount of the relief which can in this way be afforded (and no doubt it is often considerable), inasmuch as it is independent of the natural channels of supply which have just been described, it might appear at first sight to be an unqualified gain to the distressed people. But, unfortunately, it is not so. Apart from the disturbance of social and economical relations, which is effected by large labour undertakings of temporary duration, the preparations which Government has to make for unusual work themselves very greatly hinder ordinary traffic in rural lines of route; boats and carts, &c., have to be collected—even impressed—in all directions, and become locked up, so to speak, for days and weeks, before they are actually wanted, in order that they may be certainly ready when needed. And thus, not only while Government is importing, but also long before it commences to do so, private enterprise is left almost without a vehicle. Moreover, the

Government method of proceeding, by drawing away as many persons as possible from their homes (and those the able-bodied rather than the infirm) as well as by supplying grain, directly tends to remove the pressure upon the village *mahajans* and *modis*, and to make the market which they supply even more uncertain, and less to be counted upon, than it was before. And it probably may with strict accuracy be concluded, that as soon as Government announces its anticipation of a famine and its intention to take extraordinary measures of prevention, all natural effort at the village end of the system ceases. Some of the wealthy zamindars, however, here and there do much to furnish an artificial substitute very nearly resembling it in effect, by causing their local *amla* to lay in stores for the benefit of their ryots. And this wholesome action is capable of being most extensively applied. The village *panchayat* suggested in an earlier page as a means of effecting an equitable local taxation would appear to be also an instrument which might be employed for the direct stimulation of the ordinary machinery of supply. But as yet, unfortunately, this side of the great problem which the occurrence of a period of scarcity forces upon the Government has remained practically untouched.

THE AGRICULTURAL COMMUNITY IN CEYLON.

I.

THE VILLAGE ECONOMY.

THE more primitive and less changed form of the Singhalese agricultural community is to be found in the interior of the Island of Ceylon, which, as is well known, in shape and position resembles a pear, pendent, with a slightly curved stalk to the southern end of the Indian peninsula on its eastern side. A mass of mountains rising in some instances to the elevation of 7,000 or 8,000 feet, bordered at its base with a margin of lower land which continues to the coast on all sides, occupies the circular portion of the pear, and the elongated extension of this margin towards the north amounts to a moiety of the entire island.

The new North Central Province which was constituted on the 6th September, 1873, for administrative purposes, mainly at the expense of the former Northern Province, but with some contributions from the North-Western, Central, and Eastern Provinces, covers the mid-island portion of the northern plain, abutting upon, and spreading outwards to the north from the great umbilical knot of the southern mountainous district.

The whole of this new Province may be said to be one vast forest.

In looking down upon it from the top of such rocky eminences as Dambulla or Mehintale, which here and there arise abruptly out of it, or even from the dome of an Anuradhapura dagoba, the eye sees only interminable jungle in a state of nature, dotted very sparsely with tiny specks of yellow-green cultivation. Some few pools of water, or tanks, may also sometimes be detected glittering in the dense and dark mass of extended forest. The hidden surface of the country is, however, not absolutely flat. In places it exhibits considerable undulation. In others it is broken by low ridges or rounded bosses of gneiss. As a rule, the pools seem to be by origin merely accumulations of water in such natural depressions of the ground as have no outlet sufficiently low to drain them, a state of things which seems to be favoured by the forest condition of the country. But their depth and size have been, in most instances, artificially increased by the expedient of an earthen bund or embankment, thrown across the lower side of the depression. In the drier seasons of the year, as the water bulk shrinks back towards the bund,— *i.e.* towards the deeper side,—it withdraws from the greater portion of the tank space, so that the jungle is enabled to flourish there (as it also does over the embankment itself) just as vigorously as every other where in the surrounding tracts. The result is, that it is no easy task to obtain a view of a tank even when you are in close proximity to it. And when a tank is satisfactorily full, much of it closely resembles a circuit of flooded forest.

Anuradhapura, the classic city of the Mahawansa, for seven or eight centuries the metropolis of the dynasties which in succession ruled over the larger portion of Ceylon, and for as many left to decay under the powerful disintegrating forces of a luxuriant tropical vegetation, is very nearly the middle point of the new Province, and the population of the district, such as it is—for at the census of 1871 it only numbered sixteen to the square mile (the inhabitants of the rural villages and modern bazar all counted together)—has for a very long period of time, until lately, been preserved by the remoteness and inaccessibility of its situation from the disturbing action of foreign influences of any kind, and may be safely taken, even at this day, to furnish us with an actual living specimen typical of an agricultural economy and civilisation which probably characterised the Ceylon of very early times.

The people are Singhalese, and class themselves with the Kandyan, or highlanders, as distinguished from the low-country Singhalese who border the coast on either side. They are of robust frame, commonly of fine open countenance, though somewhat harsh in feature, and of a peculiar yellow brown tint, in strong contrast to the comparatively slight-limbed, black-complexioned Tamils, who are their neighbours on the north and east, and who, indeed, constitute the population of the northern portion of the island.

The Singhalese language doubtless belongs to the Aryan group, and is apparently sprung from a root closely allied to the Sanscritic prakrits of Northern India. But the Singhalese people themselves generally have the appearance of being the result of at least an intermixture of an Aryan with some other, yellow-tinted, coarsely-built, ethnic element.

It is remarkable that they are broad-shouldered, deep-chested, and muscular, with a pronounced calf to the leg, like all Mongolian peoples, and unlike the Aryans of India.[1] But their most striking pecu-

---

[1] The description "delicate in limbs and features," given in Keith Johnston's *Physical Geography*, p. 321, only applies to certain of the low country Singhalese of the maritime provinces, who appear to be of a mixed race.

liarity, perhaps, is the excessive hairiness of both male and female. The chest of the man often resembles a door-mat, and the hair of his head reaches low down his back, a feature which attracted the notice of the earliest Greek geographers. The lower part of the abdomen also, both in male and female, is profusely hairy. This extraordinary capillary development is certainly the reverse of what we see in those Mongolian peoples with whom we are best acquainted. It seems, however, that the Ainos, a Turanian race on the extreme east of Asia, possess it even to a greater extent than the Singhalese, and that they at an early historical period were widely spread over the islands and tracts of country now covered by the Japanese, Chinese, and Malays. Can it be that the Singhalese are, by blood, in a large measure traceable to an Aino or a cognate origin, and that they owe little more than their language, literature, and religion to the invasion of Aryans from Upper Bengal, of which history tells us?

On the other hand, the Tamil inhabitants of the Northern Province, undistinguishable as a whole from their brethren of the mainland of India, with their slight build, black skin, thick lips, open nostrils, and coarse hair, belong unmistakably to the Dravidian race.

Naturally enough, too, on the marches of the Tamil and Singhalese districts, low caste villages are to be found in which no pure type of either kind is preserved; but these are exceptional.

The distribution of the population of the district is by agricultural villages, except only the cases of the petty and often ephemeral bazars which have sprung up at convenient places along the highways —gradually as these have have been opened out through the forest—and which are perhaps never kept by the Kandyans, but by low country Singhalese, Moormen, or Tamils.

The principal and controlling element of the village is the paddy tract or paddy field, which itself is (to use mathematical language) a function of the supply of water.

Usually the field is, so to speak, attached, or appended to, a tank, and often is strikingly tiny relative to the size of the entire tank. It is irrigated by the flow of water which passes out from the tank through a masonry culvert piercing the lowest part of the retaining bund, or more often through a breach or cutting made in the bund itself. And the lie of the field will be such that the outflow of water can be made to flood the whole of it in a succession of flats from the upper part of its slope next the tank, to the lowest and most remote from it; the line of soil surface from side to side being almost always horizontal throughout. According to the local character of the ground the field will be of more or less irregular shape, with its longer extension stretching away from the tank bund. In all other respects it is a simple clearing in that universal jungle which prevails on all sides, and which even covers up, as has been already mentioned, the actual bund of the tank, and very much even of the tank bottom itself.

With each field corresponds a *gama* or village i.e., the group of homesteads in which live the people who cultivate the field. It is sometimes the case, though not often, that a village can boast of more than one field. The group stands in the jungle by the side of the field, obscured by the trees and next the bund. It usually exhibits little if any order of arrangement. A single homestead, if its owner be well to do, consists of a low, thatched, mud-wattled hut, of perhaps two unlighted rooms opening upon the diminutive veranda which has the earth platform of the hut for floor, and its projecting eaves for a roof. In front of this hut will be small mud-plastered *attawas*, or roofed cylinders of wicker-work, raised upon supports (equivalent to the *golas* of Bengal) for storage of grain. On one side, too, will stand a large open shed, with its little loft for cattle (if the cottier possesses any) implements, curry grinder, rice pounder (the *dhenki* of Bengal),

&c. Under the back eaves of the hut also will be found a place for ploughs, the surface-smoother, harrows, &c. And abutting upon the little homestead's curtilage, or partially enclosing it, will be a garden or loosely cultivated plot for fruit trees, condiments, curry vegetables (*sāg* of Bengal), &c. The whole is usually most ill kept and neglected. And the different homesteads of the village group are separated from each other by irrregular, ill-defined, muddy tracks.

The people who constitute the inhabitants of such a village are related and subordinated, in a peculiar connection with the land, to a territorial head, who, in these modern days is commonly spoken of as the proprietor of the village, though the term does not seem to be in all respects accurate. This head doubtless is, as will be presently explained, the historical successor and representative of the primitive chieftain. He may take the shape of the Crown, or of a religious foundation, or of a private Singhalese gentleman; and there are, nowadays, certain diversities in the incidents of these three several cases such as render this triple distinction noteworthy.

The village field, or paddy tract, is shared among the families of the village in the following manner, namely, it is divided into portions by parallel balks drawn across it from side to side at right angles to the line of water-flow. And each such portion is the hereditary share, qualified by the special incidents to be next mentioned, of some one person or family resident in or belonging to the village.

The principal portion, or share, falls to, and is termed the *Mottettuwa* (*ziraat* in Bengal), of the head of the village; and all the other shares, although the tenure of them is permanent and hereditary, are charged with some obligation of subjection on the part of the shareholder to that head, *i e.*, the shareholder is in each case bound either to make to the head some contribution of produce in kind, or to render him some defined and specific service, domestic or agricultural. This distinction of tenure, or subjection, corresponds very closely with the *lakhiraj* and *raiotti* conditions of holding in Bengal. Only that in Bengal the *raiotti* holding, *i.e.*, the holding by contribution of share of produce, is the prevalent form, and the *lakhiraj* holding is the exception, while in Ceylon the holding by rendering of service *nilakariya* is (or rather was) all but universal, and the other the exception. There is a further difference, also, namely, that in Bengal the service of the *lakhiraj* holding is always free and honourable, such as that of the priest, the doctor, the watchman, and so on; but in Ceylon, that of the *nilakariya* is usually menial.

It is generally the case that a plurality of villages have a common head, and formerly the household establishment and personal retinue of a wealthy native chieftain used to be kept up by a method of turns of menial service discharged by villagers, who were drawn for the purpose from the many villages belonging to him in due order upon the footing of their land tenure obligation.

Changes in the state of society have caused much of this to become obsolete, and the corresponding service tenure to become, so to speak, freehold. But where a Buddhist Vihara, or temple, is the head or proprietor of the village, as happens frequently in the North Central Province, the personal service which in this instance takes special forms, such as tom-tom beating on specified occasions, maintaining illuminations, thatching or doing other repairs to the *pansala* (*i.e.*, the Buddhist priest's residence), &c., is still in full activity.

The administrative organisation which is needed to secure to the head of the village the perception of all these service advantages and profits consisted of one or two officials, namely, the *Gamerale*, or emphatically the village man, the *Lekham*, writer or accountant, &c. And some of the more wealthy of the shareholders in the village field, probably by reason of being by family origin of the same blood with the chieftain, hold their share by the service of filling hereditarily one of these offices, or of yielding hospitality to the head of the village when he comes, or to any other visitors whom the village receives.

A *penuma* or present, which has its exact equivalent in the Bengali *nazar*, is due from every service renderer upon presenting himself for the performance of his service, and often the like when his term of service is completed.

Some services consist in doing for the village head such work as smiths', carpenters', dhobis' work or even that of the doctor (*Vederale*). And in the village these persons get paid in their turn by their fellow villagers for the exercise of their professional or artisan's functions and skill (when needed), either by labour done for them in the tilling of their shares of the village field, or by a quota of the paddy on the payer's threshing-floor, measured out and delivered when the harvest is completed.

Other service again consists in supplying the village head with oil, betel-nuts, or with honey from the jungle, or with game, &c.

Besides services such as have been mentioned, rendered to the village head alone, the exigencies of cultivation under the primitive conditions which obtain in the North Central Province, and indeed throughout Ceylon generally, necessitate certain combined action on the part of the villagers for their joint benefit, *e.g.* fencing the village field every season against the wild animals of the jungle which surrounds it. The whole work much exceeds anything that any one shareholder could execute unaided. And if there be a flaw in it anywhere every shareholder's plot is open to invasion. Every shareholder is thus directly interested in this work, and must bear his portion of it in proportion to his share in the field. Similarly if any breach in the bund has to be filled up, or some repair to be done to it, or a channel to be cut across it, this is done by all the shareholders jointly furnishing out of their families or dependents, each in due proportion, a continual supply of labour in successive relays until the work is done.

Again, although each shareholder in the village paddy field, has a certain hereditary right of property in his plot, and of exclusively cultivating it, yet the primitive method of cultivation which is generally pursued connects him, whether he will or no, in almost every step of his tilling with his neighbours, above and below, either in a dominant or a serviant character. The process of preparing and clearing the soil for the seed sowing or planting, of killing the weeds and keeping them down, and of promoting the growth of the paddy-plant, is from beginning to end in a large degree effected by the aid of successive submersions of the plot, which have to be varied as regards the depth of water required according to the process and the stage of it. There are commonly so many as three prolonged submersions in the course of tilling, and seven shorter ones during the growth of the plant. And as the submergence of a relatively lower plot generally means the submergence of the plots above it, while the paddy plant cannot be depended upon to grow equally fast in all the plots, therefore, in order that there be no risk of one shareholder's operations destroying the young plants of his neighbours, the usual rule is that the shareholder at the lower end of the field should commence the operations of the tilling season in his plot before any one else, and so get a safe start of the man next above him. And the like order is followed by all the others in succession.

If, too, in any year, either from deficiency in the supply of water or other cause a portion only of the village paddy field can be effectively cultivated, that limited portion is taken as the whole, and is divided among the village shareholders, as the original entirety was. And whether this is to be done or not is determined upon by the shareholders as a body. This does not now seem to be everywhere known in practice, but it is provided for often enough in the newly framed *gansabawa* rules, at the instance of the villagers themselves, to indicate that it was a deeply rooted ancient custom.

There is, thus, much matter for internal administration in the village, in the interest of the shareholders themselves, *i.e.*, independently of their relations to the head of the village, which calls for an organisation for the purpose. And consequently, in addition to the officers of the village head, concerned only to look after, and secure to him his rights, there are in each village of the North Central Province (and indeed this feature of primitive agricultural economies prevails universally), the *vel vidahne* and others chosen by the shareholders to control and carry out the system of fencing, ploughing, sowing, shifting of allotment, when necessary, &c., or generally the internal agricultural economy of the village.

The rice production of the irrigated fields is not sufficient even to form the principal portion of the shareholder's support in the greater number of the villages of this Province. The ordinary staple of life is the dry grain, *korakkan*, grown upon the upland as it is called, *i.e.*, on merely unwatered ground, or ground which the flow of water cannot be made to reach. A piece of the forest which surrounds the village and the village paddy field, is felled and burnt, and a crop of *korakkan* is raised thereon for a couple of consecutive years at most, when the clearing is allowed to relapse into jungle again; and the process is not repeated on the same spot for another ten years at least.

This process of *chena* clearing is often done in the North Central Province by the joint action of the village shareholders, under the management of their own officers: and sometimes the whole course of cultivation which follows is also joint, with a partition only of the produce. But sometimes, too, after the clearing is effected, the land is divided and allotted previously to the cultivation. And this is always done in the case of the plots required for the growth of each household's vegetables or curry stuff.

In the maritime provinces this system of joint clearing seems to be absolutely unknown. There every one who has *chena* land, appears to own it absolutely, and either clears and cultivates it himself at long intervals, or gets this done for him on some terms of *anda* letting.

In some few instances there is, it is said, forest and *chena* ground recognised as appurtenant to the village, in this sense, at least, that the shareholders of the village paddy field can, without question on the part of either the village head or of the Government, clear and cultivate in the manner just described any portion of it at their discretion on the foundation of, and in proportion to, their village holdings. But generally the Crown asserts a paramount claim to all jungle and waste land, wherever situated, which has not been before appropriated to actual use; and no tree can be felled or *chena* cultivated thereon except under license from Government.

The actual work of tilling is usually done on the portion of each shareholder by the hands of the members of his family. The occupation of cultivating paddy is in an especial degree respectable, and has almost a sacred character. Women even are not worthy enough to take part in all its operations, and in particular they cannot be seen on the threshing floor—at any rate while the so-called hill paddy, or more highly valued sort of rice grain, is being threshed.

In cases, however, such as those where the shareholder is a woman without children, or where he has other employment, or is well off enough to be able to abstain from manual labour and others of a like kind, it is a common arrangement that his share should be cultivated for him by another person upon the terms of this latter, the person who actually cultivates, rendering to the shareowner a specified share of the produce. This is designated a letting in *ande,* i.e. *half share;* and as a rule, perhaps almost always, the agreed upon share amounts to half the produce both in straw and paddy, the cultivator having also to give a share to the responsible servant who is usually sent by the shareowner to remain on the ground and look after his interests from the day of reaping to the day of partition, and having moreover to feed this man during the interval.

Very nearly all vicarious cultivation assumes this shape, for no such thing is known as the letting of the land for a money rent, and there is no class of agricultural labourers, working on the land of another for money hire. In truth it may be said that in the purely agricultural village of Ceylon there is practically no money in use. Perhaps the majority of the sharers in the village field are deficient in the capital necessary for carrying on the cultivation of their plots. They have not paddy enough to last them for food till next season of harvest or for seed, or they have no plough, or no oxen. These they obtain when and as they are required, from the capitalist of the village, on the terms of setting apart for him on the threshing floor a certain stipulated quantity or share of the produce in return for each item of loan. In the same way (as has been already mentioned) the services of the *Vederale*, or of the village blacksmith and other artizans, will be remunerated. And the like may be done sometimes in the matter of land labour also, but the general custom is for neighbouring shareholders to mutually assist one another in this particular when needed.

The head of the village is more advantageously situated in respect of his *muttettuwa* because he is entitled to have that cultivated for him gratuitously under the supervision of his officers by the turns of tillage service due to him from those of the village shareholders, whose tenures involve that service. And when he carries on the cultivation in this manner he of course appropriates the whole of the produce at the harvest. But he, too, often finds it the more convenient and even the more profitable course to dispense with these services, and to let out the *muttettuwa* land in *ande, i.e.*, on terms of receiving a specified (originally half) share of the produce.

The form and condition of village economy and of agricultural industry, which has been here treated as typical, and which has been mainly described from examples furnished by the North Central and Kandyan provinces, does not of course prevail to the exclusion of every other in all parts of the Island. Nor does it by any means always present itself, in every instance, complete in all its features. Disintegrating influences have been, in modern times at least, silently but surely at work within the village itself. And on the outside of it by a process which may be termed the converse of that which led to the establishment of a regal hierarchy on the basis of the village, the sovereign power, when once constituted, in course of time became the instrument for generating and developing entirely new conditions and notions of property in land.

II.

LAND TENURE AND STATE ECONOMY.

It is very commonly supposed that the king, as theoretical proprietor of all land, from time to time granted to his chieftains such as Adigars, Dessaves, &c., tracts of land in consideration of the grantees rendering him military and civil services. That these Adigars and other grantees sublet the land so granted to them, to peasant cultivators, who paid their rent in services. And that it was in this sort of *de haut en bas* method of proceeding that the Ceylon agricultural village with its peculiar incidents came into being. But it is not difficult to satisfy oneself that agricultural villages must have been very generally distributed over the country and must have attained an advanced stage of development before there were any Dessaves, or king, to initiate this process. And the safer inference from history seems to be that royal and feudal grants of the kind imagined, made in the earlier times by a chieftain or king to his officers or companions, were grants of dominion over populations, not grants of property in land, as we now understand it, which in truth is, comparatively speaking, the conception of a relatively modern stage of society.

The primary result of these feudal grants was to confer upon the grantee the chieftain's customary rights over the villages and unappropriated lands which formed the subject of the grant; and so, doubtless, arose the *Nindegama* (or village under private ownership) as opposed to the royal or *Gabada-gama*.

Sub-infeudation never seems to have had place in Ceylon to any considerable extent. In this respect the Singhalese land system offers much contrast to that of Bengal. But there seems to be difference enough in the data of the two cases to account for this diversity of consequence. Personal service, which was the ordinary tenure obligation of the Singhalese cultivator, is not so readily transferable as a debt of money or of contribution in kind such as the Bengalee raiat owed to his village chief. And moreover the Bengal sub-tenures did not attain their extraordinary modern development until after the Permanent Settlement had given the zamindars an absolute right of property in all the land of their *Zamindaries*—a right which is without parallel in Ceylon. Both the royal and the private seignior however, in the latter island, made immediate grants of unappropriated or waste land. Some of these became cultivating settlements, having the grantee (not, be it observed, the grantor) at their head, the grantor having no other connection with the new community than the link of service which bound the grantee to him, and which often in course of time wore out, or became unenforceable. Others perhaps were from the very beginning exclusive and free of continuing obligation.

To these several origins may perhaps be referred with some degree of probability the very numerous cases of cultivators, and even of non-cultivating proprietors, who own lands by a right of an absolute and independent character, free of all corporate relations whatever, and of every feudal ingredient, which are to be found in all parts of the country, especially in the maritime provinces; though probably in these latter the measures of the Dutch dominant authority, which will be spoken of below, effected the larger part of the change which has taken place in modern times.

And in a sense an agricultural labourers' class is now coming into existence; for wealthy native gentlemen who have obtained the command of money by other pursuits than that of agriculture, have found themselves able to obtain the labour of the poorer village proprietors for daily money wages, and by that means to "farm" their own lands extensively in the English meaning of the word—a practice which is probably spreading to the great advantage of the public.

The joint family system is as conspicuous in Ceylon as it is in Bengal, though perhaps family groups in the former are seldom seen of the large dimensions which are common enough in the latter. It is, however, distinguished by a very remarkable feature: two, or possibly more, brothers living together under one roof will have one wife between them. This is evidently a survival from an early stage of civilisation, and seems to point to much difficulty in the way of securing the necessaries of life, and to some artificial restriction on the number of women. The practice has been discouraged for the future by English legislation in regard to marriage, but it is as yet by no means extinct, and still enters as a curious factor in the law of inheritance, which has to be administered by the civil courts.

The enjoyment of property by all the members of the joint family together has in law very much the incidents of the English tenancy in common. But in the details of actual daily use it varies with the subject, the custom of the district, the will of the most influential coparceners and other circumstances. The affair is managed by the agreement, express or implied, of the whole of the adult joint sharers in the family property, who often separate themselves into smaller groups each taking its own plot of land. The arrangement, however, for the common enjoyment, whatever it be and however long it may have subsisted, is liable to be upset by any dissentient sharer claiming to have his share divided off for him; and indeed it is only by the exercise of this right of partition that a sharer aggrieved by the acts of his copartners can obtain relief.

In the cases of cocoa-nut or areca-nut plantations, of jak trees, and even of paddy fields, it is usual that every gathering of the crop should be made in the presence of all the sharers, and the produce then and there divided according to the shares. In such cases all the sharers together do the necessary work incidental to the cultivation or to the keeping up of the plantation and constitute in fact a cooperative society. Another practice is for the sharers to let out the land or plantation in *anda* either to an outsider, or to one or more of themselves. In this case, also, all the sharers ought to be present at the division of the produce, which is effected in two steps, *i.e.* first division into moieties, and then a division of one moiety among the sharers.

Sometimes the enjoyment of the property is by *tatta maru* succession. The subject is supposed to be divided into as many equal parts as will just admit of the proportionate share of each coparcener being represented by an integral number of these parts; and then instead of an actual division being made accordingly, and every sharer obtaining his proper number of *parts*, each takes the *entirety* for the same number of seasons as he is entitled to parts, giving it up at the end of such period of time to the sharer who stands next in the rota, in order that he may similarly hold it for his own number of seasons; and so on for all the shareholders in turn. Thus if A, B, and C were jointly entitled to a paddy field in undivided shares proportionate to 2, 3 and 4, *i.e.*, to a 2/9th, 1/3rd, 4/9th share of the whole respectively, then by this method of enjoyment A would take the whole field for two years, after him B for three years, and after B again C would take it for four years; and then the set of turns would be repeated in the same order, for successive periods of nine years, until some sharer should insist upon having an actual partition of the field.

A similar sort of succession is adopted in some villages on the coast for the enjoyment by the villagers of the fishing grounds belonging to the village: these are divided into localities; and the recognised boats of the village fish these localities by turns which are settled by *gansabawa* arrangement. Each of these boats with its nets is a valuable piece of property, belonging to many co-sharers jointly, who are commonly members of one family, and have become entitled to their shares by inheritance.[1] The mode in which the copartners share in the earnings of a boat is interesting. On a day's fishing the produce is drawn ashore, is divided in a sufficient number of lots, each estimated to be worth the same assigned value; and these lots are then so distributed that:—

$\frac{1}{50}$th, say, goes to the owner of the land on which the fish are brought ashore,

$\frac{1}{4}$th to those engaged in the labour,

$\frac{1}{5}$th for the assistance of extra nets, &c., rendered by third parties in the process of landing and securing the fish,

which together $= \dfrac{2 + 25 + 20}{100} = \dfrac{47}{100}$;

and the remaining $\frac{53}{100}$ths go to the owners of the boat and net according to their shares therein.

---

[1] Some interesting facts of village organisation, survivals of early practices, are given by Mr. Nell in a valuable note which forms the Appendix to Part I. of *Grenier's Reports* (Ceylon) for 1874.

III.

CEYLON AND BENGAL.

The sketch, which has been attempted in the foregoing pages, seems to be sufficient to disclose a very close parallelism between the agricultural village of Ceylon, and the agricultural village of Bengal or Upper India. The village head proprietor or seignior of Ceylon is the zamindar of Bengal. The *muttettuwa* of the former is the *ziraat* of the latter. The Singhalese *nilakaraya* with his *panguwa* or share of the village paddy field is the Bengalee *ryot* with his *jot*—with this difference, that the *nilakariya's* right in his land is almost universally hereditary and absolute, subject only to the rendering of the special service to the lord, while the *ryot's* tenure does not generally nowadays rise above a right of occupation with liability to variation of rent. Also the middlemen, or under-tenure holders of Bengal, are absent in Ceylon, mainly (as has been above suggested) because in this island personal service to the lord early took the place of the original contribution of produce, or of its equivalent in later days, namely a money commutation in lieu thereof; and also possibly because the development of the Bengalee tenures was the outcome of an idea of property in the *zamindari*, which has never yet been reached in regard to the relation between the *nilakaraya*, and the head of the Ceylon village.

The cultivation in *ande* of the one people is also the precise counterpart of the *batai* cultivation of the other. And the deputing of the right to cultivate the soil, as distinguished from the letting out land as a commodity for a price, seems to characterise both agricultural systems. The usufructuary mortgage, it may be added, which flows from this conception, is the prevailing form of dealing with both the *panguwa* and the *jot* respectively, as commodities.

Lastly we see in Ceylon as in Bengal the double set of village officers, to which the relation between the members of the little village republic on the one hand, with their lord on the other, gives rise, namely, the *gamerale*, *lekhama*, *kankaname* answering to the *naib*, the *patwari*, the *gomashta;* and the *vel vidane* equivalent to the *mandal*.

The ways of life, customs, and laws of the two populations are almost identical; their methods and behaviour in the English Courts of Justice the same. And the constitution and corporate characteristics of the Buddhist religious foundations agree most closely with those of the Bihar *maths*.

Reference has already been made to the assumption that the existing system of land tenure in Ceylon is primarily attributable to grants of land made by the king as lord paramount of the soil, subject to conditions of service or other obligation.

But in view of the corresponding system of Bengal it seems to accord better with the social facts of the present day, and such little evidence bearing upon primitive Aryan civilisation as remains to us, to suppose that the Singhalese society first developed itself, clearing by clearing in separate village communities, isolated from each other and scattered over the land very much, as they even now still are in the existing condition of the North Central Province. *Each* cultivating settlement developed for itself insensibly its own internal organisation, *all* doing so after the same type, as a necessary consequence of the almost complete identity of materials, process, and circumstances, by which they were severally affected. The aggregation of a plurality of villages together under a common head or seignior must, however, have very soon followed upon the establishment of the village organisation. After the consolidation of the village unit, and the complete appropriation of the local tilling resources, a flourishing community would throw out new settlements, or cultivation clearings, generally in the neighbourhood of the parent village, to which they would be reckoned as affiliations. By marriage, too, and often perhaps by high-handed measures, one family would become the dominant and privileged family of several villages. And when the petty chieftain is thus reached, a progress of the like kind, though possibly displaying the larger and more regal features of fighting and spoliation, and involving every diversity of incident, leads easily to the rajah and the king.

There is nothing, however, in this process to introduce any new notions of territorial proprietorship, such as those of which we of Western Europe find it difficult to disabuse our minds. The right to exclusively cultivate, (whether by his own hands or vicariously,) and to enjoy the usufruct of a certain specified share of the village culturable land as incident to his membership in the village community, and subject to an ascertained obligation towards the village chief, constituted the extent of the villager's idea of proprietorship. The chieftain himself had the like right in respect of his *muttettuwa*, coupled with the right to exact the obligations which were due to him from the other shareholders. The common lands of the village, chiefly pasturage, were almost universally kept in the direct management of the village itself, by the hand of its officials. And the jungle was pretty well left to itself, uncared for, each member of the village probably at first taking out of it such wood as he from time to time had need for, and gathering honey and other wild products according as he had opportunity. In process of time, however, the chieftain, as leader in the constant war of the cultivator against wild animals, early came to have recognised privilege in respect to the game of the forest, and from thence advanced to general rights over the forests themselves, and over purely waste lands; and on a footing of this kind he eventually managed to secure to himself tolls for ferries, stallage in markets and the like.

The larger development of the chieftain into the Rajah or any other form of sovereign personage did not bring any new proprietary element into the political system. The chieftainship of all the villages came to reside in the new centre of power, except so far as, either from favour or convenience, it might in some instances be left in the hands of the old possessors, or bestowed upon new men, in either case in consideration of services to be rendered, or it might even be given over gratuitously, from motives of piety, to religious institutions in hopes solely of advantages to be derived in a future state of existence.

In this way we arrive at a state economy in which the Crown is paramount village head or chieftain, with certain lay village heads holding under it, generally on obligation of military or other service of honour, and also ecclesiastical village heads, similarly holding under it, though without any positive obligations, and therefore virtually independent.

The services and aids receivable from the lay headman, and the services and contributions due directly from the shareholders of those villages, in respect to which no middleman existed, together with the produce of the chieftain's *muttettuwa* lands therein, constituted the principal revenues and means of the supreme power; though these were supplemented, especially in relatively modern times, by dues of very various kinds levied simply by the exercise of sovereign authority.

It is remarkable that while in the Aryan village system of India the obligation of the raiat to the zamindar almost universally took the form of contribution of a specified share of the produce, or the discharge of a village office, or of a religious duty, in that of Ceylon the contribution of a share of the produce is the exception, and the tenure obligation is far the most commonly one of personal service.

IV.

THE GRAIN TAX.

IN the preceding description one universally prevailing obligation, resting throughout Ceylon on the cultivator at the present day, has been omitted, namely, the obligation to pay to the Crown a tithe or share of his paddy crop if he has any, and, in some parts of the country, also of his other grain crops. Many of the witnesses, both Native and European, who gave their evidence before the recent Government Grain Commission, seemed inclined to identify this obligation with that which is spoken of in Manu and the other Hindu Shasters as the duty of every cultivator to contribute a share of his produce to the lord or to the state. And nearly all thought it stood upon some very ancient custom. But it can hardly be doubted that in Ceylon the services and the liability to make special contributions to the village head which have been already described, are the equivalent, and the representative of that ancient contribution in kind, which comprises the modern revenue of India; and that consequently the Government tithe of Ceylon must be attributed to some other source. And on a close scrutiny of historical facts its origin appears to be of comparatively modern date. Upon the basis of the village organisation the sovereign power of the state, which was, so to speak, the concentration in one regal person of the seigniorial rights over each of the village units, enjoyed those rights through more than one channel, or in diverse forms and methods.

In very many cases, as has been already mentioned, the seigniorship of the village was bestowed upon, or allowed to fall into the hands of, religious foundations, free of any obligation to the state, the public advantage derivable from the maintenance of the religious institutions constituting ample consideration for the alienation; in others the seigniorship was granted to influential men, or to royal favourites or connections, in consideration of feudal or other services on the part of the grantee, or even sometimes gratuitously.

In far the greater number of cases, however, the exercise and perception of the seignioral rights was delegated to local Government officers, heads of districts, into which the country was parcelled, who were endowed with an executive or administrative character as representatives of the Crown, but who no doubt generally contrived in the end to make their office hereditary and to convert and attach to it some portion of seignioral rights as personal profit.

And lastly, in very many instances villages were kept in hand by the Crown (held *khas* as it is phrased in India) for the especial support of the central establishments : the *muttetuwa* therein was service-tilled, or let out in *ande*, as the case might be, under the direction of royal servants; the produce thus accruing was deposited in kind in royal storehouses (*gabedawa*), arsenals (*awudege*), or treasuries (*arramudale*), according to its sort, and the personal services due were rendered at the palace or elsewhere, to meet some immediate royal requirement. The Crown villages or lands were known under various designations, as *ratninda* or *ande*, original Crown lands, *nillapalla*, those which had fallen into the Crown from failure of the office to which they were attached, *mallapalla*, those which reverted to the Crown from death of the grantee.

The whole period throughout which the Portuguese exercised any authority in the island was marked by great disorganisation of the state machinery. Several independent native powers at times maintained a separate simultaneous existence in the different provinces. And there was but little continuity of general municipal administration of any kind. The village system, however, was still in activity, even in the low part of the country near the coast, *i.e.*, the part of the country most affected by foreign influence and other disturbing forces; and it was by the services and contributions derivable from this source that, first the native powers of the low country, and after them the Portuguese, recruited their military forces and obtained the means of government. The Portuguese, when they had become supreme over the southern maritime circuit of the island, took up the position of the native kings, whom they superseded, and adopted their fiscal and administrative machinery as it stood.

The Dutch, on the other hand, after turning out the Portuguese, and upon being settled in power throughout the maritime provinces, displaced all the native local heads and officials; and their Government assumed to itself the direct collection and benefit of the various dues, cesses, and services, which the previous course of things had had the result of fastening upon the holder of land, as the incident of his tenure, to whomsoever these had been hitherto rendered.

The English in assuming the government of the maritime provinces from the Dutch at first merely stepped into the shoes of their predecessors, availing themselves, and making use, of the services of those who held land on tenure of service (and on that account duty free), also receiving at the store-houses, &c., the seignior's share of produce in kind, from the *Mallapalla*, *Nillapalla*, *Ratninda*, or *Ande* lands, and thirdly taking immediately such benefits as were derivable from holders of land on other and uncertain tenures, inclusive of, among other things, the payment of quotas of produce, and of measures of paddy.

These third set of dues were converted by Royal Proclamation of May 3, 1800, into a tax of 1-10th of the produce. What they previously were, or what was the territorial extent to which they related, does not appear in the statute book, but from the phraseology of the proclamation it would seem that they had respect to lands which formed the residue of the maritime provinces after exception made of the Government lands, and the lands held on tenure of service to Government. Evidently the private seignior and the vihara headship had both alike disappeared before the Dutch.

In the following year (1801, September 3) by proclamation the obligation to service on *tenure of land* throughout the maritime provinces was abolished (as from 1st May, 1802), and land held duty free on account of that service was subjected to payment to Government of 1-10th of the produce if high land, and 1-5th of the produce if low land.

At the same time the payment of ¼ of the produce in respect of *Mallapalla, Nillapalla, Ratninda* or *Ande* lands was reserved.

But though the obligation to service was thus divorced from the land, power was still reserved to the governor to exact it by special order from persons of whatever caste and condition for adequate pay to be given therefor. The exigencies of the Kandyan war afterwards led to a renewal of the general claim of Government to the services of the people, this time without reference to the possession of land, but on the ground of custom and caste, payment to be made at rates fixed by Government. And in 1809 the making of roads was declared to be gratuitous service, lying on the inhabitants of the district through which they passed.

These enactments applied only to the maritime provinces of the island acquired from the Dutch. In 1815, however, the English also obtained by conquest and treaty the government of the Central or Kandyan Province, which up to that time had been solely under the administration of native powers. And in 1818, by the proclamation of the 21st November, it was enacted that all duties theretofore payable into the royal store-house, treasury, or arsenal, and all duties or other taxes whatever were abolished, and in lieu thereof a tax of 1-10th of the produce on all paddy lands was substituted, reduced to 1-14th in certain specified Korles.

This was evidently a step of no very discriminating character. The dues and cesses which were abolished were payable out of very various subjects, and on some diversity of obligations. And the substitution which is thus made for them is a general average levy, not even from all lands, but from all paddy lands. At the same time the services due in respect of service tenure lands, on which mainly this new tax must have fallen as well as on others, were retained, though it was stipulated that the services should be generally paid for at an established rate, the repair and making of roads only being, as in the maritime provinces, gratuitous.

The liability of certain inhabitants of temple lands to perform service to Government was also retained (cl. 21, of Procl. 21st November, 1818).

On the 24th of December, 1831, Lt.-Col. Colebrooke made his report to the Secretary of State after the inquiry into the administration of the

Government of Ceylon which he and Mr. Cameron had been commissioned to carry out; and on the footing of this report an Order of Council dated 12th April, 1832, declared that none of His Majesty's native or Indian subjects within the island should be or were liable to render any service to His Majesty in respect to the tenure of their land, or in respect of their caste or otherwise to which His Majesty's subjects of European birth or descent were not liable, any law, custom, or regulation notwithstanding.

But even this proclamation contained the reservation of services to the Crown of holders of land in royal villages in the Kandyan Province, and the like for vihara and private owners in the same province.

The results of all these measures may be summarised thus;—on taking over the maritime provinces from the Dutch, the English found the lands held under one or other of three general classes of tenure, namely:—

1st. Lands held on tenure of service.

2nd. Lands held in *ande*, which were formerly Crown lands.

3rd. Lands held on any other tenure, spoken of in the proclamation as uncertain, or clogged with inconveniences.

And they converted tenure No. (1) into a tax of 1-10th of the produce if the lands were high lands and 1-5th of the produce if they were low lands; tenure No. (2) into a tax of $\frac{1}{4}$ of the produce; and tenure No. (3) into a tax of 1-10th of the produce.

On assuming the Government of the Kandyan Province, they did not inquire into and discriminate the tenures there existing, but abolished at one stroke all duties payable in kind to Government, and all other duties and taxes whatever, and substituted in their stead a tax of 1-10th of the annual produce upon all paddy lands.

And while doing away with all services due to Government, as they thus eventually did, they reserved the services of tenants of lands in the royal villages of the Kandyan Province, which were tacitly treated as lands still belonging immediately to the Crown. According to Ribeyro, Knox, and Valentyn, the fact seems to have been that in the Portuguese and earlier times there was almost no money in the country. All trade which was not a Crown monopoly was effected by barter. Paddy was the commodity which commonly filled the place of coin. Most of the presents which, as we have seen, accompanied all service, took the form of paddy, and nearly all obligations by way of remuneration or duty were discharged by a measure of grain drawn from the contents of the thrashing-floor at harvest.

So that, to generalize somewhat, when the English came the demesne lands of the Crown, as they may be termed, comparatively limited in extent, were cultivated by tenants, upon the condition of rendering from $\frac{1}{4}$ to $\frac{1}{2}$ of the produce into the Crown store-houses; most of the remaining cultivable land of the country was held upon some service more or less skilled (as is described very graphically by Ribeyro), and such other occupiers of land as there were, were obliged, without any very definite principle, also to make contributions of paddy, which were generally in lieu of, and practically stood as a money commutation for, some less acceptable service: and all occupiers alike were subjected to irregular cesses in kind at the time of harvest.

The English administration reformed this state of things by (sooner or later) sweeping away all these obligations except that of the tenants of the demesne lands; and by replacing them with a tax of 1-10th of all the produce of the soil in the maritime provinces, and of 1-10th of the paddy in the Kandyan provinces. In the latter arrangements they do not seem to have recognised the fact that the paddy payments which they thus replaced by a tax of 1-10th of the paddy crop were in their character generally money commutations of dues payable in respect of all kinds of crop.

[1] The earliest mention of any tax, or any contribution of the people towards the support of a royal person which is to be found in the historical books of Ceylon, occurs in the Aggauna Sutta in Digha Nitraya, and in the commentary thereon called Sumangala Vilasani.

The Aggauna Sutta is a sermon by Buddha himself, and the commentary is the work of the well-known and learned Buddhist divine Buddhagosha.

The passage in the sermon is "Salinam Bhagam Anupa dassama." In English, "We shall give a portion of our paddy."

Buddhagosha's commentary on this is: "Mayam Ekakassa Khettalo Amanam Ammanam Aharitva Tuiham Sali-bhagam dassama. Yan Jaya Kinchi Kammamua Katabbam Iwam Amhakam Iettaratthane Iitthati." In English, "We shall give you at the rate of ammunan of paddy from each field of

---

[1] For the following information I am indebted to the learned Suriyagoda Unanse, Librarian of the Malagava, Kandy.

ours. You need not follow any trade. But be you our chief."

The word "Sali" which is here used signifies literally a particular kind of rice. but it is understood to be intended in these places to stand for all grain produce.

No other tax, or obligation towards the governing power is noticed. And it does not seem unreasonable to infer that this contribution of one ammunam of grain produce per field (whatever that amounted to) was nothing more than the Singhalese form, in the time of Buddha's teaching, of the ancient Indo-Aryan land tenure. The growth of the system of services, which in modern times very largely displaced it, must have taken place subsequently. And the paddy cesses, which ultimately were often again super-imposed upon the services, probably came in later still, with an increase in the central power of exaction.

The Singhalese word "otu," by which the Government tax or claim is commonly designated, means "one"; and is probably equivalent only to *one portion*, or *one share*, without indicating anything with regard to the proportion of the share to the entirety.

How the proportion, therefore, of 1-10th in the English impost was arrived at is not very clear, though it seems to have been founded upon the practice of the Dutch in granting out Crown lands.

The grain tax appears consequently to be no older than the century, and if it be justified as being in effect a return, under some modification, to the earliest and most widely prevalent form of national revenue which was developed from the basis of the village organization among the Aryan races, it is noteworthy as a characteristic of the Ceylon Aryans that from the same basis they produced the service system in its stead.

EVOLUTION OF THE INDO-ARYAN SOCIAL AND LAND SYSTEM.

FROM THE JOINT FAMILY TO THE VILLAGE.

MANY years ago I ventured to describe in this place[1] some of the more prominent features of the Hindu joint-family as they appeared to one who had then recently arrived in this country. At that time I was unacquainted with the labours of Nasse, Sir H. Maine and others, who have shown the true character of this still living institution and the place it has held in the progress of Aryan civilization.

[1] The following pages reproduce a paper which was read at a meeting of the Bethune Society, Calcutta, in 1872. At that time the writer had no knowledge of Ceylon, and the paper has been allowed to retain its original form because of the completeness with which it seems to account for the facts of the Singhalese agricultural village, to which it was not directed, as well as those of the Bengallee village for which its explanation is designed.

I may now assume that its historical value is generally well understood.

On inquiring into the growth in India of proprietary rights in land, we find the joint-family at its very origin. The village was at first, and still is in a large degree, a group of such families, often all sprung from or appendant to a central family. They were seldom, however, even from the very outset, all of equal rank.

The mode in which this came about may be taken to be pretty accurately ascertained, for the founding of a new village in waste and unoccupied ground has always been, even down to the present day, a not uncommon occurrence. In the days of Manu, according to the Institutes, it was quite probable in any given case that persons might be alive who remembered the foundation of the village; and at the present time every settlement report sent in to Government will be found to furnish instances, and to describe the circumstances, of newly created agricultural communities. We shall hardly be wrong if we assume that the process which we see in operation now-a-days does not differ essentially from that which gave rise to the village in archaic times. I imagine that one or two enterprising persons more or less connected together by ties of relationship, started the little colony. Of these, doubtless, one would, in some special manner, be leader, and would together with his family after him maintain a pre-eminence in the new society. Next would come the family of the man who was especially learned in, or who became charged with the care of, religious matters—precepts and ceremonies—in other words, who was the repositary of the higher law of the small community.

Very soon other persons would be allowed to cultivate land, and to have place within the ambit of the new settlement upon terms prescribed to them as to the situation of their allotment, performing work on the land of the leaders, and other conditions of subordination. Others again would merely obtain the comparatively civilized shelter afforded by the village against the perils of the outside wilderness, pursuing therein convenient handicrafts, or performing servile tasks.

Land was not conceived of as the subject of property in the modern sense, or as belonging to any individual. Each village had its boundaries, which early came to be most precise, and the entire space within these belonged to the whole village. Every family, however, appropriated to itself or became the owner of the homestead which it occupied, and the garden or orchard attached thereto, and often too its particular tank. So much of the land within the village boundaries as was needed for cultivation was apportioned among the recognised families. At first this was done merely for the year's tilling, then at longer intervals, and later still only on the occasions of considerable changes in the families, and so on. The grazing ground, the waste, and the woodland (or jungle) was common to all alike In the early days of village civilization, the agricultural element was comparatively small, and it was both easy and advantageous that the culturable plots should be changed, as just mentioned, at more or less frequent periods. As, however, larger areas came to be taken into cultivation, and increased skill and labour to be applied to the reclamation and culture of the soil, and non-annual crops to be grown, it followed naturally that the different families ultimately got to retain permanently in their hands either the whole or the better portion of their respective allotments.

The cultivation of the family plot was effected, as a rule, by the members of the family alone. But the leading family and the priest or cultured family, no doubt, from the beginning inherited and enjoyed much prestige and priority of consideration which enabled them to attain to a position of privilege. They seem generally to have cultivated more or less by servants, or by the means of *batai* agreements—*i.e.* agreements under which the tilling is done by a person not the owner—in consideration of a definite share of the produce being yielded to the owner.

And it is not improbable that, originally at any rate, their servants and *batai* occupants were drawn from the, so to speak, interloper portions of the inhabitants of the village—*i.e.* those who could not claim their part in the village soil by derivative rights from the founder.

Thus there grew to be, even from the commencement, a gradation of respectability and employment within the village itself; and it is especially noticeable that there were two privileged heads of the village, the secular and the religious or clerical.

As population increased and became more fixed, the cultivation of cereals and pulses became more necessary and engrossing; and the value of cattle became greater, as being both the cultivating power and the means of exchange. For reasons already suggested, the recognised founder's family and the priests' families, doubtless, obtained advantages in the allotment of *khets*, or culturable plots, both in regard to situation and quantity, and became the wealthiest members of the community—*i.e.* possessors of the largest herds, and cultivators of the biggest *khets* with the least expenditure of manual labour. They were also the principal guides and directors of village affairs. And so it came about that to own and look after cattle (the symbol of wealth) was respectable, and, in modern phraseology, the occupation of a gentleman, as distinguished from the manual labour of the field.

After these we have the remainder of those families who were entitled, as of old right, to participation in the village lands, and were essentially agricultural in occupation.

And lastly there is the class of relative strangers or outsiders, namely, artizans and petty traders, followed by a servile class, hewers of wood, drawers of water, scavengers, &c.

Thus far we encounter no indication that any real approach has been made towards personal *property* in land. We have found that each family in time got the right to retain continuously year after year its own particular plots for cultivation; or at any rate did so in the case of those plots which they had respectively by especial pains reclaimed from a state of waste, or which had other peculiarities; and we have arrived at the conclusion that the leading families, out of all the families entitled to the village lands, got the better of their neighbours in these matters. Subsequently, again, as families broke up, it came to be acknowledged that the members of each had a right to distribute among themselves the family *khets* for cultivation.

But still the proprietary conception went no further than this, namely, that the particular plot of land which the family or individual claimed was that part of the village land which he or it was entitled to cultivate, or to have cultivated for his own benefit.

At the same time the business of allotment (so long as the practice of allotting obtained), the order of cultivation, the maintenance of the water supply, the keeping up of fences, and all other affairs of common interest to the little community, were managed by the heads of families, entitled to their share of the village lands, in *panchayat* assembled.

A further development of the social system, and a new source of land rights, was brought about by the attrition of village with village.

The exclusiveness of the Aryan family was its marked characteristic. In the earliest beginnings to which we can get back, to use the words of a recent historian of Greece,[1] "the house of each man was to him what the den is to the wild beast which dwells in it; something, namely, to which he only has a right, and which he allows his mate and his offspring to share, but which no other living thing may enter except at the risk of life." The same spirit can be perceived animating the Hindu family throughout all its stages, even down to the present time ; and so it was necessarily the governing principle of the group of families which constituted the

[1] Cox's *Greece*, p. 13.

village, in its relation to its neighbours as soon as it had any.

Each little colony or *abad* held itself aloof from and independent of all others; jealous of its rights, and quick to resent, as well as to defend itself from encroachment. As villages thickened, causes of quarrel increased, for instance,—pasturage grounds —reclamations — profitable jungle tracts — fuel — thatching grass—bamboo clumps, &c. &c.—until at last, it may be said, the normal relation between the *abads* was one of chronic hostility.

Collision on these points led to fights, in which no doubt the head of the leading family in the village was the director, and the different members of that family, both from their position and from their comparative independence of manual occupation, were the principal actors.

The common consequence of these fights was that the successful party not merely vindicated its own rights, but seized and occupied some of the best lands of its antagonist, and carried off his herds.

And as in those early days fighting was mainly an affair of personal prowess, these acquisitions were appropriated by those whose strong arms had won them. The conquered *khets* came to belong, in a new sense, to the leader of the expedition, and those to whom he awarded them. And we may safely assume that he appropriated to himself the lion's share of the captured cattle. Thus was introduced a peculiar cause of aggrandisement of the leading family and its adherents. Already distinguished by family blood, by wealth, and by hereditary position and partial immunity from hard labour, they now acquired great additional wealth from the outside, became possessors of *nij*, or private, lands in foreign villages; and above all became invested with that personal influence and authority which attaches to successful fighters. The beaten villages, at first, probably only suffered the loss of the appropriated *khet* and of the stolen herds. But this must have had the effect of impoverishing some of its inhabitants, and of increasing the numbers of the dependent population. So that the invaders would at once find it easy to enforce or procure the cultivation of their newly-acquired lands upon *batai* terms. But cultivation by servants, or on *batai* conditions, was not in itself novel; it was only extended as the result of these proceedings. The really new ingredient of tenure which came in through them was the complete independence of the village community even in theory which characterised the victor's retention of these lands.

Results such as these, of course, tended very soon to give rise to fighting expeditions for their own sake, and upon an enlarged scale. Time and distance were involved in them; and the fighters had then to be maintained while away from home. At first this would be managed out of the principal man's wealth: he assigned portions of his land to the more prominent among them, generally on conditions of service, and supported others out of his own stores, flocks, and herds. Then the non-fighters of the primary village would contribute rations in kind. And next, perhaps even before this step, each subdued village would be made to pay a permanent tribute of produce in kind.

Here we have before us the growth of a chieftainship and a fighting class, mostly sprung in the first instance from the village founder's family, but also including others who had won their place by the side of these through strength of arm. And when in this way an energetic and relatively powerful family had gained supremacy over many villages, its head became a hereditary local chief, and the fighting men constituted a diminutive aristocracy, most of them actually and all reputedly of the same blood as the chief. The causes which led to this development were of universal operation; and so, sooner or later, all villages fell under this kind of dominion, and the originally free *abads* became subordinated in groups to chiefs and rajahs. Also the chiefs and rajahs with their several little attached aristocracies, each hereditarily separate from their people, came to be collectively regarded as a noble military governing race, such as the rajpoot of historical times. If the celebrated Kshatria caste ever had more reality than belongs to mere mention in Brahmanical pages (and it certainly has no reality now) it doubtless arose in this fashion.[1]

Similarly, from those of the original settlers, who discharged in each *abad* the functions of priest and moral teacher, came the great clerkly race-caste of Brahman. They were in the first instance generally, no doubt, closely connected with the head of the colony himself, and like him obtained advantages in the allotment of land, and in getting it tilled for them. Thus freed from the necessity of manual toil, and devoted to the humanizing pursuit of religion, law, and advancement of knowledge, they ultimately came to constitute, by hereditary separation, a singular class of aristocracy —seldom wealthy, but always of vast influence in their several communities.

[1] See Growse's *Mathura*.

As their generations widened, their increasing wants were met by assignments of land made by the chief and others.

And being the repositaries of all learning, and in possession of priestly powers, as society progressed they gradually monopolised all that existed in the way of public offices, and attained an importance which, as a rule, much exceeded that of an ordinary member of the fighting or warrior class, and closely approached that of the chief himself. The aggregate of these everywhere were *Brahmans*. It is possible that out of the same materials a third hereditary class, also reputed to be of pure and unmixed descent from the founders of the settlement, may have developed itself and acquired a social status of privilege. For it is conceivable that besides the fighting men and the teachers, some few others of the original settlers or their descendants may by good fortune in husbandry, or likely enough by joining trade therewith, have contrived to distinguish themselves in wealth above their fellows, and to free themselves from the toil of agricultural labour; and may at the same time have avoided the ranks of the chief's adherents. I confess I think this last supposition extremely improbable, for in the stage of civilisation which is here being considered an unlettered man of leisure and wealth could scarcely have found a respectable alternative to that which for want of a better term we may call the profession of arms, and which must have been looked upon as the gentleman's occupation. If, however, such a segregation could have originally taken place, and if notwithstanding the want of the compacting force which is incident to community of employment, purity of family blood could be maintained in this body, then like the fighting and the clerkly classes it would enjoy an aristocratic pre-eminence, and would answer to the caste which has been described by Brahmanical writers under the designation *Vaisya*, but the existence of which, so far as I know, has never been otherwise evidenced.

The great bulk, however, of the descendants of

the original settlers (speaking of villages in the mass) were unable to rise above the common level, were less careful of purity of blood, or of preserving any mark of descent from the immigrant race. With them gradually came to be intermixed people of all kinds, aborigines, run-aways from other *abads* from cause of pauperism, feud, or otherwise, some of whom came to be even allowed a portion of the village lands.

The social development which I suppose to have been thus effected may be concisely and roughly described as follows :—

(1.) The immigrant and growing population in each different tract or district of country, although made up of village units, in course of time acquired as a whole a certain homogeneity of physical appearance and of character, peculiar to itself, being the product of various influences, such as circumstances of the district, general habits of life of the people, infiltration of foreign ingredients, and so on.

(2.) A hereditary aristocratic class rose to the top of each community or people (so distinguished), and established over it a domination which bore characteristics resembling those of feudalism in Europe.

(3.) And a clerkly class in substance hereditary known everywhere as the Brahmans, in like manner came into social pre-eminence, and managed to appropriate to itself the influence and authority of the priest and the teacher.

I may venture here to say (though my opinion in itself is worth very little) that I quite agree with Mr. Growse in thinking that there never was at any time in Indian Aryan society a hereditary *Vaisya* class; and as I have already mentioned, I cannot perceive in the conditions under which I imagine that society to have been developed any cause adequate to its production. Probably the *Brahman*, *Kshatria*, *Vaisya*, and *Sudra* of the Brahmanical codes were only the Utopian class distinctions of a prehistoric More.

From the Joint Family to the Village. 251

Although there may be some difficulty in conceiving the exact nature of the process by which the result (1) is produced, there can be no doubt, I apprehend, that, in some stages of society at any rate, it is a reality of very active operation. In quite recent times, we have familiar to us under the designation of Yankee an instance of the origination, by immigration into a new country, of a novel and very distinct type of people, marked by physical and intellectual characteristics of the highest order.

And a glance over the ground which is covered by the Aryan race in India will show, that while there can be no question as to a certain community of race character possessed by the different populations, there have also been at work upon them respectively strong local influences and special modifying causes. To take large divisions, it is impossible not to see that the population of the Punjab differs uniformly and materially from that of the Kumaon, and similarly the latter again from the populations of Bengal and Orissa. I will make no endeavour now to seek out these influences and causes for each case, because to do so would carry me somewhat wide of my present purpose.

On the theory put forward, the two privileged classes (2) and (3) ought to be distinguished from the commoner local population by such marks as purity of descent (*i.e.* descent preserved from the freer intermixture prevailing around), together with the relatively elevating habits a leisured life can confer; and yet should participate with that population in the general characteristics which serve to separate them from the population of other localities. And that this is so in India is, I think, as a rule, abundantly apparent. In the Chapter of the Star of India lately held in Calcutta, the small groups of noblemen who stood around, say, for example, the Maharaja of Pattiala, the Maharaja of Gwalior, and the Maharaja of Rewah respectively, were as markedly different from each other in feature of countenance and bodily proportions, and could be as readily recognised separately, as if the comparison were made between them and the like number of Englishmen. And the same assertion may be made relative to the Brahman.

The general results in regard to rights of property in land, of the social progress and course of change which I have endeavoured to represent, were very simple. The village community stood out with great distinctness as a self-governing agricultural corporation. Every family in it except those which were purely servile or which had never become recognised as sharers in the customary rights, had its allotment of village land for cultivation; it had also the right to pasture its cattle over the belt surrounding the village and on other pasture grounds of the village, if any; and a right to take what it wanted of the jungle products within the village limits.

The local chieftain had a portion of lands in *all* the villages subordinate to him which was in a special manner his own, and was additional to the substantial share which he had of the communal rights. The other members of the warrior class often had, besides their own village lands, an assignment of land from the chief in some village, not necessarily their own, which they held in more or less dependence upon him. And the chief, further, had a tribute of a certain portion of the produce of every village allotment (exclusive of those of the Brahman and the warrior) which he could use as he pleased for the support of himself or his followers, and which he often no doubt assigned pretty freely to favourites and others on conditions of service and otherwise.

The chief and the other members of the warrior class (or feudal aristocracy) and the Brahman seldom or perhaps never took any personal part in cultivation. They either tilled their lands through servants, or oftener allowed other persons to occupy and till them upon condition of yielding up a portion of the produce, they themselves probably (at least in the earlier days of the practice) furnishing cattle, seed, and other agricultural capital. And arrangements of this kind could be altered by the persons concerned at their convenience. But the land allotment generally was an affair of the village, and although the ordinary village cultivator was obliged to pay tribute in kind in respect of his share to the chief, he could not be disturbed in the possession thereof by him. There never was, so far as I can discover, any assumption on the part of the chief of a right of possession in respect of the cultivators' share of the village land or of a right to disturb that possession. And all questions of right, and all disputes within the village, were settled on a basis of custom and equity by the village *panchayat*, wherein the chief, either in person or represented by a superior servant, had a voice. In all this there is at most conceived only the right to cultivate land, and a deputing of that right to another in consideration of a share in the produce. And little or no approach had up to this stage been made to the idea of property in land as a commodity, and of power to alienate it, or even to hire out the use of it for a money payment. The chief was in a sense lord of the villages which were subordinate to him, and entitled to a share of the produce from every cultivator therein: but he was not *owner* in the modern English sense, and had no power to dispose of the possession of any land except his *nij*, or private, land; and with regard to this he only had the right to cultivate by himself or by his servants, or to get somebody else to do it on condition of dividing the produce. No other practice was known or thought of, and it need hardly be remarked that in early stages of society, practice or custom precedes and is the measure of right.

At first sight the distinction which I am endeavouring to draw may appear to be without a difference; the produce of the land must have been in effect divided much in the same way between the cultivators and the chief, who took tribute in kind as if the parties were true landlord and tenant.

But on looking closer it will be found that the two relations differ very materially, and that the one I am dwelling upon is anterior to the latter as a matter of progress. It is especially important to remember that the share of produce which the Chief could take was not regulated by his own pleasure, or by the making a bargain, but by custom, or practice, in regard to which the village *panchayat* was the supreme authority, and that the Chief had no power to turn the cultivator out of possession.

When these quotas of produce were in the course of progress turned into money payments, or their equivalent (an event which has not happened universally even yet), they still did not become rent paid for occupation and use of land as an article belonging to and at the disposal of the person paid, but were dues payable to a superior ruling authority by the *subjects* of that authority. The Chief, though zamindar of *all* the land within the zamindary, was at most landlord (and that in the very qualified sense of one merely having the right to dispose of the occupation and tilling of the soil) of so much of it as was his *nij* land, and in some instances probably of the wastes. The machinery of this system was the zamindar's *ka-chahri*, the centre of local authority, side by side with which was the *panchayat*, i.e. the old *abad* self-government.

I am unable to adduce the direct evidence of any historical writer in favour of this view, but there is a good deal in the old codes which tends to support it indirectly.

In the Institutes of Manu, not perhaps a very ancient compilation in the form under which it has come down to us, though probably as old and respectable an authority as we can go to, there is nowhere any mention of land as a subject of property in the modern English sense. Private ownership of cultivated plots is recognised, but it is simply the ownership of the cultivator. The land itself belongs to the village. There is no trace of rent. The owner is only another name for cultivator He is indeed under obligation to cultivate lest the Rajah's or lord's dues in kind be shortcoming. But he might cultivate by servants, of whose doings he knew little or nothing, or arrange with some one else to cultivate on a division of crops (*i.e.* the *batai* system, a form of metayer).

In another place of Manu we find every one enjoined to keep a supply of grain sufficient for his household for three years. And it is evident that almost everybody is supposed to be an actual cultivator.

Although the practice of *batai* is very like the small end of a wedge, which might have disrupted the primitive system, yet it did not in fact lead to the letting of land: and *rent* in any form seems to be altogether unknown to Manu.

Selling of land, or even of the use of land, does not appear to be anywhere directly alluded to. Contract of sale in some variety is spoken of, but nowhere, so far as I remember, in immediate reference to land. Appropriating a field, giving a field, and seizing a field, have all a place in Manu's pages, but not buying or selling a field. The passage in p. 303 § 114 of Sir W. Jones's translation (4to. ed.) when rightly rendered, does not give rise to the inference that land was there contemplated as a subject of purchase.

Somewhat later in time, no doubt, according to the Mitakshara, separated kinsmen had acquired uncontrolled power of disposing of their respective shares of the family allotment. This, however, did not amount to a dealing with a specific portion of land as a thing of property, but was a mere transfer of a personal cultivating right, incidental to personal status in the village community, and subject to an obligation to render to the lord his share of the produce. And for this cause it was necessary that the transaction should be accompanied by specified public formalities: and an out-and-out sale was discountenanced except for

From the Joint Family to the Village. 261

necessity. Moreover, when the transfer was not absolute, but conditional by way of security for the repayment of a debt, it always took the form of what is now called a usufructuary mortgage.

It seems to me pretty clear that the usufruct of land by actual tillage on the footing of a right of partnership in the village cultivating community, and not the land itself, constituted the object to which the words of ownership occurring in the Hindu law-writers relate.

The same story is brought down to modern times by copper-plates of title, old sanads, and other evidence of the like kind. These disclose the pretty frequent grant or assignment of the right to make collections and other zamindari rights proceeding from a superior lord, or the gift of a plot from the waste, or out of the zamindar's *ziraat,* to a Brahman or other deserving person. But I know of no instance of private transfer by purchase and sale of actual land, or even of the lease of land for a term of years in consideration of a rent.[1]

The land system at which we have thus arrived is one of power or authority on the one side, and subjection on the other, rather than of property; and I may venture to say generally that it is the zamindar and *raiyat* system of Aryan India at the present day.

I have not now the time to illustrate this proposition adequately by examples. The state of things in Bengal has been so affected by direct legislation, and the spread of English real property notions, that I cannot appeal to it for this purpose without more explanation than I have here space for. But I will venture to say that Mr. La Touche's very interesting Settlement Report of Ajmere and

---

[1] I am indebted to the learned Sanscrit scholar, Dr. Rajindralala Mitra for notice of the Sanchi tablet, of which a translation is given in the Journal of the Asiatic Society of Bengal, vol. vi. p. 456. But I do not imagine that the transaction therein spoken of was a purchase and sale of land as between private owners. It reads to me more like an enfranchisement of some sort (such as redemption of liability to pay revenue to the lord) with the view to the land becoming *debattar*.

Mhairwarra, recently published, supplies facts which serve to establish it for that district, notwithstanding that Mr. La Touche very often uses language which broadly declares the State's *right of ownership* in all lands constituting the territory of the State. Mr. La Touche, I admit, appears to employ these words "right of ownership" in their widest English meaning; but I do not think that his facts require anything nearly so large. In his first passage on the "Tenures" of Ajmere, he says: "The soil is broadly divided into two classes—khalsa, or the private domain of the Crown, and land held in estates, or baronies, by feudal Chiefs originally under an obligation of military service," and I cannot help thinking that he has been misled by an analogy which his phraseology borrowed from feudal Europe suggests, and which, to say the best of it, is only imperfect.

As I understand the report, the general result may be stated thus: Certain members of the village community enjoy the permanently cultivated or improved lands of the village by some recognised hereditary or customary right of cultivation, which is sometimes termed ownership and sometimes proprietorship; that if they pay the customary share of the produce to the person entitled to receive it, they consider themselves entitled to continue undisturbed in the occupation and cultivation of their land, or even to transfer it to another; that there is no such thing as the letting of land on terms of profit; that private sales of land are practically unknown, and that the sale of land by the Civil Court (an English innovation) has been prohibited because it is so opposed to ancient custom as to be incapable of being carried into effect; that mortgages are almost all of an usufructuary kind, and in Mhairwarra there is a kind of *metayer* system established between the mortgagor and mortgagee; that the State, as representative of the former superior Chief, collects the revenue (which is the modern equivalent to the old *customary share of the produce*) from the cultivators by certain agency machinery, and exercises other recognised Chief's rights, except over lands in respect to which the Chief''s rights to collect dues, and of other kind, were assigned by him to minor Chiefs, designated as istamrardars or jaghirdars, on conditions of military service, or for other consideration; that amongst the rights so exercised by the State and its assignees, was the right to dispose of waste land; and finally, that although within the State area of collection the revenue is settled in the form of a money payment, in all jaghir estates the revenue is collected by an estimate of the produce, and money assessments are unknown.

If this concise statement of facts, drawn from Mr. La Touche's report, be approximately correct, as I think it is, provided the report be read cleared of expressions which seem due merely to Mr. La Touche's implied theory of original State ownership, it accords singularly well with, and justifies almost to the word, the proposition which I have just ventured to make.

And this example is the more forcible, because

Mr. La Touche says that "the land tenures are, as might be expected, entirely analogous to those prevailing in the adjacent Native States," an assertion which the result of my own personal inquiries enables me to confirm.

But the true relation between the Indo-Aryan land system and the modern form of absolute right of ownership of land which obtains in England, will be best explained by drawing attention to the point at which the latter diverged from the former.

In Europe the course of change from the initial joint family village onwards was at first much the same in character as that which occurred in India, but it early exhibited a very remarkable difference. In the conflict of villages the strongest party did not limit itself, I imagine, as appears to have been the case in the East, to making appropriations from the waste, and to imposing a produce tribute on the cultivators of the defeated village, leaving them otherwise undisturbed in their possessions and in the management of their village affairs; but it turned the cultivators out of their land, taking the cultivation into its own hands, and reducing the former cultivators to the condition of labourers or serfs. The root of the village government and administration was thus destroyed; and in place of the produce tribute was substituted a dominion over the soil—a difference which was all-important, and pregnant with the most weighty political consequences.

There was still, I conceive, at this stage no idea of ownership of, or property in, land, other than the idea of right to cultivate, no idea of right to land independent of the purposes of cultivation or other actual use of it. Thus the dominant party, by its leader and chief, took over the cultivation, distributing it probably in parcels amongst themselves, the Chief no doubt ultimately getting by far the largest share, and being especially the authority to distribute, while the subjected people became bound to labour for their masters, and on this condition were allowed to retain or occupy a homestead—and, so to speak, subsistence—plot of land. From this beginning grew up the manor, corresponding in some degree, though remotely, to the oriental *mauzah*, or village. The lord's demesne, or cultivation, comprised the bulk of the land, or at any rate the best of it; some portions of land became the cultivation of free men of the lord's race or belonging allied to him by military ties and by blood, and the rest was the subsistence land of the serfs, bound to labour on the lord's land.[1] From the serf holdings again, at a later period, the copyhold tenures developed.

But meanwhile and for a long time the lord was only owner of his land in the sense of cultivator and user of it. He cultivated his land in his various manors through the intervention of a bailiff in each manor. In the course of social and economic change, the expense of this vicarious management became so great as to leave little or no profit for the lord, and a new expedient suggested itself. The bailiff

---

[1] For the freemen's obligations to the lord, see Sir H. Maine's paper in a recent number of the *Fortnightly Review*.

was dispensed with, and the cultivation of the land was given out in portions to the more substantial serfs and others, on the terms of the lord providing the cattle, implements, and other cultivating capital (including seed grain), and the cultivator (now become farmer) remunerating the lord partly by money payments and partly by a share of the produce.

In some parts of Europe this led to a permanent *metayer* system, but in England it did not last long. The farming class speedily acquired capital enough to find themselves in cattle, &c., and to take in hire the cultivation or use of the land for a simple annual payment of money, *i.e.* rent. And thus the ownership of land became permanently distinguished from the use and cultivation of it under contract with the owner; and the landlord and farmer became two grades of persons dealing with the same commodity, namely, the owner of it unskilled in using it, and the hirer of it for use.

On the other hand, those serfs who did not

succeed in rising to the position of the farmer in the end sunk to be mere labourers, subsisting solely on wages earned by doing for the farmer, and under his directions and control, the manual work of tilling the soil.

As long as right to land was inseparably associated with personal use of it, there was no thought of alienating it at the will of the person to whom the use belonged, but when it became a mere commodity, which was only valuable for as much as it would bring on being let out, then of course it also became freely alienable like any other commodity.

This stage seems never to have been reached in the course of the purely oriental development. It is, however, hardly too much to say that in India the tendency of the natural economic and social forces of the country, if allowed free play and given time, would have been to make the land a commodity in the hands of the village cultivator, or perhaps even of the mahajan, rather than in those of the zamindar.

But in Bengal the Permanent Settlement which gave an artificial right to the zamindars and the English civil courts which recognise the power of alienating every personal right capable of definition, have introduced disturbing forces of immense effect; and it would be rash indeed to attempt to foretell the ultimate result which may be expected in the course of progress if the Legislature should not again interfere. All that can be safely said is that the present is eminently a period of transition. The political consequences to which I just now referred would alone afford a very large subject for discussion.

In the East, under the village system, the people practically governed themselves, and the contest for power among the Chiefs of the noble class was mainly a struggle for command of the *kachahri tahsils*, the contents of which were spent in personal indulgence, royal magnificence, and splendid monuments to the glory of the successful competitor.

In the West, such government of the people and administration of public affairs as there was, fell to the lord and his courts. There were no collections, and a great portion of the means of maintaining and working the machinery of authority had to be obtained by some system of levy and taxation.

These two differing sets of conditions led necessarily to intrinsically different political developments; and the presence of Turkey in Europe has caused the comparative analysis of them to be deserving of more attention than it has yet received.

APPENDIX.

T

APPENDIX.

NOTE A.

AFTER the text was written, the following memorandum was received by the author from Baboo Ram Sundar Basack, of Dacca. It very clearly describes the means of agricultural families in Eastern Bengal, and deserves to be printed in full :—

Ordinary ryots may be divided into three classes in consideration of their household assets.

1st.—Those who cultivate fifteen bigas and upwards and have a family, say of one or two brothers and four or five grown-up sons.

2nd.—Those who cultivate about eight or ten bigas and have about three or four male adults in the family.

3rd.—Those who have one son or brother or nobody to assist them and cannot therefore cultivate more than four or five bigas.

Often a ryot having no other adult male in the family to assist him has capital enough to employ labourers, in which case he belongs to the first or second class.

The number of first class ryots is very small, of second class there is a larger number. The majority belong to the third class.

Below the third class there is a large number who may be regarded as labourers more properly than as regular cultivators, who have one or two bigas of land, but sustain themselves and family principally by working for others on hire.

The first class have generally four thatched houses in good condition to inclose the quadrangle together, with three or four out-houses to serve as the dhenkighur, cowshed, and gola. The principal one among the four houses inclosing the quadrangle generally cost Rs. 30 or 40, the labour being supplied by themselves. The other houses cost generally about Rs. 20 or 25. On the whole, therefore, the amount spent on the erection of the houses belonging to such a family may be valued at Rs. 150 or 175.

In a second class family the number of out-houses besides the four forming the quadrangle is not more than one or two. On the whole, their value may be estimated at Rs. 100 or 125.

A third class ryot has one or two houses with a cowshed, or one or two single thatched houses to serve as kitchen, dhenkighur, &c. The value of these houses may be put down at Rs. 30 or 40.

These values are estimated at the cost of erection; if sold in good condition they generally fetch less than those amounts, but their sale price varies exceedingly in consideration of their condition, situation, and demand, &c.

A first class ryot has generally a brass kalsi, three or four lotahs, four or five thalas, one or two batis, one boughna, one or two iron pans.[1]

The quantity of brass forming these utensils would be about twelve or fifteen seers. When bought the cost per seer varies from Re. 1 8a. to Rs. 2. When sold the price varies from annas 12 to Re. 1 4a. per seer. On the whole the value of these utensils may be put down at Rs. 20.

The iron basins and one or two china plates in the case of Muhammadans, and country earthenware pots and dishes, may be valued at a couple of rupees.

Baskets and other utensils made of bamboos or cane-work, such as jhakee, dalli, kula, dalla, and katta (काठी) and dhama, or measure of capacity, may be valued at one rupee.

---

[1] Kalsi—a large water-pot.
Lotah or pali—a tumbler.
Thalas—plates.
Bati—a cup.
Boughnas—brass vessels.

In the case of second class ryots the total quantity of brass would be about eight or ten seers, and may be valued at Rs. 8 12 or 15. The other class of utensils may be valued at Rs. 2.

A third class ryot has generally one or two brass lotahs, one or two thalas, sometimes a boughna. The total quantity may be put down at five seers and be valued at Rs. 8.

The earthen and bamboo-work utensils may be estimated at Rs. 2, *i.e.* the same as the second class; for the want of brass utensils has to be supplied by a larger number of these.

Among ryots of the first class a few only have anything like the sinduk, which is an invariable accompaniment of the house of a trading class in the village. The price of one varies from Rs. 15 to 20. Instead of the regular family sinduks,[1] most of the ryots of this class have one small chest of mangoe or other inferior wood, and one or two petaras (constructed of matted cane). The price of these varies from Rs. 2 to 4, and the petaras also cost the same amount. In addition to these, most ryots or their females have one or two small wooden or tin boxes to keep cash, ornaments, or other valuables. The price of these would be about a rupee and a half. On the whole, therefore, the total value of these chests, boxes, &c., may be set down at Rs. 6 or 8.

[1] Sinduks—wooden chests.

Second class families have generally a petara and a small box or two valued at about Rs. 3 or 4.

Third class ryots may be said not to have any of these, except jhaels or small petaras in some cases, valued at about a rupee and a half.

The general custom is to keep the valuables hidden in earthenware pots kept either under the ground or outside.

With the exception of a very few, the ryots have no chowkees or charpoys, the general custom being with the ryots in churs to have fixed manchaus or fixed bamboo platforms, &c., in the case of ryots living in Ashali land to spread moulas, hoglas, chatais, patees or sowp on the floor at night for the bedding. A moula cost about three annas, and a patee or sowp six or eight annas. The number depends on the number of persons in a family. One rupee for each family may be taken as the average value of spreadings for all classes of ryots. All ryots use chhalas or gunny bags to sit upon, which are, when occasion requires, used also to hold grains.

There are seats of various kinds made of bamboo slips, canes, and splinters of betel-nut tree, and of small planks called peera (পিঁড়া) or low stools. These are so small in size that they can hold only one man on each.

Each ryot, male or female, has two dhutees [1] of

---

[1] ধুতি (Dhutee) a piece of Manchester cloth, known in the bazaar as longcloth or American drill.

coarse Manchester cloth for ordinary use while out of work about twelve feet long and three feet broad. Besides these well-to-do families, especially the females among them, have country sharees and zenana coats, and men chaddars, sometimes peerans. For the winter season the elderly men and women have chaddars of thick cloth, while at work they use very narrow and short gamchas or worn-out clothes turned into smaller size. There is no difference among the different classes with respect to the clothes possessed by a family except so far as depends upon the number of individuals in each. The average value of clothes belonging to each individual, male or female, may be set down at Rs. 2. In a first class family consisting of about twelve persons, four of whom may be left out of consideration, in consideration of the different persons wearing the same clothes, the value may be put down at Rs. 15 or 16.

In second class families consisting of about seven persons, of whom three may be left out of consideration, the average value of clothes may be put down at Rs. 8 or 9.

- সাড়ি (Shari) a piece of cloth put on by women having borders of different colours.
- চাদর (Chadars) or sheet—a piece of American drill or longcloth measuring about nine feet in length.
- পিরাণ (Peeran) or shirt—a coat newly introduced into fashion of American drill or longcloth.
- গামছা (Gamcha) or napkin, or a piece of cloth short in breadth and length.
- কাঁথা (Kantha) quilt stuffed with rags.

In third class families consisting of two or three individuals, the value of clothes may be put down at Rs. 4 or 5.

In addition to these Rs. 3, 2, and 1 may be taken as the average value of leps (quilt), kanthas, and pillows belong to a family of first, second, and third class ryot respectively.

Adult males use no ornaments. Boys have sometimes brass or silver bangles for the hands and mandulees or patta to hang from the neck. Women use ornaments [1] of various kinds made of gold or silver and sometimes of brass. On the whole, the value of ornaments belonging to a first class family may be set down at Rs. 40 or 50. Women whose husbands are living, when Muhammadans use churi of silver or of lac, and when Hindu, a pair of shell bracelets.

Second class family about Rs. 30, and third class family about Rs. 10 or 15.

---

[1] নথ (Nath) a ring for the nose.

বেসর (Besar) an ornament hung from the nose.

দানা (Dana) beads for the neck used by Hindus, but very seldom.

কালসি (Kalse) for arms.

বালা (Balla) bangles.

মল (Mul) or kharu-anklets.

চুড়ি (Churi) bracelet used by Muhammadans.

হাসলি (Hasli) a large ring round the neck.

In the cookhouse[1] there is scarcely any article except *pata* and *puta* for grinding condiments in addition to brass and earthen pots. These, along with *dhenki*, ukti, and mosal (a large wooden mortar and pestle), may be valued at about Rs. 3 in each family.

Ryots generally keep, according to their circumstances, quantity of rice, mustard, &c., for consumption during the year, and seeds for next year's cultivation. The value may be set down for a first-class family, Rs. 90 or 100, for second class, Rs. 40 or 50, for a third class, Rs. 25.

A first class family possesses about eight or ten cows and bullocks, sometimes a couple of goats or sheep. In the case of Muhammadans a number of fowls. A second class family possesses four or five cows, and a third class, two or three.

The value of cattle in a first class family may be

---

[1] পাটা (Pata)—a flat stone.

পুতা (Puta)—a stone mullar.

ঘটী (Ghotee)—a brass or earthen water-pot.

রাইং (Raing)—an earthen pot used in cooking rice.

পাতিল (Patil)—an earthen basin used in cooking curry.

শরা (Shara)—an earthen cover for a pot.

ঝাঁজরি (Jhajree)—an earthen vessel for straining water when washing rice, &c.

হাতা (Hatta)—an iron or wooden ladle or spoon used in cooking.

বাউনি (Bowlee) an iron tongs used in catching pots when warm.

তাগারি (Tagaree) a wooden bowl for holding things cooked.

put down at Rs. 70, in a second class family, Rs. 40, and in a third class family, Rs. 20.

A first class family possesses about eight or ten ploughs and three or four harrows, valued at Rs. 8.

The value for a second and third class family may be put down at Rs. 5 and 3 respectively.

A first class family possesses generally three daos, four or five kachees, two kodalees or spades, one khuntee (a digging hoe) and an axe. The value may be put down at Rs. 5.

Second and third class families possess these articles in less numbers, and the value may be put down at Rs. 3 and 2 respectively.

The ryots living in low lands and fields, &c., watered by annual inundation, and on river side, have generally a dingee (a small boat), the value of which may be set down at Rs. 10 to 30.

The first and second class ryots only possess such dingee, but third class ryots very seldom.

With respect to the large class below the third, it may be said generally that they have a single house, a brass lota or thalla, or a stone or wooden plate and cane or bamboo basket, &c., and nothing in the way of a sinduk or charpoys; one or two mats and kanthas and pillows and a couple of dhutees, a plough, a harrow, a dao, a kodalee, a kachee and sometimes a cow or two. The value of all these in average may be estimated at Rs. 25.

Table showing the total value of property possessed by different Classes of Ryot.

Classes of Ryots.	House.	Household Utensils.	Sinduks.	Charpoys.	Clothes including Kantha and Pillow.	Ornaments.	Articles in Cookroom.	Gola articles.	Cattle.	Ploughs.	Daos, &c.	Boat.	Total.
	Rs. As. P.	Rs. As. P.	Rs. As. P.	Rs. As. P.	Rs. As. P.	Rs. As. P.	Rs. As. P.	Rs. As. P.	Rs. As. P.	Rs. As. P.	Rs. As. P.	Rs. As. P.	Rs. As. P.
1st Class...	162 8 0	0 32 0	4 0 0	1 0 0	18 8 0	45 0 0	3 0 0	95 0 0	80 0 0	8 0 0	5 0 0	25 0 0	477 4 0
2nd Class...	112 8 0	0 15 0	3 0 0	0 10 0	30 8 0	0 3 0	0 45 0	40 0 0	5 0 0	3 0 0	15 0 0	...	283 0 0
3rd Class...	35 0 0	0 10 0	0 12 0	0 5 0	11 8 0	0 3 0	0 25 0	20 0 0	3 0 0	2 0 0	...	...	116 4 0
Last Class.	...	...	...	...	...	...	...	...	...	...	...	...	25 0 0

NOTE B.

A FULL representation of a *jama bandi* in its completest form could only be given on a folded page of inconvenient size, but perhaps some idea of it may be conveyed by the following explanation.

Suppose a given ryot to be one Moti Lall Gopi, and the different items of his rent for the current year to be exhibited thus :—

Description of land.	Quantity.	Rate.	Amount of Rent.
	Big. Cot	Rs. As. P.	Rs. As. P.
Sali, rice land, first quality...	2 10 0	4 0 0	10 0 0
Ditto, second quality ...	1 1 0	3 0 0	3 2 2
Ditto, third quality	0 7½ 0	2 4 0	0 13 10
Bamboo	0 6 0	15 0 0	4 8 0
Waste	0 2 15	1 0 0	0 2 4
Homestead	0 1 0	20 0 0	1 0 0
Compound	0 1 0	15 0 0	0 12 0
Excavation	0 5½ 0	1 0 0	0 4 8
	4 14 15	...	20 11 0

In the *jama bandi* all these will be given in parallel columns; thus the first column will give the name, next come four columns containing respectively, description of land, quantity, rate, and rent in respect of the Sali, first quality ; then four more for the Sali, second quality, and so on; in all, this will make thirty-three columns; then will come a column for the total quantity of land, *namely*, four bigas, fourteen cottas, fifteen gandas; after this the column for the total rent; next again two columns for the total land and total rent for the previous year; then a column for the amount of rent paid in respect of that year; then a column for arrears, and finally a column for the total rent due, say forty columns altogether. And there may be even more than this number, if, as is the case in some zamindaries, the alteration in each particular item of land, as compared with the corresponding item of the preceding year, and alteration in the rates of rent, if any, and also the different subjects of arrears are all entered separately. And if the *jama bandi* is that made on behalf of an undivided shareholder of a tenure, all the separate shares, the amount payable by each ryot towards each of them, and so on, will also be given in proper columns. The names of the ryots are written in succession, one under the other, and all the columns are appropriately filled up against each name. Against a subtenure-holder only the name of his tenure, the amount of the rent, and the portions payable to each shareholder, are entered.

The *jama bandi* thus furnishes at a glance all the facts in classified detail, relevant and incidental to the collection of the rent of the estate for the current year.

GLOSSARY.

GLOSSARY.

Ail.—An earthen balk or ridge, dividing one plot of cultivated ground from another—generally very narrow, but sometimes broad enough for a trackway.

Amla.—The servants or officers, either individually or collectively, of a zamindar's kachahri or estate-office.

Arhar.—A kind of pulse (*cytisus cajan*) grown for food.

Asan, or Ashan.—A square piece of carpet.

Badmáash.—One who is disreputable.

Bahangi.—A bamboo furnished with cords at each end, by means of which luggage is carried slung across the shoulder.

Baithakhanah.—The sitting-room, or public portion of a native dwelling-house.

Bári.—A dwelling-house—homestead.

Bau.—Young married girl.

Bhadra log.—Respectable well-to-do people.

Bhát.—Boiled rice.

Bigha.—A measure of land: in Bengal it is equivalent to about one-third of an acre.

Bonti.—A broad sickle-shaped knifeblade, fixed vertically

into a heavy wooden stand. In use, the stand is held firm by the feet, and the fish, vegetable, straw or other article to be cleaned, sliced, or cut up, is with the hand duly worked against the concave cutting edge thus made fast.

Broto.—A self-imposed exercise of a devotional character—obligation, vow.

Chadr, or Chadar.—A sheet, or cloth.

Charpoy.—A frame of wood, having a web of tape or cord stretched across it, and resting upon four short legs.

Chaukidar.—The village watchman, or constable.

Chela.—A disciple of a Mohant.

Chittha.—Memorandum—name of a business book used in the management of a zamindar's property, in which measurements and other like information are entered.

Chulha.—A fireplace built up of clay.

Cowrie.—See Kauri.

Daftarkhana.—An office or room in which books of account and registers are kept.

Dahi.—Thickened milk.

Dana.—Grain.

Dakait.—One of a gang of robbers.

Dakaiti.—Gang robbery.

Dál.—Split peas, or any other split pulse.

Dalán.—Hall.

Dao.—Billhook, or cleaver.

Deorhi.—Anteroom at the entrance door or gateway of a house, where the daftarkhana usually is.

Dhán.—The rice plant, or the rice grain unhusked.

Dhenki.—An instrument, which in its essential parts is a pestle and mortar; it is chiefly used to husk and clean rice.

Dhoti.—The cloth worn round the loins.
Gaddi.—A seat.
Gamla.—An open earthen vessel.
Ghara.—A necked, narrow-mouthed, earthen vessel.
Ghát.—The landing slope, or steps, on the bank of a river, or of a tank, the pass up a mountain or ridge of hills, sometimes the line of hill itself.
Goála.—One who keeps cows and sells milk.
Gola.—A hut, or place in which grain is stored ; generally *circular* in form.
Gomashta.—Generally agent, one who carries on business for another—a zamindar's servant employed in collecting village rents is often so called.
Gour.—See Gurh.
Gurh.—Coarse sugar of date tree, &c., hardened into a cake—molasses.
Hát.—A market.
Hookha.—See Hukha.
Hukha, or *Hookka.*—A form of pipe for smoking tobacco.
Jágir, Jághir.—A service tenure of land or revenue.
Jalkar-wála.—One who has rights of fishing.
Jamma, or *Jama.*—The aggregate of payments made for land in the year—the total rent.
Jama-bandi.—The assessment or detailed representation of the rents settled in an estate, village, or district.
Jama-wásil-báki.—An account paper showing simultaneously the full rent, the amount collected and the amount of arrears, in respect of an estate, village, or district.
Jangal, or *Jungle.*—Forest, a wood, any tract, small or great,

in which the natural growth of trees, bushes, and vegetation is undisturbed.

Jote, or Jot.—Both the land, which the cultivator tills, and his tenure of it are often termed his jote.

Kabiráj.—A Hindu physician.

Kabulyat.—The counterpart of a pottah, or lease, given by the tenant to his landlord.

Kachahri, Cutcherry.—A court or office where public business, or the business of a zamindar's estate, is done.

Kachcha.—Untranslatable. Raw, crude, immature, incomplete.

Karta.—The member of the joint-family who manages the family property.

Kathak.—A professional story-teller; one who recites traditional poems, &c.

Kauri (Cowrie).—A small shell (*cypræa*) used as money.

Khál.—A water channel.

Khatiyán.—An account book of the nature of a ledger.

Khet.—A plot of cultivated arable land.

Kist.—An instalment, portion of a whole; annual rent and revenue is almost universally paid in fixed kists in the course of the year.

Kodál, or Kodáli.—A hoe, by means of which the work of the spade, the shovel, and the hoe alike is done.

Láthi, or Láttee.—A stick or bludgeon, usually of bamboo, heavily ringed and feruled with metal.

Mafassal, or Mofussil.—Quite untranslatable. The country as opposed to the town. The subordinate as opposed to the principal.

Mahájan.—Merchant, money-dealer — one who makes it a

business in the villages to advance money and grain to the cultivator on the pledge of crops.

Mahalla.—A division of a town, a quarter.

Maidán.—An open grass-covered space.

Majlis.—An assembly.

Mandal.—The village headman.

Mandap.—An open-sided roofed structure, or building.

Mandir.—A temple.

Mantra.—A passage from the Veda; a prayer.

Masála.—Spice, seasoning.

Masjid.—A mosque.

Math.—An endowed temple or shrine.

Máth.—The open arable plain, which forms the cultivated land of the village.

Mauzu.—A village and its lands.

Modi.—Village shopkeeper.

Mohant.—The superior of a math.

Mokarari.—That which is fixed or established—permanent.

Morha.—A stool.

Mulla, or Mulána.—One who has charge of the village mosque, Muhammadan schoolmaster.

Náib.—Deputy or representative—the head officer or steward representing the zamindar in the management of large zamindaries.

Nirkh.—A standard or customary rate, as of rent, &c.

Oothán.—See Uthán.

Pakka.—The opposite to *kachcha*, and equally untranslatable. Ripe, mature, complete.

Pálla.—A turn, as of worship, or enjoyment of property.

Pancháyat.—Untranslatable. Literally a set of five persons, it has come to designate a body of caste men, of villagers or others, who deal with and settle disputes relating to caste, occupation, and so on.

Patta, or *Pottah.*—A lease.

Patwári.—One who keeps the collection papers of a mouzah or village; and commonly also makes the collections of the village.

Peon—for Piada, footman.— It is the usual designation of inferior servants of a zamindar or landholder.

Pitára.—A wickerwork, or otherwise slightly-constructed box of peculiar shape.

Puja (Poojah).—Worship.

Purohit.—The family priest.

Rabi, or *Rubbee.*—The March and April period of the year; the harvest season of the crops which were sown or planted after the cessation of the monsoon rains in September or October of the preceding year.

Raiyat.—Originally a subject, but now the universal term for cultivator of the soil—peasant.

Rubbee.—See Rabi.

Ryot.—See Raiyat.

Sandúk, or *Sinduk.*—A wooden chest.

Shádi.—Nuptial ceremony.

Shámiána.— Tent canvas stretched horizontally across, as a covering, from side to side of a quadrangle, or from top to top of poles, firmly fixed in the ground—awning.

Shráddha.—An obsequial ceremony in which food and water are offered to deceased ancestors.

Takhtaposh.—A low platform or sitting-place.

Táluq.—A dependency.

Tári, or *Tádi,* vulgarly toddy.—The juice of the palm tree, both fermented and unfermented. Spirit made from other sources is also called Tari.

Tehsildar, or Tahsildar.—One who collects rents or revenue.

Thákur.—A representation of the deity, an idol, also title of honour, lord, chief.

Thákurbári.—Chamber or house occupied by an idol.

Thál.—A metal plate or dish.

Top, or Tope, or Topu.—A grove or group of fruit-bearing trees.

Utbandi-jama.—Rent according to the land actually tilled, when land tilled one year is allowed to lie fallow the next.

Uthán.—The open house-space inclosed by the huts of a homestead.

Zamindar.—Landholder

THE END.

LONDON:
R. CLAY, SONS, AND TAYLOR,
BREAD STREET HILL, E.C.

BEDFORD STREET, STRAND, LONDON, W.C.
December, 1879.

MACMILLAN & CO.'S CATALOGUE of Works in the Departments of History, Biography, Travels, Critical and Literary Essays, Politics, Political and Social Economy, Law, etc.; and Works connected with Language.

HISTORY, BIOGRAPHY, TRAVELS, &c.

Albemarle.—FIFTY YEARS OF MY LIFE. By GEORGE THOMAS, Earl of Albemarle. With Steel Portrait of the first Earl of Albemarle, engraved by JEENS. Third and Cheaper Edition. Crown 8vo. 7s. 6d.

"*The book is one of the most amusing of its class. . . . These reminiscences have the charm and flavour of personal experience, and they bring us into direct contact with the persons they describe.*"—EDINBURGH REVIEW.

Anderson.—MANDALAY TO MOMIEN; a Narrative of the Two Expeditions to Western China, of 1868 and 1875, under Colonel E. B. Sladen and Colonel Horace Browne. By Dr. ANDERSON, F.R.S.E., Medical and Scientific Officer to the Expeditions. With numerous Maps and Illustrations. 8vo. 21s.

"*A pleasant, useful, carefully-written, and important work.*"—ATHENÆUM.

Appleton.—Works by T. G. APPLETON:—

A NILE JOURNAL. Illustrated by EUGENE BENSON. Crown 8vo. 6s.

SYRIAN SUNSHINE. Crown 8vo. 6s.

Arnold (M.)—ESSAYS IN CRITICISM. By MATTHEW ARNOLD. New Edition, Revised and Enlarged. Crown 8vo. 9s.

Arnold (W. T.)—THE ROMAN SYSTEM OF PROVINCIAL ADMINISTRATION TO THE ACCESSION OF CONSTANTINE THE GREAT. Being the Arnold Prize Essay for 1879. By W. T. Arnold, B.A. Crown 8vo. 6s.

Atkinson.—AN ART TOUR TO NORTHERN CAPITALS OF EUROPE, including Descriptions of the Towns, the Museums, and other Art Treasures of Copenhagen, Christiania, Stockholm, Abo, Helsingfors, Wiborg, St. Petersburg, Moscow, and Kief. By J. BEAVINGTON ATKINSON. 8vo. 12s.

Bailey.—THE SUCCESSION TO THE ENGLISH CROWN. A Historical Sketch. By A. BAILEY, M.A., Barrister-at-Law. Crown 8vo. 7s. 6d.

Baker (Sir Samuel W.)—Works by Sir SAMUEL BAKER, Pacha, M.A., F.R.S., F.R.G.S.:—

CYPRUS AS I SAW IT IN 1879. With Frontispiece. 8vo. 12s. 6d.

ISMAILIA: A Narrative of the Expedition to Central Africa for the Suppression of the Slave Trade, organised by Ismail, Khedive of Egypt. With Portraits, Map, and fifty full-page Illustrations by ZWECKER and DURAND. New and Cheaper Edition. With New Preface. Crown 8vo. 6s.

"*A book which will be read with very great interest.*"—TIMES. "*Well written and full of remarkable adventures.*"—PALL MALL GAZETTE. "*Adds another thrilling chapter to the history of African adventure.*"—DAILY NEWS. "*Reads more like a romance.... incomparably more entertaining than books of African travel usually are.*"—MORNING POST.

THE ALBERT N'YANZA Great Basin of the Nile, and Exploration of the Nile Sources. Fifth Edition. Maps and Illustrations. Crown 8vo. 6s.

"*Charmingly written;*" says the SPECTATOR, "*full, as might be expected, of incident, and free from that wearisome reiteration of useless facts which is the drawback to almost all books of African travel.*"

THE NILE TRIBUTARIES OF ABYSSINIA, and the Sword Hunters of the Hamran Arabs. With Maps and Illustrations. Sixth Edition. Crown 8vo. 6s.

The TIMES *says:* "*It adds much to our information respecting Egyptian Abyssinia and the different races that spread over it. It contains, moreover, some notable instances of English daring and enterprising skill; it abounds in animated tales of exploits dear to the heart of the British sportsman; and it will attract even the least studious reader, as the author tells a story well, and can describe nature with uncommon power.*"

Bancroft.—THE HISTORY OF THE UNITED STATES OF AMERICA, FROM THE DISCOVERY OF THE CONTINENT. By GEORGE BANCROFT. New and thoroughly Revised Edition. Six Vols. Crown 8vo. 54s.

Barker (Lady).—Works by LADY BARKER :—

A YEAR'S HOUSEKEEPING IN SOUTH AFRICA. With Illustrations. New and Cheaper Edition. Crown 8vo. 6s.

" *We have to thank Lady Barker for a very amusing book, over which we have spent many a delightful hour, and of which we will not take leave without alluding to the ineffably droll illustrations which add so very much to the enjoyment of her clear and sparkling descriptions.*"—MORNING POST.

Beesly.—STORIES FROM THE HISTORY OF ROME. By Mrs. BEESLY. Extra fcap. 8vo. 2s. 6d.

" *A little book for which every cultivated and intelligent mother will be grateful for.*"—EXAMINER.

Bismarck—IN THE FRANCO-GERMAN WAR. An Authorized Translation from the German of Dr. MORITZ BUSCH. Two Vols. Crown 8vo. 18s.

The TIMES *says* :—" *The publication of Bismarck's after-dinner talk, whether discreet or not, will be of priceless biographical value, and Englishmen, at least, will not be disposed to quarrel with Dr. Busch for giving a picture as true to life as Boswell's 'Johnson' of the foremost practical genius that Germany has produced since Frederick the Great.*"

Blackburne.—BIOGRAPHY OF THE RIGHT HON. FRANCIS BLACKBURNE, Late Lord Chancellor of Ireland. Chiefly in connexion with his Public and Political Career. By his Son, EDWARD BLACKBURNE, Q.C. With Portrait Engraved by JEENS. 8vo. 12s.

Blanford (W. T.)—GEOLOGY AND ZOOLOGY OF ABYSSINIA. By W. T. BLANFORD. 8vo. 21s.

Brontë.—CHARLOTTE BRONTË. A Monograph. By T. WEMYSS REID. With Illustrations. Third Edition. Crown 8vo. 6s.

Brooke.—THE RAJA OF SARAWAK : an Account of Sir James Brooke, K.C.B., LL.D. Given chiefly through Letters or Journals. By GERTRUDE L. JACOB. With Portrait and Maps. Two Vols. 8vo. 25s.

Bryce.—Works by JAMES BRYCE, D.C.L., Regius Professor of Civil Law, Oxford :—

THE HOLY ROMAN EMPIRE. Sixth Edition, Revised and Enlarged. Crown 8vo. 7s. 6d.

" *It exactly supplies a want : it affords a key to much which men read of in their books as isolated facts, but of which they have hitherto had no connected exposition set before them.*"—SATURDAY REVIEW.

Bryce.—*continued.*

TRANSCAUCASIA AND ARARAT: being Notes of a Vacation Tour in the Autumn of 1876. With an Illustration and Map. Third Edition. Crown 8vo. 9s.

"*Mr. Bryce has written a lively and at the same time an instructive description of the tour he made last year in and about the Caucasus. When so well-informed a jurist travels into regions seldom visited, and even walks up a mountain so rarely scaled as Ararat, he is justified in thinking that the impressions he brings home are worthy of being communicated to the world at large, especially when a terrible war is casting a lurid glow over the countries he has lately surveyed.*"—ATHENÆUM.

Burgoyne.—POLITICAL AND MILITARY EPISODES DURING THE FIRST HALF OF THE REIGN OF GEORGE III. Derived from the Life and Correspondence of the Right Hon. J. Burgoyne, Lieut.-General in his Majesty's Army, and M.P. for Preston. By E. B. DE FONBLANQUE. With Portrait, Heliotype Plate, and Maps. 8vo. 16s.

Burke.—EDMUND BURKE, a Historical Study. By JOHN MORLEY, B.A., Oxon. Crown 8vo. 7s. 6d.

Burrows.—WORTHIES OF ALL SOULS: Four Centuries of English History. Illustrated from the College Archives. By MONTAGU BURROWS, Chichele Professor of Modern History at Oxford, Fellow of All Souls. 8vo. 14s.

"*A most amusing as well as a most instructive book.*—GUARDIAN.

Cameron.—OUR FUTURE HIGHWAY. By V. LOVETT CAMERON, C.B., Commander R.N. With Illustrations. 2 vols. Crown 8vo. [*Shortly.*

Campbell.—LOG-LETTERS FROM THE "CHALLENGER." By LORD GEORGE CAMPBELL. With Map. Fifth and cheaper Edition. Crown 8vo. 6s.

"*A delightful book, which we heartily commend to the general reader.*"—SATURDAY REVIEW.

"*We do not hesitate to say that anything so fresh, so picturesque, so generally delightful, as these log-letters has not appeared among books o travel for a long time.*"—EXAMINER.

Campbell.—MY CIRCULAR NOTES: Extracts from Journals; Letters sent Home; Geological and other Notes, written while Travelling Westwards round the World, from July 6th, 1874, to July 6th, 1875. By J. F. CAMPBELL, Author of "Frost and Fire." Cheaper Issue. Crown 8vo. 6s.

Campbell.—TURKS AND GREEKS. Notes of a recent Excursion. By the Hon. DUDLEY CAMPBELL, M.A. With Coloured Map. Crown 8vo. 3s. 6d.

Carpenter.—LIFE AND WORK OF MARY CARPENTER By the Rev. J. E. CARPENTER. With Portrait engraved by JEENS. Crown 8vo. [*Shortly*.

Carstares.—WILLIAM CARSTARES: a Character and Career of the Revolutionary Epoch (1649—1715). By ROBERT STORY, Minister of Rosneath. 8vo. 12s.

Chatterton: A BIOGRAPHICAL STUDY. By DANIEL WILSON, LL.D., Professor of History and English Literature in University College, Toronto. Crown 8vo. 6s. 6d.

Chatterton: A STORY OF THE YEAR 1770. By Professor MASSON, LL.D. Crown 8vo. 5s.

Clark.—MEMORIALS FROM JOURNALS AND LETTERS OF SAMUEL CLARK, M.A., formerly Principal of the National Society's Training College, Battersea. Edited with Introduction by his WIFE. With Portrait. Crown 8vo. 7s. 6d.

Clifford (W. K.)—LECTURES AND ESSAYS. Edited by LESLIE STEPHEN and FREDERICK POLLOCK, with Introduction by F. POLLOCK. Two Portraits. 2 vols. 8vo. 25s.

The TIMES of October 22, 1879, says:—"*Many a friend of the author on first taking up these volumes and remembering his versatile genius and his keen enjoyment of all realms of intellectual activity must have trembled lest they should be found to consist of fragmentary pieces of work, too disconnected to do justice to his powers of consecutive reasoning and too varied to have any effect as a whole. Fortunately those fears are groundless . . . . It is not only in subject that the various papers are closely related. There is also a singular consistency of view and of method throughout . . . . It is in the social and metaphysical subjects that the richness of his intellect shows itself most forcibly in the variety and originality of the ideas which he presents to us. To appreciate this variety, it is necessary to read the book itself, for it treats, in some form or other, of nearly all the subjects of deepest interest in this age of questioning.*"

Combe.—THE LIFE OF GEORGE COMBE, Author of "The Constitution of Man." By CHARLES GIBBON. With Three Portraits engraved by JEENS. Two Vols. 8vo. 32s.

"*A graphic and interesting account of the long life and indefatigable labours of a very remarkable man.*"—SCOTSMAN.

Cooper.—ATHENÆ CANTABRIGIENSES. By CHARLES HENRY COOPER, F.S.A., and THOMPSON COOPER, F.S.A. Vol. I. 8vo., 1500—85, 18s.; Vol. II., 1586—1609, 18s.

Correggio.—ANTONIO ALLEGRI DA CORREGGIO. From the German of Dr. JULIUS MEYER, Director of the Royal Gallery, Berlin. Edited, with an Introduction, by Mrs. HEATON. Containing Twenty Woodbury-type Illustrations. Royal 8vo. Cloth elegant. 31s. 6d.

Cox (G. V.)—RECOLLECTIONS OF OXFORD. By G. V. Cox, M.A., New College, late Esquire Bedel and Coroner in the University of Oxford. *Cheaper Edition.* Crown 8vo. 6s.

Cunynghame (Sir A. T.)—MY COMMAND IN SOUTH AFRICA, 1874—78. Comprising Experiences of Travel in the Colonies of South Africa and the Independent States. By Sir ARTHUR THURLOW CUNYNGHAME, G.C.B., then Lieutenant-Governor and Commander of the Forces in South Africa. Third Edition. 8vo. 12s. 6d.

The TIMES *says :—"It is a volume of great interest, ... full of incidents which vividly illustrate the condition of the Colonies and the character and habits of the natives. . . . . It contains valuable illustrations of Cape warfare, and at the present moment it cannot fail to command wide-spread attention."*

"Daily News."—THE DAILY NEWS' CORRESPONDENCE of the War between Germany and France, 1870—1. Edited with Notes and Comments. New Edition. Complete in One Volume. With Maps and Plans. Crown 8vo. 6s.

THE DAILY NEWS' CORRESPONDENCE of the War between Russia and Turkey, to the fall of Kars. Including the letters of Mr. Archibald Forbes, Mr. J. E. McGahan, and other Special Correspondents in Europe and Asia. Second Edition, enlarged. Cheaper Edition. Crown 8vo. 6s.

FROM THE FALL OF KARS TO THE CONCLUSION OF PEACE. Cheaper Edition. Crown 8vo. 6s.

Davidson.—THE LIFE OF A SCOTTISH PROBATIONER; being a Memoir of Thomas Davidson, with his Poems and Letters. By JAMES BROWN, Minister of St. James's Street Church, Paisley. Second Edition, revised and enlarged, with Portrait. Crown 8vo. 7s. 6d.

Deas.—THE RIVER CLYDE. An Historical Description of the Rise and Progress of the Harbour of Glasgow, and of the Improvement of the River from Glasgow to Port Glasgow. By J. DEAS, M. Inst. C.E. 8vo. 10s. 6d.

Denison.—A HISTORY OF CAVALRY FROM THE EARLIEST TIMES. With Lessons for the Future. By Lieut.-Col. GEORGE DENISON, Commanding the Governor-General's Body Guard, Canada, Author of "Modern Cavalry." With Maps and Plans. 8vo. 18s.

Dilke.—GREATER BRITAIN. A Record of Travel in English-speaking Countries during 1866-7. (America, Australia, India. By Sir CHARLES WENTWORTH DILKE, M.P. Sixth Edition. Crown 8vo. 6s.

"*Many of the subjects discussed in these pages,*" *says the* DAILY NEWS, "*are of the widest interest, and such as no man who cares for the future of his race and of the world can afford to treat with indifference.*"

Doyle.—HISTORY OF AMERICA. By J. A. DOYLE. With Maps. 18mo. 4s. 6d.

"*Mr. Doyle's style is clear and simple, his facts are accurately stated, and his book is meritoriously free from prejudice on questions where partisanship runs high amongst us.*"—SATURDAY REVIEW.

Drummond of Hawthornden: THE STORY OF HIS LIFE AND WRITINGS. By PROFESSOR MASSON. With Portrait and Vignette engraved by C. H. JEENS. Crown 8vo. 10s. 6d.

Duff.—Works by M. E. GRANT-DUFF, M.P., late Under Secretary of State for India:—

NOTES OF AN INDIAN JOURNEY. With Map. 8vo. 10s. 6d.

MISCELLANIES POLITICAL AND LITERARY. 8vo. 10s. 6d.

Eadie.—LIFE OF JOHN EADIE, D.D., LL.D. By JAMES BROWN, D.D., Author of "The Life of a Scottish Probationer." With Portrait. Second Edition. Crown 8vo. 7s. 6d.

"*An ably written and characteristic biography.*"—TIMES.

Elliott.—LIFE OF HENRY VENN ELLIOTT, of Brighton. By JOSIAH BATEMAN, M.A. With Portrait, engraved by JEENS. Extra fcap. 8vo. Third and Cheaper Edition. 6s.

Elze.—ESSAYS ON SHAKESPEARE. By Dr. KARL ELZE. Translated with the Author's sanction by L. DORA SCHMITZ. 8vo. 12s.

English Men of Letters. Edited by JOHN MORLEY. A Series of Short Books to tell people what is best worth knowing as to the Life, Character, and Works of some of the great English Writers. In crown 8vo. Price 2s. 6d. each.

English Men of Letters.—*continued.*

I. DR. JOHNSON. By LESLIE STEPHEN.
"*The new series opens well with Mr. Leslie Stephen's sketch of Dr. Johnson. It could hardly have been done better; and it will convey to the readers for whom it is intended a juster estimate of Johnson than either of the two essays of Lord Macaulay*"—PALL MALL GAZETTE.

II. SIR WALTER SCOTT. By R. H. HUTTON.
"*The tone of the volume is excellent throughout.*"—ATHENÆUM.
"*We could not wish for a more suggestive introduction to Scott and his poems and novels.*"—EXAMINER.

III. GIBBON. By J. C. MORISON.
"*As a clear, thoughtful, and attractive record of the life and works of the greatest among the world's historians, it deserves the highest praise.*"— EXAMINER.

IV. SHELLEY. By J. A. SYMONDS.
"*The lovers of this great poet are to be congratulated on having at their command so fresh, clear, and intelligent a presentment of the subject, written by a man of adequate and wide culture.*"—ATHENÆUM.

V. HUME. By Professor HUXLEY.
"*It may fairly be said that no one now living could have expounded Hume with more sympathy or with equal perspicuity.*"—ATHENÆUM.

VI. GOLDSMITH. By WILLIAM BLACK.
"*Mr. Black brings a fine sympathy and taste to bear in his criticism of Goldsmith's writings as well as in his sketch of the incidents of his life.*" ATHENÆUM.

VII. DEFOE. By W. MINTO.
"*Mr. Minto's book is careful and accurate in all that is stated, and faithful in all that it suggests. It will repay reading more than once.*" ATHENÆUM.

VIII. BURNS. By Principal SHAIRP, Professor of Poetry in the University of Oxford.
"*It is impossible to desire fairer criticism than Principal Shairp's on Burns's poetry . . . . None of the series has given a truer estimate either of character or of genius than this little volume . . . . and all who read it will be thoroughly grateful to the author for this monument to the genius of Scotland's greatest poet.*"—SPECTATOR.

IX. SPENSER. By the Very Rev. the DEAN OF ST. PAUL'S.
"*Dr. Church is master of his subject, and writes always with good taste.*"—ACADEMY.

X. THACKERAY. By ANTHONY TROLLOPE.
"*Mr. Trollope's sketch is excellently adapted to fufil the purpose of the series in which it appears.*"—ATHENÆUM.

XI. BURKE. By JOHN MORLEY.
"*Perhaps the best criticism yet published on the life and character of*

English Men of Letters.—*continued.*
Burke is contained in Mr. Morley's compendious biography. His style is vigorous and polished, and both his political and personal judgment, and his literary criticisms are just, generous, subtle, and in a high degree interesting."—SATURDAY REVIEW.

MILTON. By MARK PATTISON. . [*Just ready.*]
HAWTHORNE. By HENRY JAMES.
SOUTHEY. By Professor DOWDEN.
CHAUCER. By Professor WARD.
COWPER. By GOLDWIN SMITH. } [*In preparation.*]
BUNYAN. By J. A. FROUDE.
WORDSWORTH. By F. W. H. MYERS.
Others in preparation.

Eton College, History of. By H. C. MAXWELL LYTE, M.A. With numerous Illustrations by Professor DELAMOTTE, Coloured Plates, and a Steel Portrait of the Founder, engraved by C. H. JEENS. New and cheaper Issue, with Corrections. Medium 8vo. Cloth elegant. 21*s.*
" *We are at length presented with a work on England's greatest public school, worthy of the subject of which it treats. . . . A really valuable and authentic history of Eton College.*"—GUARDIAN.

European History, Narrated in a Series of Historical Selections from the best Authorities. Edited and arranged by E. M. SEWELL and C. M. YONGE. First Series, crown 8vo. 6*s.*; Second Series, 1088–1228, crown 8vo. 6*s.* Third Edition.
" *We know of scarcely anything,*" *says the* GUARDIAN, *of this volume,* "*which is so likely to raise to a higher level the average standard of English education.*"

Faraday.—MICHAEL FARADAY. By J. H. GLADSTONE, Ph.D., F.R.S. Second Edition, with Portrait engraved by JEENS from a photograph by J. WATKINS. Crown 8vo. 4*s.* 6*d.*
PORTRAIT. Artist's Proof. 5*s.*

Forbes.—LIFE AND LETTERS OF JAMES DAVID FORBES, F.R.S., late Principal of the United College in the University of St. Andrews. By J. C. SHAIRP, LL.D., Principal of the United College in the University of St. Andrews; P. G. TAIT, M.A., Professor of Natural Philosophy in the University of Edinburgh; and A. ADAMS-REILLY, F.R.G.S. 8vo. with Portraits, Map, and Illustrations, 16*s.*

Freeman.—Works by EDWARD A. FREEMAN, D.C.L., LL.D. :—
HISTORICAL ESSAYS. Third Edition. 8vo. 10*s.* 6*d.*
CONTENTS :—*I.* "*The Mythical and Romantic Elements in Early English History;*" *II.* "*The Continuity of English History;*" *III.* "*The Relations between the Crowns of England and Scotland;*" *IV.*

Freeman—*continued*.

"St. Thomas of Canterbury and his Biographers;" V. "The Reign of Edward the Third;" VI. "The Holy Roman Empire;" VII. "The Franks and the Gauls;" VIII. "The Early Sieges of Paris;" IX. "Frederick the First, King of Italy;" X. "The Emperor Frederick the Second;" XI. "Charles the Bold;" XII. "Presidential Government."

HISTORICAL ESSAYS. SECOND SERIES. 8vo. 10s. 6d.

The principal Essays are:—"Ancient Greece and Mediæval Italy:" "Mr. Gladstone's Homer and the Homeric Ages:" "The Historians of Athens:" "The Athenian Democracy:" "Alexander the Great:" "Greece during the Macedonian Period:" "Mommsen's History of Rome:" "Lucius Cornelius Sulla:" "The Flavian Cæsars."

HISTORICAL ESSAYS. Third Series. 8vo. 12s.

CONTENTS:—"First Impressions of Rome." "The Illyrian Emperors and their Land." "Augusta Treverorum." "The Goths at Ravenna." "Race and Language." "The Byzantine Empire." "First Impressions of Athens." "Mediæval and Modern Greece." "The Southern Slaves." "Sicilian Cycles." "The Normans at Palermo."

COMPARATIVE POLITICS.—Lectures at the Royal Institution. To which is added the "Unity of History," the Rede Lecture at Cambridge, 1872. 8vo. 14s.

THE HISTORY AND CONQUESTS OF THE SARACENS. Six Lectures. Third Edition, with New Preface. Crown 8vo. 3s. 6d.

HISTORICAL AND ARCHITECTURAL SKETCHES: chiefly Italian. With Illustrations by the Author. Crown 8vo. 10s. 6d.

HISTORY OF FEDERAL GOVERNMENT, from the Foundation of the Achaian League to the Disruption of the United States. Vol. I. General Introduction. History of the Greek Federations. 8vo. 21s.

OLD ENGLISH HISTORY. With *Five Coloured Maps*. Fourth Edition. Extra fcap. 8vo., half-bound. 6s.

"*The book indeed is full of instruction and interest to students of all ages, and he must be a well-informed man indeed who will not rise from its perusal with clearer and more accurate ideas of a too much neglected portion of English history.*"—SPECTATOR.

HISTORY OF THE CATHEDRAL CHURCH OF WELLS, as illustrating the History of the Cathedral Churches of the Old Foundation. Crown 8vo. 3s. 6d.

"*The history assumes in Mr. Freeman's hands a significance, and, we may add, a practical value as suggestive of what a cathedral ought to be, which make it well worthy of mention.*"—SPECTATOR.

Freeman—*continued.*

THE GROWTH OF THE ENGLISH CONSTITUTION FROM THE EARLIEST TIMES. Crown 8vo. 5s. Third Edition, revised.

GENERAL SKETCH OF EUROPEAN HISTORY. Being Vol. I. of a Historical Course for Schools edited by E. A. FREEMAN. New Edition, enlarged with Maps, Chronological Table, Index, &c. 18mo. 3s. 6d.

"*It supplies the great want of a good foundation for historical teaching. The scheme is an excellent one, and this instalment has been accepted in a way that promises much for the volumes that are yet to appear.*"—EDUCATIONAL TIMES.

THE OTTOMAN POWER IN EUROPE : its Nature, its Growth, and its Decline. With Three Coloured Maps. Crown 8vo. 7s. 6d.

Galileo.—THE PRIVATE LIFE OF GALILEO. Compiled principally from his Correspondence and that of his eldest daughter, Sister Maria Celeste, Nun in the Franciscan Convent of S. Matthew in Arcetri. With Portrait. Crown 8vo. 7s. 6d.

Geddes.—THE PROBLEM OF THE HOMERIC POEMS. By W. D. GEDDES, LL.D., Professor of Greek in the University of Aberdeen. 8vo. 14s.

Gladstone—Works by the Right Hon. W. E. GLADSTONE, M.P.:—
JUVENTUS MUNDI. The Gods and Men of the Heroic Age. Crown 8vo. cloth. With Map. 10s. 6d. Second Edition.

"*Seldom,*" says the ATHENÆUM, "*out of the great poems themselves, have these Divinities looked so majestic and respectable. To read these brilliant details is like standing on the Olympian threshold and gazing at the ineffable brightness within.*"

HOMERIC SYNCHRONISM. An inquiry into the Time and Place of Homer. Crown 8vo. 6s.

"*It is impossible not to admire the immense range of thought and inquiry which the author has displayed.*"—BRITISH QUARTERLY REVIEW.

Goethe and Mendelssohn (1821—1831). Translated from the German of Dr. KARL MENDELSSOHN, Son of the Composer, by M. E. VON GLEHN. From the Private Diaries and Home Letters of Mendelssohn, with Poems and Letters of Goethe never before printed. Also with two New and Original Portraits, Facsimiles, and Appendix of Twenty Letters hitherto unpublished. Crown 8vo. 5s. Second Edition, enlarged.

"... Every page is full of interest, not merely to the musician, but to the general reader. The book is a very charming one, on a topic of deep and lasting interest."—STANDARD.

Goldsmid.—TELEGRAPH AND TRAVEL. A Narrative of the Formation and Development of Telegraphic Communication between England and India, under the orders of Her Majesty's Government, with incidental Notices of the Countries traversed by the Lines. By Colonel Sir FREDERIC GOLDSMID, C.B., K.C.S.I., late Director of the Government Indo-European Telegraph. With numerous Illustrations and Maps. 8vo. 21s.

"The merit of the work is a total absence of exaggeration, which does not, however, preclude a vividness and vigour of style not always characteristic of similar narratives."—STANDARD.

Gordon.—LAST LETTERS FROM EGYPT, to which are added Letters from the Cape. By LADY DUFF GORDON. With a Memoir by her Daughter, Mrs. Ross, and Portrait engraved by JEENS. Second Edition. Crown 8vo. 9s.

"The intending tourist who wishes to acquaint himself with the country he is about to visit, stands embarrassed amidst the riches presented for his choice, and in the end probably rests contented with the sober usefulness of Murray. He will not, however, if he is well advised, grudge a place in his portmanteau to this book."—TIMES.

Gray.—CHINA. A History of the Laws, Manners, and Customs of the People. By the VENERABLE JOHN HENRY GRAY. LL.D., Archdeacon of Hong Kong, formerly H.B.M. Consular Chaplain at Canton. Edited by W. Gow Gregor. With 150 Full-page Illustrations, being Facsimiles of Drawings by a Chinese Artist. 2 Vols. Demy 8vo. 32s.

"Its pages contain the most truthful and vivid picture of Chinese life which has ever been published."—ATHENÆUM.

"The only elaborate and valuable book we have had for many years treating generally of the people of the Celestial Empire."—ACADEMY.

Green.—Works by JOHN RICHARD GREEN :—

HISTORY OF THE ENGLISH PEOPLE. Vol. I.—Early England—Foreign Kings—The Charter—The Parliament. With 8 Coloured Maps. 8vo. 16s. Vol. II.—The Monarchy, 1461—1540; the Restoration, 1540—1603. 8vo. 16s. Vol. III. —Puritan England, 1603—1660; the Revolution, 1660—1688. With 4 Maps. 8vo. 16s. [*Vol. IV. in the press.*

"Mr. Green has done a work which probably no one but himself could have done. He has read and assimilated the results of all the labours of students during the last half century in the field of English history, and has given them a fresh meaning by his own independent study. He has fused together by the force of sympathetic imagination all that he has so

Green.—*continued.*

collected, and has given us a vivid and forcible sketch of the march of English history. His book, both in its aims and its accomplishments, rises far beyond any of a similar kind, and it will give the colouring to the popular view to English history for some time to come."—EXAMINER.

A SHORT HISTORY OF THE ENGLISH PEOPLE. With Coloured Maps, Genealogical Tables, and Chronological Annals. Crown 8vo. 8s. 6d. Sixty-third Thousand.

" *To say that Mr. Green's book is better than those which have preceded it, would be to convey a very inadequate impression of its merits. It stands alone as the one general history of the country, for the sake of which all others, if young and old are wise, will be speedily and surely set aside.*"

STRAY STUDIES FROM ENGLAND AND ITALY. Crown 8vo. 8s. 6d. Containing : Lambeth and the Archbishops—The Florence of Dante—Venice and Rome—Early History of Oxford —The District Visitor—Capri—Hotels in the Clouds—Sketches in Sunshine, &c.

" *One and all of the papers are eminently readable.*"—ATHENÆUM.

Guest.—LECTURES ON THE HISTORY OF ENGLAND. By M. J. GUEST. With Maps. Crown 8vo. 6s.

" *The book is pleasant reading, it is full of information, much of it is valuable, most of it is correct, told in a gossipy and intelligible way.*"— ATHENÆUM.

Hamerton.—Works by P. G. HAMERTON :—

THE INTELLECTUAL LIFE. With a Portrait of Leonardo da Vinci, etched by LEOPOLD FLAMENG. Second Edition. Crown 10s. 6d. 8vo.

" *We have read the whole book with great pleasure, and we can recommend it strongly to all who can appreciate grave reflections on a very important subject, excellently illustrated from the resources of a mind stored with much reading and much keen observation of real life.*"— SATURDAY REVIEW.

THOUGHTS ABOUT ART. New Edition, revised, with an Introduction. Crown 8vo. 8s. 6d.

" *A manual of sound and thorough criticism on art.*"—STANDARD.

Hill.—THE RECORDER OF BIRMINGHAM. A Memoir of Matthew Davenport Hill, with Selections from his Correspondence. By his Daughters ROSAMOND and FLORENCE DAVENPORT-HILL. With Portrait engraved by C. H. JEENS. 8vo. 16s.

Hill.—WHAT WE SAW IN AUSTRALIA. By ROSAMOND and FLORENCE HILL. Crown 8vo. 10s. 6d.

"*May be recommended as an interesting and truthful picture of the condition of those lands which are so distant and yet so much like home.*"—SATURDAY REVIEW.

Hodgson.—MEMOIR OF REV. FRANCIS HODGSON, B.D., Scholar, Poet, and Divine. By his Son, the Rev. JAMES T. HODGSON, M.A. Containing numerous Letters from Lord Byron and others. With Portrait engraved by JEENS. Two Vols. Crown 8vo. 18s.

"*A book that has added so much of a healthy nature to our knowledge of Byron, and that contains so rich a store of delightful correspondence.*"—ATHENÆUM.

Hole.—A GENEALOGICAL STEMMA OF THE KINGS OF ENGLAND AND FRANCE. By the Rev. C. HOLE, M.A., Trinity College, Cambridge. On Sheet, 1s.

A BRIEF BIOGRAPHICAL DICTIONARY. Compiled and Arranged by the Rev. CHARLES HOLE, M.A. Second Edition. 18mo. 4s. 6d.

Hooker and Ball.—MAROCCO AND THE GREAT ATLAS: Journal of a Tour in. By Sir JOSEPH D. HOOKER, K.C.S.I., C.B., F.R.S., &c., and JOHN BALL, F.R.S. With an Appendix, including a Sketch of the Geology of Marocco, by G. MAW, F.L.S., F.G.S. With Illustrations and Map. 8vo. 21s.

"*It is long since any more interesting book of travels has issued from our press.*"—SATURDAY REVIEW. "*This is, without doubt, one of the most interesting and valuable books of travel published for many years.*"—SPECTATOR.

Hozier (H. M.)—Works by CAPTAIN HENRY M. HOZIER, late Assistant Military Secretary to Lord Napier of Magdala:—

THE SEVEN WEEKS' WAR; Its Antecedents and Incidents. *New and Cheaper Edition.* With New Preface, Maps, and Plans. Crown 8vo. 6s.

THE INVASIONS OF ENGLAND: a History of the Past, with Lessons for the Future. Two Vols. 8vo. 28s.

Hübner.—A RAMBLE ROUND THE WORLD IN 1871. By M. LE BARON HÜBNER, formerly Ambassador and Minister. Translated by LADY HERBERT. New and Cheaper Edition. With numerous Illustrations. Crown 8vo. 6s.

"*It is difficult to do ample justice to this pleasant narrative of travel .... it does not contain a single dull paragraph.*"—MORNING POST.

HISTORY, BIOGRAPHY, TRAVELS, ETC. 15

Hughes.—Works by THOMAS HUGHES, Q.C., Author of "Tom Brown's School Days."
ALFRED THE GREAT. New Edition. Crown 8vo. 6s.
MEMOIR OF A BROTHER. With Portrait of GEORGE HUGHES, after WATTS. Engraved by JEENS. Crown 8vo. 5s. Sixth Edition.
" *The boy who can read this book without deriving from it some additional impulse towards honourable, manly, and independent conduct, has no good stuff in him.*"—DAILY NEWS.

Hunt.—HISTORY OF ITALY. By the Rev. W. HUNT, M.A. Being the Fourth Volume of the Historical Course for Schools. Edited by EDWARD A. FREEMAN, D.C.L. 18mo. 3s.
" *Mr. Hunt gives us a most compact but very readable little book, containing in small compass a very complete outline of a complicated and perplexing subject. It is a book which may be safely recommended to others besides schoolboys.*"—JOHN BULL.

Irving.—THE ANNALS OF OUR TIME. A Diurnal of Events, Social and Political, Home and Foreign, from the Accession of Queen Victoria to the Peace of Versailles. By JOSEPH IRVING. *Fourth Edition.* 8vo. half-bound. 16s.
ANNALS OF OUR TIME. Supplement. From Feb. 28, 1871, to March 19, 1874. 8vo. 4s. 6d.
ANNALS OF OUR TIME. Second Supplement. From March, 1874, to the Occupation of Cyprus. 8vo. 4s. 6d.
" *We have before us a trusty and ready guide to the events of the past thirty years, available equally for the statesman, the politician, the public writer, and the general reader.*"—TIMES.

James.—Works by HENRY JAMES, Jun. FRENCH POETS AND NOVELISTS. Crown 8vo. 8s. 6d.
CONTENTS:—*Alfred de Musset; Théophile Gautier; Baudelaire; Honoré de Balzac; George Sand; The Two Ampères; Turgenieff, &c.*

Johnson's Lives of the Poets.—The Six Chief Lives—Milton, Dryden, Swift, Addison, Pope, Gray. With Macaulay's "Life of Johnson." Edited, with Preface, by MATTHEW ARNOLD. Crown 8vo. 6s.

Killen.—ECCLESIASTICAL HISTORY OF IRELAND, from the Earliest Date to the Present Time. By W. D. KILLEN, D.D., President of Assembly's College, Belfast, and Professor of Ecclesiastical History. Two Vols. 8vo. 25s.
" *Those who have the leisure will do well to read these two volumes. They are full of interest, and are the result of great research.* . . . *We*

have no hesitation in recommending the work to all who wish to improve their acquaintance with Irish history."—SPECTATOR.

Kingsley (Charles).—Works by the Rev. CHARLES KINGSLEY, M.A., Rector of Eversley and Canon of Westminster. (For other Works by the same Author, *see* THEOLOGICAL and BELLES LETTRES Catalogues.)

ON THE ANCIEN RÉGIME as it existed on the Continent before the FRENCH REVOLUTION. Three Lectures delivered at the Royal Institution. Crown 8vo. 6s.

AT LAST : A CHRISTMAS in the WEST INDIES. With nearly Fifty Illustrations. Sixth Edition. Crown 8vo. 6s.
Mr. Kingsley's dream of forty years was at last fulfilled, when he started on a Christmas expedition to the West Indies, for the purpose of becoming personally acquainted with the scenes which he has so vividly described in "Westward Ho!" These two volumes are the journal of his voyage. Records of natural history, sketches of tropical landscape, chapters on education, views of society, all find their place. "We can only say that Mr. Kingsley's account of a 'Christmas in the West Indies' is in every way worthy to be classed among his happiest productions."—STANDARD.

THE ROMAN AND THE TEUTON. A Series of Lectures delivered before the University of Cambridge. New and Cheaper Edition, with Preface by Professor MAX MÜLLER. Crown 8vo. 6s.

PLAYS AND PURITANS, and other Historical Essays. With Portrait of Sir WALTER RALEIGH. New Edition. Crown 8vo. 6s.
In addition to the Essay mentioned in the title, this volume contains other two—one on "Sir Walter Raleigh and his Time," and one on Froude's "History of England."

Kingsley (Henry).—TALES OF OLD TRAVEL. Renarrated by HENRY KINGSLEY, F.R.G.S. With *Eight Illustrations* by HUARD. Fifth Edition. Crown 8vo. 5s.
"We know no better book for those who want knowledge or seek to refresh it. As for the 'sensational,' most novels are tame compared with these narratives."—ATHENÆUM.

Lang.—CYPRUS : Its History, its Present Resources and Future Prospects. By R. HAMILTON LANG, late H.M. Consul for the Island of Cyprus. With Two Illustrations and Four Maps. 8vo. 14s.
"The fair and impartial account of her past and present to be found in these pages has an undoubted claim on the attention of all intelligent readers."—MORNING POST.

HISTORY, BIOGRAPHY, TRAVELS, ETC.

Laocoon.—Translated from the Text of Lessing, with Preface and Notes by the Right Hon. Sir Robert J. Phillimore, D.C.L. With Photographs. 8vo. 12s.

Leonardo da Vinci and his Works.—Consisting of a Life of Leonardo Da Vinci, by Mrs. Charles W. Heaton, Author of "Albrecht Dürer of Nürnberg," &c., an Essay on his Scientific and Literary Works by Charles Christopher Black, M.A., and an account of his more important Paintings and Drawings. Illustrated with Permanent Photographs. Royal 8vo, cloth, extra gilt. 31s. 6d.

Liechtenstein.—HOLLAND HOUSE. By Princess Marie Liechtenstein. With Five Steel Engravings by C. H. Jeens, after Paintings by Watts and other celebrated Artists, and numerous Illustrations drawn by Professor P. H. Delamotte, and engraved on Wood by J. D. Cooper, W. Palmer, and Jewitt & Co. Third and Cheaper Edition. Medium 8vo. cloth elegant. 16s.

Also, an Edition containing, in addition to the above, about 40 Illustrations by the Woodbury-type process, and India Proofs of the Steel Engravings. Two vols. medium 4to. half morocco elegant. 4l. 4s.

Lloyd.—THE AGE OF PERICLES. A History of the Arts and Politics of Greece from the Persian to the Peloponnesian War. By W. Watkiss Lloyd. Two Vols. 8vo. 21s.

"*No such account of Greek art of the best period has yet been brought together in an English work. . . . . Mr. Lloyd has produced a book of unusual excellence and interest.*"—Pall Mall Gazette.

Loch Etive and the Sons of Uisnach.—With Illustrations. 8vo. 14s.

"*Not only have we Loch Etive of the present time brought before us in colours as true as they are vivid, but stirring scenes which happened on the borders of the beautiful lake in semi-mythical times are conjured up with singular skill. Nowhere else do we remember to have met with such a well-written account of the invasion of Scotland by the Irish.*"—Globe.

Loftie.—A RIDE IN EGYPT FROM SIOOT TO LUXOR, IN 1879; with Notes on the Present State and Ancient History of the Nile Valley, and some account of the various ways of making the voyage out and home. By the Rev. W. J. Loftie. With Illustrations. Crown 8vo. 10s. 6d.

"*We prophesy that Mr. Loftie's little book will accompany many travellers on the Nile in the coming winters.*"—Times.

Lubbock.—ADDRESSES, POLITICAL AND EDUCATIONAL. By Sir JOHN LUBBOCK, Bart., M.P., D.C.L., F.R.S. 8vo. 8s. 6d.

Macdonell.—FRANCE SINCE THE FIRST EMPIRE. By JAMES MACDONELL. Edited with Preface by his Wife. Crown 8vo. [*Shortly.*

Macarthur.—HISTORY OF SCOTLAND, By MARGARET MACARTHUR. Being the Third Volume of the Historical Course for Schools, Edited by EDWARD A. FREEMAN, D.C.L. Second Edition. 18mo. 2s.

"*It is an excellent summary, unimpeachable as to facts, and putting them in the clearest and most impartial light attainable.*"—GUARDIAN.
"*No previous History of Scotland of the same bulk is anything like so trustworthy, or deserves to be so extensively used as a text-book.*"—GLOBE.

Macmillan (Rev. Hugh).—For other Works by same Author, see THEOLOGICAL and SCIENTIFIC CATALOGUES.

HOLIDAYS ON HIGH LANDS; or, Rambles and Incidents in search of Alpine Plants. Second Edition, revised and enlarged. Globe 8vo. cloth. 6s.

"*Botanical knowledge is blended with a love of nature, a pious enthusiasm, and a rich felicity of diction not to be met with in any works of kindred character, if we except those of Hugh Miller.*"—TELEGRAPH.

Macready.—MACREADY'S REMINISCENCES AND SELECTIONS FROM HIS DIARIES AND LETTERS. Edited by Sir F. POLLOCK, Bart., one of his Executors. With Four Portraits engraved by JEENS. New and Cheaper Edition. Crown 8vo. 7s. 6d.

"*As a careful and for the most part just estimate of the stage during a very brilliant period, the attraction of these volumes can scarcely be surpassed. . . . Readers who have no special interest in theatrical matters, but enjoy miscellaneous gossip, will be allured from page to page, attracted by familiar names and by observations upon popular actors and authors.*"—SPECTATOR.

Mahaffy.—Works by the Rev. J. P. MAHAFFY, M.A., Fellow of Trinity College, Dublin:—

SOCIAL LIFE IN GREECE FROM HOMER TO MENANDER. Third Edition, revised and enlarged, with a new chapter on Greek Art. Crown 8vo. 9s.

"*It should be in the hands of all who desire thoroughly to understand and to enjoy Greek literature, and to get an intelligent idea of the old Greek life, political, social, and religious.*"—GUARDIAN.

Mahaffy.—*continued.*
RAMBLES AND STUDIES IN GREECE. With Illustrations. Crown 8vo. 10s. 6d. New and enlarged Edition, with Map and Illustrations.
"*A singularly instructive and agreeable volume.*"—ATHENÆUM.

"**Maori."**—SPORT AND WORK ON THE NEPAUL FRONTIER; or, Twelve Years' Sporting Reminiscences of an Indigo Planter. By "MAORI." With Illustrations. 8vo. 14s.
"*Every day's adventures, with all the joys and perils of the chase, are told as only a keen and cunning sportsman can tell them.*"—STANDARD.

Margary.—THE JOURNEY OF AUGUSTUS RAYMOND MARGARY FROM SHANGHAE TO BHAMO AND BACK TO MANWYNE. From his Journals and Letters, with a brief Biographical Preface, a concluding chapter by Sir RUTHERFORD ALCOCK, K.C.B., and a Steel Portrait engraved by JEENS, and Map. 8vo. 10s. 6d.
"*There is a manliness, a cheerful spirit, an inherent vigour which was never overcome by sickness or debility, a tact which conquered the prejudices of a strange and suspicious population, a quiet self-reliance, always combined with deep religious feeling, unalloyed by either priggishness, cant, or superstition, that ought to commend this volume to readers sitting quietly at home who feel any pride in the high estimation accorded to men of their race at Yarkand or at Khiva, in the heart of Africa, or on the shores of Lake Seri-kul.*"—SATURDAY REVIEW.

Markham.—NORTHWARD HO! By Captain ALBERT H. MARKHAM, R.N., Author of "The Great Frozen Sea," &c. Including a Narrative of Captain Phipps's Expedition, by a Midshipman. With Illustrations. Crown 8vo. 10s. 6d.
"*Captain Markham's interesting volume has the advantage of being written by a man who is practically conversant with the subject.*"—PALL MALL GAZETTE.

Martin.—THE HISTORY OF LLOYD'S, AND OF MARINE INSURANCE IN GREAT BRITAIN. With an Appendix containing Statistics relating to Marine Insurance. By FREDERICK MARTIN, Author of "The Statesman's Year Book." 8vo. 14s.

Martineau.—BIOGRAPHICAL SKETCHES, 1852—1875. By HARRIET MARTINEAU. With Additional Sketches, and Autobiographical Sketch. Fifth Edition. Crown 8vo. 6s.

Masson (David).—For other Works by same Author, *see* PHILOSOPHICAL and BELLES LETTRES CATALOGUES.

Masson (David).—*continued.*

CHATTERTON : A Story of the Year 1770. By DAVID MASSON, LL.D., Professor of Rhetoric and English Literature in the University of Edinburgh. Crown 8vo. 5s.

THE THREE DEVILS: Luther's, Goethe's, and Milton's; and other Essays. Crown 8vo. 5s.

WORDSWORTH, SHELLEY, AND KEATS; and other Essays. Crown 8vo. 5s.

Mathews.—LIFE OF CHARLES J. MATHEWS, Chiefly Autobiographical. With Selections from his Correspondence and Speeches. Edited by CHARLES DICKENS.

"*One of the pleasantest and most readable books of the season. From first to last these two volumes are alive with the inimitable artist and comedian. ... The whole book is full of life, vigour, and wit, and even through some of the gloomy episodes of volume two, will repay most careful study. So complete, so varied a picture of a man's life is rarely to be met with.*"—STANDARD.

Maurice.—THE FRIENDSHIP OF BOOKS; AND OTHER LECTURES. By the REV. F. D. MAURICE. Edited with Preface, by THOMAS HUGHES, Q.C. Crown 8vo. 10s. 6d.

Mayor (J. E. B.)—WORKS edited by JOHN E. B. MAYOR, M.A., Kennedy Professor of Latin at Cambridge :—

CAMBRIDGE IN THE SEVENTEENTH CENTURY. Part II. Autobiography of Matthew Robinson. Fcap. 8vo. 5s. 6d.

LIFE OF BISHOP BEDELL. By his SON. Fcap. 8vo. 3s. 6d.

Melbourne.—MEMOIRS OF THE RT. HON. WILLIAM, SECOND VISCOUNT MELBOURNE. By W. M. TORRENS, M.P. With Portrait after Sir. T. Lawrence. Second Edition. 2 Vols. 8vo. 32s.

"*As might be expected, he has produced a book which will command and reward attention. It contains a great deal of valuable matter and a great deal of animated, elegant writing.*"—QUARTERLY REVIEW.

Mendelssohn.—LETTERS AND RECOLLECTIONS. By FERDINAND HILLER. Translated by M. E. VON GLEHN. With Portrait from a Drawing by KARL MÜLLER, never before published. Second Edition. Crown 8vo. 7s. 6d.

"*This is a very interesting addition to our knowledge of the great German composer. It reveals him to us under a new light, as the warm-hearted comrade, the musician whose soul was in his work, and the home-loving, domestic man.*"—STANDARD.

HISTORY, BIOGRAPHY, TRAVELS, ETC. 21

Merewether.—BY SEA AND BY LAND. Being a Trip through Egypt, India, Ceylon, Australia, New Zealand, and America—all Round the World. By HENRY ALWORTH MEREWETHER, one of Her Majesty's Counsel. Crown 8vo. 8s. 6d.

Michael Angelo Buonarotti; Sculptor, Painter, Architect. The Story of his Life and Labours. By C. C. BLACK, M.A. Illustrated by 20 Permanent Photographs. Royal 8vo. cloth elegant, 31s. 6d.

"*The story of Michael Angelo's life remains interesting whatever be the manner of telling it, and supported as it is by this beautiful series of photographs, the volume must take rank among the most splendid of Christmas books, fitted to serve and to outlive the season.*"—PALL MALL GAZETTE.

Michelet.—A SUMMARY OF MODERN HISTORY. Translated from the French of M. MICHELET, and continued to the present time by M. C. M. SIMPSON. Globe 8vo. 4s. 6d.

Milton.—LIFE OF JOHN MILTON. Narrated in connection with the Political, Ecclesiastical, and Literary History of his Time. By DAVID MASSON, M.A., LL.D., Professor of Rhetoric and English Literature in the University of Edinburgh. With Portraits. Vol. I. 18s. Vol. II., 1638—1643. 8vo. 16s. Vol. III. 1643—1649. 8vo. 18s. Vols. IV. and V. 1649—1660. 32s. Vol. VI. concluding the work in the press.

This work is not only a Biography, but also a continuous Political, Ecclesiastical, and Literary History of England through Milton's whole time.

Mitford (A. B.)—TALES OF OLD JAPAN. By A. B. MITFORD, Second Secretary to the British Legation in Japan. With upwards of 30 Illustrations, drawn and cut on Wood by Japanese Artists. New and Cheaper Edition. Crown 8vo. 6s.

"*These very original volumes will always be interesting as memorials of a most exceptional society, while regarded simply as tales, they are sparkling, sensational, and dramatic.*"—PALL MALL GAZETTE.

Monteiro.—ANGOLA AND THE RIVER CONGO. By JOACHIM MONTEIRO. With numerous Illustrations from Sketches taken on the spot, and a Map. Two Vols. crown 8vo. 21s.

Morison.—THE LIFE AND TIMES OF SAINT BERNARD, Abbot of Clairvaux. By JAMES COTTER MORISON, M.A. New Edition. Crown 8vo. 6s.

Moseley.—NOTES BY A NATURALIST ON THE *CHALLENGER*: being an Account of various Observations made during the Voyage of H.M.S. *Challenger*, Round the World, in 1872-76. By H. N. MOSELEY, F.R.S., Member of the Scientific Staff of the *Challenger*. 8vo. with Maps, Coloured Plates, and Woodcuts. 21s.

"*This is certainly the most interesting and suggestive book, descriptive of a naturalist's travels, which has been published since Mr. Darwin's 'Journal of Researches' appeared, more than forty years ago.*"—NATURE. "*We cannot point to any book of travels in our day more vivid in its powers of description, more varied in its subject matter, or more attractive to every educated reader.*"—SATURDAY REVIEW.

Murray.—ROUND ABOUT FRANCE. By E. C. GRENVILLE MURRAY. Crown 8vo. 7s. 6d.

"*These short essays are a perfect mine of information as to the present condition and future prospects of political parties in France. . . . It is at once extremely interesting and exceptionally instructive on a subject on which few English people are well informed.*"—SCOTSMAN.

Napier.—MACVEY NAPIER'S SELECTED CORRESPONDENCE. Edited by his Son, MACVEY NAPIER. 8vo. 14s.

The TIMES *says:*—"*It is replete with useful material for the biographers of many distinguished writers of the generation which is passing away. Since reading it we understand several noteworthy men, and Brougham in particular, far better than we did before.*" "*It would be useless to attempt within our present limits to give any adequate idea of the abundance of interesting passages which meet us in the letters of Macaulay, Brougham, Carlyle, Jeffrey, Senior, and many other well-known writers. Especially piquant are Jeffrey's periodical criticisms on the contents of the Review which he had formerly edited.*"—PALL MALL GAZETTE.

Napoleon.—THE HISTORY OF NAPOLEON I. By P. LANFREY. A Translation with the sanction of the Author. 4 vols. 8vo. Vols. I. II. and III. price 12s. each. Vol. IV. 6s.

The PALL MALL GAZETTE *says it is* "*one of the most striking pieces of historical composition of which France has to boast,*" *and the* SATURDAY REVIEW *calls it* "*an excellent translation of a work on every ground deserving to be translated. It is unquestionably and immeasurably the best that has been produced. It is in fact the only work to which we can turn for an accurate and trustworthy narrative of that extraordinary career. . . . The book is the best and indeed the only trustworthy history of Napoleon which has been written.*"

Nichol.—TABLES OF EUROPEAN LITERATURE AND HISTORY, A.D. 200—1876. By J. NICHOL, LL.D., Professor of English Language and Literature, Glasgow. 4to. 6s. 6d.

TABLES OF ANCIENT LITERATURE AND HISTORY, B.C. 1500—A.D. 200. By the same Author. 4to. 4s. 6d.

HISTORY, BIOGRAPHY, TRAVELS, ETC. 23

Nordenskiöld's Arctic Voyages, 1858-79. — With Maps and numerous Illustrations. 8vo. 16s.

"*A volume of great interest and much scientific value.*"—NATURE.

Oliphant (Mrs.).—THE MAKERS OF FLORENCE: Dante Giotto, Savonarola, and their City. By Mrs. OLIPHANT. With numerous Illustrations from drawings by Professor DELAMOTTE, and portrait of Savonarola, engraved by JEENS. Second Edition. Medium 8vo. Cloth extra. 21s.

"*We are grateful to Mrs. Oliphant for her eloquent and beautiful sketches of Dante, Fra Angelico, and Savonarola. They are picturesque, full of life, and rich in detail, and they are charmingly illustrated by the art of the engraver.*"—SPECTATOR.

Oliphant.—THE DUKE AND THE SCHOLAR; and other Essays. By T. L. KINGTON OLIPHANT. 8vo. 7s. 6d.

"*This volume contains one of the most beautiful biographical essays we have seen since Macaulay's days.*"—STANDARD.

Otte.—SCANDINAVIAN HISTORY. By E. C. OTTE. With Maps. Extra fcap. 8vo. 6s.

Owens College Essays and Addresses.—By PROFESSORS AND LECTURERS OF OWENS COLLEGE, MANCHESTER. Published in Commemoration of the Opening of the New College Buildings, October 7th, 1873. 8vo. 14s.

Palgrave (R. F. D.)—THE HOUSE OF COMMONS; Illustrations of its History and Practice. By REGINALD F. D. PALGRAVE, Clerk Assistant of the House of Commons. New and Revised Edition. Crown 8vo. 2s. 6d.

Palgrave (Sir F.)—HISTORY OF NORMANDY AND OF ENGLAND. By Sir FRANCIS PALGRAVE, Deputy Keeper of Her Majesty's Public Records. Completing the History to the Death of William Rufus. 4 Vols. 8vo. 4l. 4s.

Palgrave (W. G.)—A NARRATIVE OF A YEAR'S JOURNEY THROUGH CENTRAL AND EASTERN ARABIA, 1862-3. By WILLIAM GIFFORD PALGRAVE, late of the Eighth Regiment Bombay N. I. Sixth Edition. With Maps, Plans, and Portrait of Author, engraved on steel by Jeens. Crown 8vo. 6s.

"*He has not only written one of the best books on the Arabs and one of the best books on Arabia, but he has done so in a manner that must command the respect no less than the admiration of his fellow-countrymen.*"—FORTNIGHTLY REVIEW.

Palgrave.—*continued.*
ESSAYS ON EASTERN QUESTIONS. By W. GIFFORD PALGRAVE. 8vo. 10s. 6d.

"These essays are full of anecdote and interest. The book is decidedly a valuable addition to the stock of literature on which men must base their opinion of the difficult social and political problems suggested by the designs of Russia, the capacity of Mahometans for sovereignty, and the good government and retention of India."—SATURDAY REVIEW.

DUTCH GUIANA. With Maps and Plans. 8vo. 9s.

"His pages are nearly exhaustive as far as facts and statistics go, while they are lightened by graphic social sketches as well as sparkling descriptions of scenery."—SATURDAY REVIEW.

Patteson.—LIFE AND LETTERS OF JOHN COLERIDGE PATTESON, D.D., Missionary Bishop of the Melanesian Islands. By CHARLOTTE M. YONGE, Author of "The Heir of Redclyffe." With Portraits after RICHMOND and from Photograph, engraved by JEENS. With Map. Fifth Edition. Two Vols. Crown 8vo. 12s.

"Miss Yonge's work is in one respect a model biography. It is made up almost entirely of Patteson's own letters. Aware that he had left his home once and for all, his correspondence took the form of a diary, and as we read on we come to know the man, and to love him almost as if we had seen him."—ATHENÆUM. "Such a life, with its grand lessons of unselfishness, is a blessing and an honour to the age in which it is lived; the biography cannot be studied without pleasure and profit, and indeed we should think little of the man who did not rise from the study of it better and wiser. Neither the Church nor the nation which produces such sons need ever despair of its future."—SATURDAY REVIEW.

Pauli.—PICTURES OF OLD ENGLAND. By Dr. REINHOLD PAULI. Translated, with the approval of the Author, by E. C. OTTÉ. Cheaper Edition. Crown 8vo. 6s.

Payne.—A HISTORY OF EUROPEAN COLONIES. By E. J. PAYNE, M.A. With Maps. 18mo. 4s. 6d.

The TIMES says:—"We have seldom met with a historian capable of forming a more comprehensive, far-seeing, and unprejudiced estimate of events and peoples, and we can commend this little work as one certain to prove of the highest interest to all thoughtful readers."

Persia.—EASTERN PERSIA. An Account of the Journeys of the Persian Boundary Commission, 1870-1-2.—Vol. I. The Geography, with Narratives by Majors ST. JOHN, LOVETT, and EUAN SMITH, and an Introduction by Major-General Sir FREDERIC GOLDSMID, C.B., K.C.S.I., British Commissioner and Arbitrator.

With Maps and Illustrations.—Vol. II. The Zoology and Geology. By W. T. BLANFORD, A.R.S.M., F.R.S. With Coloured Illustrations. Two Vols. 8vo. 42s.

"*The volumes largely increase our store of information about countries with which Englishmen ought to be familiar. . . . . They throw into the shade all that hitherto has appeared in our tongue respecting the local features of Persia, its scenery, its resources, even its social condition. They contain also abundant evidence of English endurance, daring, and spirit.*"—TIMES.

Prichard.—THE ADMINISTRATION OF INDIA. From 1859 to 1868. The First Ten Years of Administration under the Crown. By I. T. PRICHARD, Barrister-at-Law. Two Vols. Demy 8vo. With Map. 21s.

Raphael.—RAPHAEL OF URBINO AND HIS FATHER GIOVANNI SANTI. By J. D. PASSAVANT, formerly Director of the Museum at Frankfort. With Twenty Permanent Photographs. Royal 8vo. Handsomely bound. 31s. 6d.

The SATURDAY REVIEW *says of them,* "*We have seen not a few elegant specimens of Mr. Woodbury's new process, but we have seen none that equal these.*"

Reynolds.—SIR JOSHUA REYNOLDS AS A PORTRAIT PAINTER. AN ESSAY. By J. CHURTON COLLINS, B.A. Balliol College, Oxford. Illustrated by a Series of Portraits of distinguished Beauties of the Court of George III. ; reproduced in Autotype from Proof Impressions of the celebrated Engravings, by VALENTINE GREEN, THOMAS WATSON, F. R. SMITH, E. FISHER, and others. Folio half-morocco. £5 5s.

Rogers (James E. Thorold).—HISTORICAL GLEANINGS : A Series of Sketches. Montague, Walpole, Adam Smith, Cobbett. By Prof. ROGERS. Crown 8vo. 4s. 6d. Second Series. Wiklif, Laud, Wilkes, and Horne Tooke. Crown 8vo. 6s.

Routledge.—CHAPTERS IN THE HISTORY OF POPULAR PROGRESS IN ENGLAND, chiefly in Relation to the Freedom of the Press and Trial by Jury, 1660—1820. With application to later years. By J. ROUTLEDGE. 8vo. 16s.

"*The volume abounds in facts and information, almost always useful and often curious.*"—TIMES.

Rumford.—COUNT RUMFORD'S COMPLETE WORKS, with Memoir, and Notices of his Daughter. By GEORGE ELLIS. Five Vols. 8vo. 4l. 14s. 6d.

Seeley (Professor).—LECTURES AND ESSAYS. By J. R. SEELEY, M.A. Professor of Modern History in the University of Cambridge. 8vo. 10s. 6d.
CONTENTS:—*Roman Imperialism:* 1. *The Great Roman Revolution;* 2. *The Proximate Cause of the Fall of the Roman Empire; The Later Empire.* — *Milton's Political Opinions* — *Milton's Poetry* — *Elementary Principles in Art* — *Liberal Education in Universities* — *English in Schools* — *The Church as a Teacher of Morality* — *The Teaching of Politics: an Inaugural Lecture delivered at Cambridge.*

Shelburne.—LIFE OF WILLIAM, EARL OF SHELBURNE, AFTERWARDS FIRST MARQUIS OF LANSDOWNE. With Extracts from his Papers and Correspondence. By Lord EDMOND FITZMAURICE. In Three Vols. 8vo. Vol. I. 1737—1766, 12s.; Vol. II. 1766—1776, 12s.; Vol. III. 1776—1805. 16s.
"*Lord Edmond Fitzmaurice has succeeded in placing before us a wealth of new matter, which, while casting valuable and much-needed light on several obscure passages in the political history of a hundred years ago, has enabled us for the first time to form a clear and consistent idea of his ancestor.*"—SPECTATOR.

Sime.—HISTORY OF GERMANY. By JAMES SIME, M.A. 18mo. 3s. Being Vol. V. of the Historical Course for Schools: Edited by EDWARD A. FREEMAN, D.C.L.
"*This is a remarkably clear and impressive History of Germany.*"—STANDARD.

Squier.—PERU: INCIDENTS OF TRAVEL AND EXPLORATION IN THE LAND OF THE INCAS. By E. G. SQUIER, M.A., F.S.A., late U.S. Commissioner to Peru. With 300 Illustrations. Second Edition. 8vo. 21s.
The TIMES says:—"*No more solid and trustworthy contribution has been made to an accurate knowledge of what are among the most wonderful ruins in the world. The work is really what its title implies. While of the greatest importance as a contribution to Peruvian archæology, it is also a thoroughly entertaining and instructive narrative of travel. Not the least important feature must be considered the numerous well executed illustrations.*"

Strangford.—EGYPTIAN SHRINES AND SYRIAN SEPULCHRES, including a Visit to Palmyra. By EMILY A. BEAUFORT (Viscountess Strangford), Author of "The Eastern Shores of the Adriatic." New Edition. Crown 8vo. 7s. 6d.

Tait.—AN ANALYSIS OF ENGLISH HISTORY, based upon Green's "Short History of the English People." By C. W. A. TAIT, M.A., Assistant Master, Clifton College. Crown 8vo. 3s. 6d.

Tait.—CATHARINE AND CRAUFURD TAIT, WIFE AND SON OF ARCHIBALD CAMPBELL, ARCHBISHOP OF CANTERBURY: a Memoir, Edited, at the request of the Archbishop, by the Rev. W. BENHAM, B.D., Vicar of Margate, and One of the Six Preachers of Canterbury Cathedral. With Two Portraits engraved by JEENS. Crown 8vo. 12s. 6d.

"*The volume can scarcely fail to be read widely and with deep interest. . . . It is difficult to put it down when once taken in hand, still more difficult to get through it without emotion. . . . We commend the volume to those who knew Catharine and Craufurd Tait as one which will bring back to their minds recollections of their characters as true as the recollections of the faces brought back by the two excellent portraits which adorn the book; while to those who knew them not, we commend it as containing the record of two noble Christian lives, which it will be a pleasure to them to contemplate and an advantage to emulate.*"—TIMES.

Thomas.—THE LIFE OF JOHN THOMAS, Surgeon of the "Earl of Oxford" East Indiaman, and First Baptist Missionary to Bengal. By C. B. LEWIS, Baptist Missionary. 8vo. 10s. 6d.

Thompson.—HISTORY OF ENGLAND. By EDITH THOMPSON. Being Vol. II. of the Historical Course for Schools, Edited by EDWARD A. FREEMAN, D.C.L. New Edition, revised and enlarged, with Maps. 18mo. 2s. 6d.

"*Freedom from prejudice, simplicity of style, and accuracy of statement, are the characteristics of this volume. It is a trustworthy text-book, and likely to be generally serviceable in schools.*"—PALL MALL GAZETTE.
"*In its great accuracy and correctness of detail it stands far ahead of the general run of school manuals. Its arrangement, too, is clear, and its style simple and straightforward.*"—SATURDAY REVIEW.

Todhunter.—THE CONFLICT OF STUDIES; AND OTHER ESSAYS ON SUBJECTS CONNECTED WITH EDUCATION. By ISAAC TODHUNTER, M.A., F.R.S., late Fellow and Principal Mathematical Lecturer of St. John's College, Cambridge. 8vo. 10s. 6d.

Trench (Archbishop).—For other Works by the same Author, see THEOLOGICAL and BELLES LETTRES CATALOGUES, and page 30 of this Catalogue.

GUSTAVUS ADOLPHUS IN GERMANY, and other Lectures on the Thirty Years' War. Second Edition, revised and enlarged. Fcap. 8vo. 4s.

PLUTARCH, HIS LIFE, HIS LIVES, AND HIS MORALS. Five Lectures. Second Edition, enlarged. Fcap. 8vo. 3s. 6d.

LECTURES ON MEDIEVAL CHURCH HISTORY. Being the substance of Lectures delivered in Queen's College, London. Second Edition, revised. 8vo. 12s.

Trench (Maria).—THE LIFE OF ST. TERESA. By MARIA TRENCH. With Portrait engraved by JEENS. Crown 8vo, cloth extra. 8s. 6d.
"*A book of rare interest.*"—JOHN BULL.

Trench (Mrs. R.)—REMAINS OF THE LATE MRS. RICHARD TRENCH. Being Selections from her Journals, Letters, and other Papers. Edited by ARCHBISHOP TRENCH. New and Cheaper Issue, with Portrait. 8vo. 6s.

Trollope.—A HISTORY OF THE COMMONWEALTH OF FLORENCE FROM THE EARLIEST INDEPENDENCE OF THE COMMUNE TO THE FALL OF THE REPUBLIC IN 1831. By T. ADOLPHUS TROLLOPE. 4 Vols. 8vo. Half morocco. 21s.

Uppingham by the Sea.—A NARRATIVE OF THE YEAR AT BORTH. By J. H. S. Crown 8vo. 3s. 6d.

Victor Emmanuel II., First King of Italy.—HIS LIFE. By G. S. GODKIN. 2 vols., crown 8vo. 16s.
"*An extremely clear and interesting history of one of the most important changes of later times.*"—EXAMINER.

Wallace.—THE MALAY ARCHIPELAGO: the Land of the Orang Utan and the Bird of Paradise. By ALFRED RUSSEL WALLACE. A Narrative of Travel with Studies of Man and Nature. With Maps and numerous Illustrations. Sixth Edition. Crown 8vo. 7s. 6d.
"*The result is a vivid picture of tropical life, which may be read with unflagging interest, and a sufficient account of his scientific conclusions to stimulate our appetite without wearying us by detail. In short, we may safely say that we have never read a more agreeable book of its kind.*"—SATURDAY REVIEW.

Ward.—A HISTORY OF ENGLISH DRAMATIC LITERATURE TO THE DEATH OF QUEEN ANNE. By A. W. WARD, M.A., Professor of History and English Literature in Owens College, Manchester. Two Vols. 8vo. 32s.
"*As full of interest as of information. To students of dramatic literature invaluable, and may be equally recommended to readers for mere pastime.*"—PALL MALL GAZETTE.

Ward (J.)—EXPERIENCES OF A DIPLOMATIST. Being recollections of Germany founded on Diaries kept during the years 1840—1870. By JOHN WARD, C.B., late H.M. Minister-Resident to the Hanse Towns. 8vo. 10s. 6d.

Waterton (C.)—WANDERINGS IN SOUTH AMERICA, THE NORTH-WEST OF THE UNITED STATES, AND THE ANTILLES IN 1812, 1816, 1820, and 1824. With Original Instructions for the perfect Preservation of Birds, etc., for Cabinets of Natural History. By CHARLES WATERTON. New Edition, edited with Biographical Introduction and Explanatory Index by the Rev. J. G. WOOD, M.A. With 100 Illustrations. Cheaper Edition. Crown 8vo. 6s.

Wedgwood.—JOHN WESLEY AND THE EVANGELICAL REACTION of the Eighteenth Century. By JULIA WEDGWOOD. Crown 8vo. 8s. 6d.

Whewell.—WILLIAM WHEWELL, D.D., late Master of Trinity College, Cambridge. An Account of his Writings, with Selections from his Literary and Scientific Correspondence. By I. TODHUNTER, M.A., F.R.S. Two Vols. 8vo. 25s.

White.—THE NATURAL HISTORY AND ANTIQUITIES OF SELBORNE. By GILBERT WHITE. Edited, with Memoir and Notes, by FRANK BUCKLAND, A Chapter on Antiquities by LORD SELBORNE, Map, &c., and numerous Illustrations by P. H. DELAMOTTE. Royal 8vo. Cloth, extra gilt. Cheaper Issue. 21s.

Also a Large Paper Edition, containing, in addition to the above, upwards of Thirty Woodburytype Illustrations from Drawings by Prof. DELAMOTTE. Two Vols. 4to. Half morocco, elegant. 4l. 4s.

"*Mr. Delamotte's charming illustrations are a worthy decoration of so dainty a book. They bring Selborne before us, and really help us to understand why White's love for his native place never grew cold.*"—TIMES.

Wilson.—A MEMOIR OF GEORGE WILSON, M.D., F.R.S.E., Regius Professor of Technology in the University of Edinburgh. By his SISTER. New Edition. Crown 8vo. 6s.

Wilson (Daniel, LL.D.)—Works by DANIEL WILSON, LL.D., Professor of History and English Literature in University College, Toronto :—

PREHISTORIC ANNALS OF SCOTLAND. New Edition, with numerous Illustrations. Two Vols. demy 8vo. 36s.

"*One of the most interesting, learned, and elegant works we have seen for a long time.*"—WESTMINSTER REVIEW.

PREHISTORIC MAN : Researches into the Origin of Civilization in the Old and New World. New Edition, revised and enlarged throughout, with numerous Illustrations and two Coloured Plates. Two Vols. 8vo. 36s.

Wilson.—*continued.*

"*A valuable work pleasantly written and well worthy of attention both by students and general readers.*"—ACADEMY.

    CHATTERTON: A Biographical Study. By DANIEL WILSON, LL.D., Professor of History and English Literature in University College, Toronto. Crown 8vo. 6s. 6d.

Yonge (Charlotte M.)—Works by CHARLOTTE M. YONGE, Author of "The Heir of Redclyffe," &c., &c. :—

    A PARALLEL HISTORY OF FRANCE AND ENGLAND: consisting of Outlines and Dates. Oblong 4to. 3s. 6d.

    CAMEOS FROM ENGLISH HISTORY. From Rollo to Edward II. Extra fcap. 8vo. Third Edition. 5s.

    SECOND SERIES, THE WARS IN FRANCE. Extra fcap. 8vo. Third Edition. 5s.

    THIRD SERIES, THE WARS OF THE ROSES. Extra fcap. 8vo. 5s.

"*Instead of dry details,*" says the NONCONFORMIST, "*we have living pictures, faithful, vivid, and striking.*"

    FOURTH SERIES. Reformation Times. Extra fcap. 8vo. 5s.

HISTORY OF FRANCE. Maps. 18mo. 3s. 6d.
                                      [*Historical Course for Schools.*

POLITICS, POLITICAL AND SOCIAL ECONOMY, LAW, AND KINDRED SUBJECTS.

Anglo-Saxon Law.—ESSAYS IN. Contents: Law Courts—Land and Family Laws and Legal Procedure generally. With Select cases. Medium 8vo. 18s.

Arnold.—THE ROMAN SYSTEM OF PROVINCIAL ADMINISTRATION TO THE ACCESSION OF CONSTANTINE THE GREAT. Being the Arnold Prize Essay for 1879. By W. T. Arnold, B.A. Crown 8vo. 6s.

Ball.—THE STUDENT'S GUIDE TO THE BAR. By WALTER W. BALL, M.A., of the Inner Temple, Barrister-at-Law. Crown 8vo. 2s. 6d.

"*The student will here find a clear statement of the several steps by which the degree of barrister is obtained, and also useful advice about the advantages of a prolonged course of 'reading in Chambers.'*"—ACADEMY.

Bernard.—FOUR LECTURES ON SUBJECTS CONNECTED WITH DIPLOMACY. By MONTAGUE BERNARD, M.A., Chichele Professor of International Law and Diplomacy, Oxford. 8vo. 9s.

"*Singularly interesting lectures, so able, clear, and attractive.*"—SPECTATOR.

Bright (John, M.P.)—Works by the Right Hon. JOHN BRIGHT, M.P.

SPEECHES ON QUESTIONS OF PUBLIC POLICY. Edited by Professor THOROLD ROGERS. Author's Popular Edition. Globe 8vo. 3s. 6d.

"*Mr. Bright's speeches will always deserve to be studied, as an apprenticeship to popular and parliamentary oratory; they will form materials for the history of our time, and many brilliant passages, perhaps some entire speeches, will really become a part of the living literature of England.*"—DAILY NEWS.

LIBRARY EDITION. Two Vols. 8vo. With Portrait. 25s.

PUBLIC ADDRESSES. Edited by J. THOROLD ROGERS. 8vo. 14s.

Bucknill.—HABITUAL DRUNKENNESS AND INSANE DRUNKARDS. By J. C. BUCKNILL, M.D., F.R.S., late Lord Chancellor's Visitor of Lunatics. Crown 8vo. 2s. 6d.

Cairnes.—Works by J. E. CAIRNES, M.A., Emeritus Professor of Political Economy in University College, London.

ESSAYS IN POLITICAL ECONOMY, THEORETICAL and APPLIED. By J. E. CAIRNES, M.A., Professor of Political Economy in University College, London. 8vo. 10s. 6d.

POLITICAL ESSAYS. 8vo. 10s. 6d.

SOME LEADING PRINCIPLES OF POLITICAL ECONOMY NEWLY EXPOUNDED. 8vo. 14s.

CONTENTS :—*Part I. Value. Part II. Labour and Capital. Part III. International Trade.*

"*A work which is perhaps the most valuable contribution to the science made since the publication, a quarter of a century since, of Mr. Mill's 'Principles of Political Economy.'*"—DAILY NEWS.

THE CHARACTER AND LOGICAL METHOD OF POLITICAL ECONOMY. New Edition, enlarged. 8vo. 7s. 6d.

"*These lectures are admirably fitted to correct the slipshod generalizations which pass current as the science of Political Economy.*"—TIMES.

Cobden (Richard).—SPEECHES ON QUESTIONS OF PUBLIC POLICY. By RICHARD COBDEN. Edited by the Right Hon. John Bright, M.P., and J. E. Thorold Rogers. Popular Edition. 8vo. 3s. 6d.

Fawcett.—Works by HENRY FAWCETT, M.A., M.P., Fellow of Trinity Hall, and Professor of Political Economy in the University of Cambridge :—

THE ECONOMIC POSITION OF THE BRITISH LABOURER. Extra fcap. 8vo. 5s.

MANUAL OF POLITICAL ECONOMY. Fifth Edition, with New Chapters on the Depreciation of Silver, etc. Crown 8vo. 12s.

The DAILY NEWS *says:* "*It forms one of the best introductions to the principles of the science, and to its practical applications in the problems of modern, and especially of English, government and society.*"

PAUPERISM : ITS CAUSES AND REMEDIES. Crown 8vo. 5s. 6d.

The ATHENÆUM *calls the work* "*a repertory of interesting and well digested information.*"

SPEECHES ON SOME CURRENT POLITICAL QUESTIONS. 8vo. 10s. 6d.

"*They will help to educate, not perhaps, parties, but the educators of parties.*"—DAILY NEWS.

Fawcett.—*continued.*

FREE TRADE AND PROTECTION: an Inquiry into the Causes which have retarded the general adoption of Free Trade since its introduction into England. Third Edition. 8vo. 7s. 6d.

"*No greater service can be rendered to the cause of Free Trade than a clear explanation of the principles on which Free Trade rests. Professor Fawcett has done this in the volume before us with all his habitual clearness of thought and expression.*"—ECONOMIST.

ESSAYS ON POLITICAL AND SOCIAL SUBJECTS. By PROFESSOR FAWCETT, M.P., and MILLICENT GARRETT FAWCETT. 8vo. 10s. 6d.

"*They will all repay the perusal of the thinking reader.*"—DAILY NEWS.

Fawcett (Mrs.)—Works by MILLICENT GARRETT FAWCETT.

POLITICAL ECONOMY FOR BEGINNERS. WITH QUESTIONS. New Edition. 18mo. 2s. 6d.

The DAILY NEWS *calls it "clear, compact, and comprehensive;" and the* SPECTATOR *says, "Mrs. Fawcett's treatise is perfectly suited to its purpose."*

TALES IN POLITICAL ECONOMY. Crown 8vo. 3s.

"*The idea is a good one, and it is quite wonderful what a mass of economic teaching the author manages to compress into a small space... The true doctrines of International Trade, Currency, and the ratio between Production and Population, are set before us and illustrated in a masterly manner.*"—ATHENÆUM.

Freeman (E. A.), M.A., D.C.L.—COMPARATIVE POLITICS. Lectures at the Royal Institution, to which is added "The Unity of History," being the Rede Lecture delivered at Cambridge in 1872. 8vo. 14s.

"*We find in Mr. Freeman's new volume the same sound, careful, comprehensive qualities which have long ago raised him to so high a place amongst historical writers. For historical discipline, then, as well as historical information, Mr. Freeman's book is full of value.*"—PALL MALL GAZETTE.

Goschen.—REPORTS AND SPEECHES ON LOCAL TAXATION. By GEORGE J. GOSCHEN, M.P. Royal 8vo. 5s.

"*The volume contains a vast mass of information of the highest value.*" —ATHENÆUM.

Guide to the Unprotected, in Every Day Matters Relating to Property and Income. By a BANKER'S DAUGHTER. Fourth Edition, Revised. Extra fcap. 8vo. 3s. 6d.

c

"*Many an unprotected female will bless the head which planned and the hand which compiled this admirable little manual. . . . This book was very much wanted, and it could not have been better done.*"— MORNING STAR.

Hamilton.—MONEY AND VALUE: an Inquiry into the Means and Ends of Economic Production, with an Appendix on the Depreciation of Silver and Indian Currency. By ROWLAND HAMILTON. 8vo. 12s.

"*The subject is here dealt with in a luminous style, and by presenting it from a new point of view in connection with the nature and functions of money, a genuine service has been rendered to commercial science.*"— BRITISH QUARTERLY REVIEW.

Harwood.—DISESTABLISHMENT: a Defence of the Principle of a National Church. By GEORGE HARWOOD, M.A. 8vo. 12s.

Hill.—OUR COMMON LAND; and other Short Essays. By OCTAVIA HILL. Extra fcap. 8vo. 3s. 6d.
CONTENTS:—*Our Common Land. District Visiting. A More Excellent Way of Charity. A Word on Good Citizenship. Open Spaces. Effectual Charity. The Future of our Commons.*

Historicus.—LETTERS ON SOME QUESTIONS OF INTERNATIONAL LAW. Reprinted from the *Times*, with considerable Additions. 8vo. 7s. 6d. Also, ADDITIONAL LETTERS. 8vo. 2s. 6d.

Holland.—THE TREATY RELATIONS OF RUSSIA AND TURKEY FROM 1774 TO 1853. A Lecture delivered at Oxford, April 1877. By T. E. HOLLAND, D.C.L., Professor of International Law and Diplomacy, Oxford. Crown 8vo. 2s.

Hughes (Thos.)—THE OLD CHURCH: WHAT SHALL WE DO WITH IT? By THOMAS HUGHES, Q.C. Crown 8vo. 6s.

Jevons.—Works by W. STANLEY JEVONS, M.A., Professor of Political Economy in University College, London. (For other Works by the same Author, see EDUCATIONAL and PHILOSOPHICAL CATALOGUES.)

THE THEORY OF POLITICAL ECONOMY. Second Edition, revised, with new Preface and Appendices. 8vo. 10s. 6d.

"*Professor Jevons has done invaluable service by courageously claiming political economy to be strictly a branch of Applied Mathematics.*"—WESTMINSTER REVIEW.

PRIMER OF POLITICAL ECONOMY. 18mo. 1s.

Laveleye. — PRIMITIVE PROPERTY. By EMILE DE LAVELEYE. Translated by G. R. L. MARRIOTT, LL.B., with an Introduction by T. E. CLIFFE LESLIE, LL.B. 8vo. 12s.

"*It is almost impossible to over-estimate the value of the well-digested knowledge which it contains; it is one of the most learned books that have been contributed to the historical department of the literature of economic science.*"—ATHENÆUM.

Leading Cases done into English. By an APPRENTICE OF LINCOLN'S INN. Third Edition. Crown 8vo. 2s. 6d.

"*Here is a rare treat for the lovers of quaint conceits, who in reading this charming little book will find enjoyment in the varied metre and graphic language in which the several tales are told, no less than in the accurate and pithy rendering of some of our most familiar 'Leading Cases.'*"—SATURDAY REVIEW.

Lubbock.—ADDRESSES, POLITICAL AND EDUCATIONAL. By Sir JOHN LUBBOCK, Bart., M.P., &c., &c. 8vo, pp. 209. 8s. 6d.

The ten speeches given are (1) on the Imperial Policy of Great Britain, (2) on the Bank Act of 1844, (3) on the Present System of Public School Education, 1876, (4) on the Present System of Elementary Education, (5) on the Income Tax, (6) on the National Debt, (7) on the Declaration of Paris, (8) on Marine Insurances, (9) on the Preservation of Ancient Monuments, and (10) on Egypt.

Macdonell.—THE LAND QUESTION, WITH SPECIAL REFERENCE TO ENGLAND AND SCOTLAND. By JOHN MACDONELL, Barrister-at-Law. 8vo. 10s. 6d.

Marshall.—THE ECONOMICS OF INDUSTRY. By A. MARSHALL, M.A., Principal of University College, Bristol, and MARY PALEY MARSHALL, late Lecturer at Newnham Hall, Cambridge. Extra fcap. 8vo. 2s. 6d.

Martin.—THE STATESMAN'S YEAR-BOOK: A Statistical and Historical Annual of the States of the Civilized World, for the year 1880. By FREDERICK MARTIN. Seventeenth Annual Publication. Revised after Official Returns. Crown 8vo. 10s. 6d.

The Statesman's Year-Book is the only work in the English language which furnishes a clear and concise account of the actual condition of all the States of Europe, the civilized countries of America, Asia, and Africa, and the British Colonies and Dependencies in all parts of the world. The new issue of the work has been revised and corrected, on the basis of official reports received direct from the heads of the leading Governments of the world, in reply to letters sent to them by the Editor. Through the valuable assistance thus given, it has been possible to collect an amount of information, political, statistical, and commercial, of the latest date, and of unimpeachable trustworthiness, such as no publication of the same kind has ever been able to furnish. "*As indispensable as Bradshaw.*"—TIMES.

Monahan.—THE METHOD OF LAW: an Essay on the Statement and Arrangement of the Legal Standard of Conduct. By J. H. MONAHAN, Q.C. Crown 8vo. 6s.

"*Will be found valuable by careful law students who have felt the importance of gaining clear ideas regarding the relations between the parts of the complex organism they have to study.*"—BRITISH QUARTERLY REVIEW.

Paterson.—THE LIBERTY OF THE SUBJECT AND THE LAWS OF ENGLAND RELATING TO THE SECURITY OF THE PERSON. Commentaries on. By JAMES PATERSON, M.A., Barrister at Law, sometime Commissioner for English and Irish Fisheries, etc. Cheaper issue. Two Vols. Crown 8vo. 21s.

"*Two or three hours' dipping into these volumes, not to say reading them through, will give legislators and stump orators a knowledge of the liberty of a citizen of their country, in its principles, its fulness, and its modification, such as they probably in nine cases out of ten never had before.*"—SCOTSMAN.

Phillimore.—PRIVATE LAW AMONG THE ROMANS, from the Pandects. By JOHN GEORGE PHILLIMORE, Q.C. 8vo. 16s.

Rogers.—COBDEN AND POLITICAL OPINION. By J. E. THOROLD ROGERS. 8vo. 10s. 6d.

"*Will be found most useful by politicians of every school, as it forms a sort of handbook to Cobden's teaching.*"—ATHENÆUM.

Stephen (C. E.)—THE SERVICE OF THE POOR; Being an Inquiry into the Reasons for and against the Establishment of Religious Sisterhoods for Charitable Purposes. By CAROLINE EMILIA STEPHEN. Crown 8vo. 6s. 6d.

"*The ablest advocate of a better line of work in this direction that we have ever seen.*"—EXAMINER.

Stephen.—Works by Sir JAMES F. STEPHEN, K.C.S.I., Q.C.

A DIGEST OF THE LAW OF EVIDENCE. Third Edition with New Preface. Crown 8vo. 6s.

A DIGEST OF THE CRIMINAL LAW. (Crimes and Punishments.) 8vo. 16s.

"*We feel sure that any person of ordinary intelligence who had never looked into a law-book in his life might, by a few days' careful study of*

Stephen.—*continued.*

this volume, obtain a more accurate understanding of the criminal law, a more perfect conception of its different bearings, a more thorough and intelligent insight into its snares and pitfalls, than an ordinary practitioner can boast of after years of study of the ordinary text-books and practical experience of the Courts unassisted by any competent guide."—SATURDAY REVIEW.

A GENERAL VIEW OF THE CRIMINAL LAW OF ENGLAND. Two Vols. Crown 8vo. [*New edition in the press.*

Stubbs.—VILLAGE POLITICS. Addresses and Sermons on the Labour Question. By C. W. STUBBS, M.A., Vicar of Granborough, Bucks. Extra fcap. 8vo. 3s. 6d.

Thornton.—Works by W. T. THORNTON, C.B., Secretary for Public Works in the India Office :—

ON LABOUR : Its Wrongful Claims and Rightful Dues ; Its Actual Present and Possible Future. Second Edition, revised, 8vo. 14s.

A PLEA FOR PEASANT PROPRIETORS : With the Outlines of a Plan for their Establishment in Ireland. New Edition, revised. Crown 8vo. 7s. 6d.

INDIAN PUBLIC WORKS AND COGNATE INDIAN TOPICS. With Map of Indian Railways. Crown 8vo. 8s. 6d.

Walker.—Works by F. A. WALKER, M.A., Ph.D., Professor of Political Economy and History, Yale College :—

THE WAGES QUESTION. A Treatise on Wages and the Wages Class. 8vo. 14s.

MONEY. 8vo. 16s.

"*It is painstaking, laborious, and states the question in a clear and very intelligible form. . . . The volume possesses a great value as a sort of encyclopædia of knowledge on the subject.*"—ECONOMIST.

MONEY IN ITS RELATIONS TO TRADE AND INDUSTRY. Crown 8vo. [*Shortly.*

Work about the Five Dials. With an Introductory Note by THOMAS CARLYLE. Crown 8vo. 6s.

"*A book which abounds with wise and practical suggestions.*"—PALL MALL GAZETTE.

WORKS CONNECTED WITH THE SCIENCE OR THE HISTORY OF LANGUAGE.

Abbott.—A SHAKESPERIAN GRAMMAR: An Attempt to illustrate some of the Differences between Elizabethan and Modern English. By the Rev. E. A. ABBOTT, D.D., Head Master of the City of London School. New and Enlarged Edition. Extra fcap. 8vo. 6s.

"*Valuable not only as an aid to the critical study of Shakespeare, but as tending to familiarize the reader with Elizabethan English in general.*"—ATHENÆUM.

Breymann.—A FRENCH GRAMMAR BASED ON PHILOLOGICAL PRINCIPLES. By HERMANN BREYMANN, Ph.D., Professor of Philology in the University of Munich late Lecturer on French Language and Literature at Owens College, Manchester. Extra fcap. 8vo. 4s. 6d.

Ellis.—PRACTICAL HINTS ON THE QUANTITATIVE PRONUNCIATION OF LATIN, FOR THE USE OF CLASSICAL TEACHERS AND LINGUISTS. By A. J. ELLIS, B.A., F.R.S., &c. Extra fcap. 8vo. 4s. 6d.

Fleay.—A SHAKESPEARE MANUAL. By the Rev. F. G. FLEAY, M.A., Head Master of Skipton Grammar School. Extra fcap. 8vo. 4s. 6d.

Goodwin.—Works by W. W. GOODWIN, Professor of Greek Literature in Harvard University.

SYNTAX OF THE GREEK MOODS AND TENSES. New Edition. Crown 8vo. 6s. 6d.

AN ELEMENTARY GREEK GRAMMAR. Crown 8vo. 6s.

"*It is the best Greek Grammar of its size in the English language.*"—ATHENÆUM.

Hadley.—ESSAYS PHILOLOGICAL AND CRITICAL. Selected from the Papers of JAMES HADLEY, LL.D., Professor of Greek in Yale College, &c. 8vo. 16s.

Hales.—LONGER ENGLISH POEMS. With Notes, Philological and Explanatory, and an Introduction on the Teaching of English. Chiefly for use in Schools. Edited by J. W. HALES, M.A., Professor of English Literature at King's College, London, &c. &c. Fifth Edition. Extra fcap. 8vo. 4s. 6d.

Helfenstein (James).—A COMPARATIVE GRAMMAR OF THE TEUTONIC LANGUAGES: Being at the same time a Historical Grammar of the English Language, and comprising Gothic, Anglo-Saxon, Early English, Modern English, Icelandic (Old Norse), Danish, Swedish, Old High German, Middle High German, Modern German, Old Saxon, Old Frisian, and Dutch. By JAMES HELFENSTEIN, Ph.D. 8vo. 18s.

Masson (Gustave).—A COMPENDIOUS DICTIONARY OF THE FRENCH LANGUAGE (French-English and English-French). Followed by a List of the Principal Diverging Derivations, and preceded by Chronological and Historical Tables. By GUSTAVE MASSON, Assistant-Master and Librarian, Harrow School. Fourth Edition. Crown 8vo. Half-bound. 6s.

"*A book which any student, whatever may be the degree of his advancement in the language, would do well to have on the table close at hand while he is reading.*"—SATURDAY REVIEW.

Mayor.—A BIBLIOGRAPHICAL CLUE TO LATIN LITERATURE. Edited after Dr. E. HUBNER. With large Additions by JOHN E. B. MAYOR, M.A., Professor of Latin in the University of Cambridge. Crown 8vo. 6s. 6d.

"*An extremely useful volume that should be in the hands of all scholars.*"—ATHENÆUM.

Morris.—Works by the Rev. RICHARD MORRIS, LL.D., Member of the Council of the Philol. Soc., Lecturer on English Language and Literature in King's College School, Editor of "Specimens of Early English," etc., etc.:—

HISTORICAL OUTLINES OF ENGLISH ACCIDENCE, comprising Chapters on the History and Development of the Language, and on Word-formation. Sixth Edition. Fcap. 8vo. 6s.

ELEMENTARY LESSONS IN HISTORICAL ENGLISH GRAMMAR, containing Accidence and Word-formation. Third Edition. 18mo. 2s. 6d.

Oliphant.—THE OLD AND MIDDLE ENGLISH. By T. L. KINGTON OLIPHANT, M.A., of Balliol College, Oxford. A New Edition, revised and greatly enlarged, of "The Sources of Standard English." Extra fcap. 8vo. 9s.

"*Mr. Oliphant's book is to our mind, one of the ablest and most scholarly contributions to our standard English we have seen for many years.*"—SCHOOL BOARD CHRONICLE. "*The book comes nearer to a history of the English language than anything we have seen since such a history could be written, without confusion and contradictions.*"—SATURDAY REVIEW.

Peile (John, M.A.)—AN INTRODUCTION TO GREEK AND LATIN ETYMOLOGY. By JOHN PEILE, M.A., Fellow and Tutor of Christ's College, Cambridge. Third and revised Edition. Crown 8vo. 10s. 6d.

"*The book may be accepted as a very valuable contribution to the science of language.*"—SATURDAY REVIEW.

Philology.—THE JOURNAL OF SACRED AND CLASSICAL PHILOLOGY. Four Vols. 8vo. 12s. 6d. each.

THE JOURNAL OF PHILOLOGY. New Series. Edited by JOHN E. B. MAYOR, M.A., and W. ALDIS WRIGHT, M.A. 4s. 6d. (Half-yearly.)

Roby (H. J.)—A GRAMMAR OF THE LATIN LANGUAGE, FROM PLAUTUS TO SUETONIUS. By HENRY JOHN ROBY, M.A., late Fellow of St. John's College, Cambridge. In Two Parts. Second Edition. Part I. containing:—Book I. Sounds. Book II. Inflexions. Book III. Word Formation. Appendices. Crown 8vo. 8s. 6d. Part II.—Syntax, Prepositions, &c. Crown 8vo. 10s. 6d.

"*The book is marked by the clear and practical insight of a master in his art. It is a book which would do honour to any country.*"—ATHENÆUM. "*Brings before the student in a methodical form the best results of modern philology bearing on the Latin language.*"—SCOTSMAN.

Schmidt.—THE RYTHMIC AND METRIC OF THE CLASSICAL LANGUAGES. To which are added, the Lyric Parts of the "Medea" of Euripides and the "Antigone" of Sophocles; with Rhythmical Scheme and Commentary. By Dr. J. H. SCHMIDT. Translated from the German by J. W. WHITE, D.D. 8vo. 10s. 6d.

Taylor.—Works by the Rev. ISAAC TAYLOR, M.A.:—

ETRUSCAN RESEARCHES. With Woodcuts. 8vo. 14s.

The TIMES *says:—*"*The learning and industry displayed in this volume deserve the most cordial recognition. The ultimate verdict of science we shall not attempt to anticipate; but we can safely say this, that it is a learned book which the unlearned can enjoy, and that in the descriptions of the tomb-builders, as well as in the marvellous coincidences and unexpected analogies brought together by the author, readers of every grade may take delight as well as philosophers and scholars.*"

WORDS AND PLACES; or, Etymological Illustrations of History, Ethnology, and Geography. By the Rev. ISAAC TAYLOR. Third Edition, revised and compressed. With Maps. Globe 8vo. 6s.

GREEKS AND GOTHS: a Study on the Runes. 8vo. 9s.

Trench.—Works by R. CHENEVIX TRENCH, D.D., Archbishop of Dublin. (For other Works by the same Author, see THEOLOGICAL CATALOGUE.)

SYNONYMS OF THE NEW TESTAMENT. Eighth Edition, enlarged. 8vo, cloth. 12s.

"*He is,*" the ATHENÆUM *says,* "*a guide in this department of knowledge to whom his readers may entrust themselves with confidence.*"

ON THE STUDY OF WORDS. Lectures Addressed (originally) to the Pupils at the Diocesan Training School, Winchester. Seventeenth Edition, enlarged. Fcap. 8vo. 5s.

ENGLISH PAST AND PRESENT. Tenth Edition, revised and improved. Fcap. 8vo. 5s.

A SELECT GLOSSARY OF ENGLISH WORDS USED FORMERLY IN SENSES DIFFERENT FROM THEIR PRESENT. Fifth Edition, enlarged. Fcap. 8vo. 5s.

Vincent and Dickson.—A HANDBOOK TO MODERN GREEK. By EDGAR VINCENT and T. G. DICKSON. Extra fcap. 8vo. 5s.

Whitney.—A COMPENDIOUS GERMAN GRAMMAR. By W. D. WHITNEY, Professor of Sanskrit and Instructor in Modern Languages in Yale College. Crown 8vo. 6s.

"*After careful examination we are inclined to pronounce it the best grammar of modern language we have ever seen.*"—SCOTSMAN.

Whitney and Edgren.—A COMPENDIOUS GERMAN AND ENGLISH DICTIONARY, with Notation of Correspondences and Brief Etymologies. By Professor W. D. WHITNEY, assisted by A. H. EDGREN. Crown 8vo. 7s. 6d.

The GERMAN-ENGLISH Part may be had separately. Price 5s.

Yonge.—HISTORY OF CHRISTIAN NAMES. By CHARLOTTE M. YONGE, Author of "The Heir of Redclyffe." Cheaper Edition. Two Vols. Crown 8vo. 12s.

Now publishing, in crown 8vo, price 2s. 6d. each.

ENGLISH MEN OF LETTERS.

Edited by JOHN MORLEY.

A Series of Short Books to tell people what is best worth knowing to the Life, Character, and Works of some of the great English Writers.

ENGLISH MEN OF LETTERS.—JOHNSON. By LESLIE STEPHEN.

"The new series opens well with Mr. Leslie Stephen's sketch of Dr. Johnson. It could hardly have been done better, and it will convey to the readers for whom it is intended a juster estimate of Johnson than either of the two essays of Lord Macaulay."—*Pall Mall Gazette*

ENGLISH MEN OF LETTERS.—SCOTT. By R. H. HUTTON.

"The tone of the volume is excellent throughout."—*Athenæum.*

"We could not wish for a more suggestive introduction to Scott and his poems and novels."—*Examiner.*

ENGLISH MEN OF LETTERS.—GIBBON. By J. C. MORISON.

"As a clear, thoughtful, and attractive record of the life and works of the greatest among the world's historians, it deserves the highest praise."—*Examiner.*

ENGLISH MEN OF LETTERS.—SHELLEY. By J. A. SYMONDS.

"The lovers of this great poet are to be congratulated on having at their command so fresh, clear, and intelligent a presentment of the subject, written by a man of adequate and wide culture."—*Athenæum.*

ENGLISH MEN OF LETTERS.—HUME. By Professor HUXLEY.

"It may fairly be said that no one now living could have expounded Hume with more sympathy or with equal perspicuity."—*Athenæum.*

ENGLISH MEN OF LETTERS.—GOLDSMITH. By WILLIAM BLACK.

"Mr. Black brings a fine sympathy and taste to bear in his criticism of Goldsmith's writings, as well as in his sketch of the incidents of his life."—*Athenæum.*

ENGLISH MEN OF LETTERS.—DEFOE. By W. MINTO.

"Mr. Minto's book is careful and accurate in all that is stated, and faithful in all that it suggests. It will repay reading more than once."—*Athenæum.*

ENGLISH MEN OF LETTERS—*Continued.*

ENGLISH MEN OF LETTERS.—BURNS. By Principal SHAIRP, Professor of Poetry in the University of Oxford.

"It is impossible to desire fairer criticism than Principal Shairp's on Burns's poetry. . . . . None of the series has given a truer estimate either of character or of genius than this little volume. . . . and all who read it will be thoroughly grateful to the author for this monument to the genius of Scotland's greatest poet."—*Spectator.*

ENGLISH MEN OF LETTERS.—SPENSER. By the Very Rev. the DEAN OF ST. PAUL'S.

"Dr. Church is master of his subject, and writes always with good taste."—*Academy.*

ENGLISH MEN OF LETTERS.—THACKERAY. By ANTHONY TROLLOPE.

"Mr. Trollope's sketch is exceedingly adapted to fulfil the purpose of the series in which it appears."—*Athenæum.*

ENGLISH MEN OF LETTERS.—BURKE. By JOHN MORLEY.

"Perhaps the best criticism yet published on the life and character of Burke is contained in Mr. Morley's compendious biography. His style is vigorous and polished, and both his political and personal judgment and his literary criticisms are just, generous, subtle, and in a high degree interesting."—*Saturday Review.*

Just ready.

MILTON. By MARK PATTISON.

In preparation.

HAWTHORNE. By HENRY JAMES.

SOUTHEY. By Professor DOWDEN.

CHAUCER. By Professor WARD.

COWPER. By GOLDWIN SMITH.

BUNYAN. By J. A. FROUDE.

WORDSWORTH. By F. W. H. MYERS.

Others in preparation.

MACMILLAN AND CO., LONDON.

LONDON:
R. CLAY, SONS, AND TAYLOR, PRINTERS,
BREAD STREET HILL.

www.ingramcontent.com/pod-product-compliance
Lightning Source LLC
Chambersburg PA
CBHW032014220426
43664CB00006B/241